line+

Shaping Changes

images
Publishing

Contents

The Practice of line+ studio:

A Sample of Contemporary Chinese Architecture

Li Xiangning

Vice President, Tongji University

Meng Fanhao (left), Zhu Peidong (right)

China's rapid urbanization has triggered an unprecedented construction boom since the 1990s. While the early phase of urban construction was marked mainly by its extensiveness, modern-day requirements of a highly commerce-oriented society, as well as the ever-changing utilization of space in the Digital Age, have created a concern for quality and renewed the recognition of it. On the one hand, quality as a spatial attribute ensures a building's suitability for function and use; on the other hand—in an era of the ever-expanding influence of social media—it has also evolved into a communicable property beyond the confines of the physical space. With the help of a photograph or a video, a building can now reach a wider audience than just its day-to-day users, and thus possesses a greater underlying power for change.

It is in this transformational context that line+ studio was founded in Hangzhou by Meng Fanhao and Zhu Peidong. The two young lead architects have been working in the industry for many years and possess extensive practical experience, as well as a keen intuition for design. This has enabled line+ studio to complete a large number of projects across a wide range of building types and practical contexts in just two years. From the Longtang Targeted Poverty Alleviation Project, a benchmark project for poverty eradication in a provincial-level impoverished village, to the revitalization of Dongximen Village in Tai'an, which deliberately leverages the role of social media against the background of "rural rejuvenation;" from Songyang Stray Birds Art Hotel, which measures only a few hundred square meters, to Zhejiang Perfect Production Factory, which covers an area of tens of thousands of square meters; and from Yunnan Dongfengyun Art Center, settled on a mountain plain in southwestern China's Yunnan Province, to iFLYTEK AI Headquarters Campus, located in a high-density urban environment, the practice of line+ studio seems difficult to box into simple categories.

Understanding why this is so requires looking back to the experience and background of the two lead architects. Unlike the previous generation of individual architects, or most individual young architects today—many of whom who would have studied overseas, outside of China, before returning to the country—the two founders of line+ studio arrived at the forefront of Chinese architectural practice after completing their studies at Nanjing University and Shanghai's Tongji University, respectively. They studied under Professor Zhang Lei at Nanjing University and Professor Huang Yiru at Tongji University, immersing themselves in the research-oriented working methods of small design studios. After graduation, they joined gad in Hangzhou, the largest and most professional architectural design firm in China. In the process of bidding for and executing large-scale projects, they experienced the demands of contemporary society first hand, got to hone their organizational skills in the complex professional division of labor, and developed their ability to control quality when faced with the frequent uncertainties in contemporary Chinese architectural practice. Perhaps it is these different experiences that predisposed line+ studio to develop a hybrid identity from the very beginning. On the one hand, the studio focuses on the fundamental qualities of architectural ontology, such as space, material, structure, and place, and the use of "concepts," as practiced by individual studios.

On the other hand, the studio also does not reject involvement in large-scale commercial projects. This hybrid nature has even led line+ studio to explore the functionality of industrial construction systems in small rural construction projects. For example, in Jiunvfeng Study and Jiunvfeng Bubble Pool in Mount Tai (Shandong Province) and the Guizhou Longtang Targeted Poverty Alleviation project in Longtang (Guizhou Province), the limitations posed by the geographical conditions and the poor construction quality in the countryside were overcome with the help of a modern-day prefabricated light steel structure system. Conversely, the studio also seeks to introduce innovations to established forms of commercial building types using the values of classical architecture. For example, in Mogan Valley, a resort project, Meng Fanhao convinced the developer to employ the concept of a "settlement" instead of simple rows of buildings, thus breaking away from the typical layout of holiday resorts in China, thereby emphasizing a harmonious relationship with the surrounding village texture and landscape. In Zhejiang Perfect Production Factory, concepts of Chinese landscape paintings and traditional gardens were applied to an industrial production facility, completely revolutionizing the plain and impersonal spatial layout of conventional box-like factory buildings.

However, all works are ultimately influenced by the zeitgeist in which they were created. Therefore, this discussion of line+ studio must also take into account the context of contemporary Chinese architectural practice. Social development in China over the last 40 years has created a large community of private owners and an emerging community of users. The former tends to focus on the commercial value of architectural projects, seeking to find a balance between market and social demands, while the latter is no longer simply satisfied with the practicality of space, possessing a strong demand for aesthetic and "interesting" spaces. It is difficult to say whether the former nurtures the latter or the latter nourishes the former, but in the collusion between the two, a new spatial demand has gradually emerged. Architecture no longer needs to be "economical, practical, and beautiful" in the traditional sense, but rather it needs to display individuality and draw attention. As the British critic Rowan Moore has pointed out, architecture is both a tool that meets practical needs, and a symbol. In China today, the latter role of architecture has perhaps long surpassed the former. Architecture no longer simply solves functional requirements, but has also become a medium for communicating one's understanding of culture. Faced with this evolved role of architecture today, line+ studio does not restrict itself to the traditional solutions of classical architecture, but rather strives to answer directly the needs of the market and the young generation's new ways of using spaces, and their aesthetic interests. This is precisely what makes the practice of line+ studio unique.

Both the structural and material considerations of classical architecture, together with the formal language valued by contemporary consumer culture, become a means to an end—to create a space which responds to these new demands and to evoke greater energy through space. Thus, we can see that in the Songyang Stray Birds Art Hotel project, the architecture not only balances traditional forms with modern lifestyles, but it also entices a younger generation of villagers to return, even attracting young entrepreneurs and artists from across the country to settle and work there. Jiunvfeng Study on Mount Tai turned a previously little-known village into a viral tourist destination that is popular with the younger generation, who flock to the venue for the great photo ops. In these projects, architects become the nexus connecting resources from governments, investors, media, and local residents. With the space as a medium, this approach moves the architects' role upward from the end of design, allowing them to regain the right to participate in the process of shaping changes.

In my 2005 article "Expedient Architecture," I pointed out that poor construction quality, low cost, and rapid construction are all inescapable problems for contemporary Chinese architects. Trying to turn these issues into an advantage is a problem that Chinese architects still need to address today. Since I wrote the article, twenty years have passed, and the unprecedented popularization of the mobile internet has added a new dimension to the contemporary context: speed—not only with the speed of construction, but also the speed of communication. With the power of the internet, architects' influence has increased dramatically; they also experience a rapid feedback loop with online communication. Thus, revealing how to respond to our present time using a new architectural language, and how to embrace this new era of architecture, is what line+ studio, as well as other contemporary Chinese architects, can contribute to the changing global architectural community.

Shaping Changes exhibition at line+ studio's office

Perspectives

Liu Yuyang

Founder and Principal,
Atelier Liu Yuyang Architects

D. Kenneth Sargent Visiting Critic,
School of Architecture, Syracuse University

In my opinion, there are two key words that best describe the practice of line+ studio. The first is culture, which relates to an open attitude. This has a lot to do with the education and messages that the studio's two founders received, being from the generation that they were, and the very market-oriented business environment that they operate in. This has led them to not only take a more open and tolerant stance in dealing with different design requirements, as well as various stakeholders, government leaders, and ultimate users, but also to show a range of flexible solutions to the contemporary cultural context. When confronted with the impoverished villages in Tai'an City, Shandong Province, during one of their projects, the studio didn't settle on low-cost buildings that reflect the living conditions of the local villagers, but instead led with a very refined and contrasting design that uses visually powerful imagery to overcome the local poverty. I believe that line+ studio is challenging who or what architecture is meant to serve, and what it needs to tackle.

The second key word is professionalism. When working on large projects, there needs to be both a high rate of completion and a delicate approach when handling projects. A firm with eighty people needs to be managed professionally and expertly in order to operate efficiently at all times. Accumulating experience in a large commercial firm before founding one's own studio—as line+ studio did—offers a new path and model for future generations of young architects. Exiting from the small-scale studio of a renowned master to open an individual studio isn't the only option anymore; an architect can also blaze their own trail for development in different ways. I think line+ studio's professional journey can serve as a great inspiration for my generation and younger architects as well.

Lu Andong

Vice Dean, Professor, and Doctoral Supervisor,
School of Architecture and Urban Planning,
Nanjing University

We are living in a time of substantial changes, where new technologies create new needs. These shifting demands are the real driving force behind architecture, and have led to fundamental transformations in the discipline. Technological changes have reshaped the way people perceive architecture's imagery, and the way they now discover places to visit. This change will radically alter architecture's most basic composition of values and elements. So the challenge for today's architecture is to redefine, filter, and reconstruct its ontology.

Architecture has always had multiple core qualities; it's only that we have been blinded by constructiveness for too long to notice them. From the very beginning, architecture has always acted as a mediator. As a type of project, it is an action-oriented intervention into reality and operation. The architect's job is to plan and direct interventions—to create an interventionistic shape. Design is a set of projects with action as their core logic. Modern technology has allowed some of the hidden and suppressed qualities of architecture to reappear. If we think of contemporary architecture as an action-oriented intermediary pointed toward change, then architectural empowerment becomes a mechanism to exert influence through action. In some of the studio's projects, we can see that they intertwine communication logic with construction logic, enabling construction to act as a mobilizer of resources to reach and influence groups. This is a new course of action. Within this changed contemporary framework, we need to re-examine architecture as a mechanism of action. And we will find that its inherent qualities as a medium and symbol will redefine its original properties in terms of construction, space, and the quality of life. This will result in a new ontological system for the people's new state of life in the Digital Age, and we hope to find a new formal language in it.

Zhang Bin

Founder and Principal Architect,
Atelier Z+

line+ studio has followed in the footsteps of one of the traditions of the current generation of Chinese architects, which is to mature early. At a very young age, they had already had the opportunity to work on highly important projects, and the broader environment for their architectural practice has become more professional and systematic than what our generation faced. Over the past few years, the proliferation of the internet has opened up more diverse areas of practice, and allowed many new opportunities that come with these. In the past, a firm with a high rate of completed projects and a high degree of professionalism was often limited to doing large projects without the ability to use its resources and work model to complete smaller projects. line+ studio's exploration has proven to be a positive approach for facing diverse types of projects, and in terms of the professionalization of Chinese architects, they have set a strong benchmark.

Zhuang Shen

Co-founder and Principal Architect,
Atelier Archmixing
Professor,
School of Design,
Shanghai Jiaotong University

The current state of China's architectural practice and the phenomena arising from it are unique. Therefore, we need to examine some of these unfolding trends and actions with a fresh eye. Among the practicing architects in China, there are those who are at the forefront of action, who have a very keen sense; their understanding far exceeds mere theory. And I think, Meng Fanhao and Zhu Peidong have reached a state where a metamorphosis is very much a possibility. It's evident in the work of the studio that they are able to use all the available resources and platforms and tie it in with their own abilities to complete a wide range of projects. They have found a working model which initially started from commercial real estate, but which was much more than just that, thereby enabling them to successfully enter the broader market. They have received a lot of positive feedback, which has opened up new possibilities for their own practice, and which in turn could be used to deliver more diverse values, and even a common value.

Zhang Lei

Co-founder and Principal Architect,
azLa (Allied Zhang & Lei Architects)
Professor,
School of Architecture and Urban Planning,
Nanjing University

The two lead architects at line+ studio are very good at mobilizing and utilizing existing frameworks and resources. From the perspective of a professional architect, this is a very good start. Based on this, even bigger breakthroughs need to made, either through work at different stages, or in terms of social responsibility, either in the creation of public space, or in the study of architectural ontology.

Zhou Rong

Associate Professor,
School of Architecture,
Tsinghua University

In the past, Chinese architects could be clearly divided into four categories: individual architects, who started to emerge with the opening of China in the 1990s; architects working in large, such as state-run, design institutes; private architects, who focused on smaller projects; and commercial architects. In the past, the boundaries between these four categories were comparatively distinct. However, following the permeation of mobile internet in the last decade, the former, relatively clear and slowly evolving social structure "converged" to a great extent. This led to the "publicization" of all forms of architecture and their inclusion into public discourse. As a result, new forms of architecture were needed. Architects who had clung to any of the four categories of the past are now unable to meet the enormously complex and integrated requirements of contemporary "publicized" architecture. This "publicized" architecture I refer to is not necessarily a public building in itself, but more architecture that is being discussed in wide circles among the public. This also characterizes the context that gave rise to line+ studio. The studio built not only on the education and training received from individual architects, but also on the sound practice of commercial studios, achieving a level of publicness that had previously been beyond architects' reach. In this new contemporary "smorgasbord," it is our duty to overcome the previously inflexible and narrow positioning of architects, and to reunify and connect the four categories of the past in order to face the changing tides.

An Architecture of Everything

Aric Chen

Curator, Writer and Director of the Zaha Hadid Foundation

Yunnan Dongfengyun Art Center

Suffice to say, the dominant credo propelling architecture these days is not any movement, style or ideology, but rather the "-ism" of capitalism, whether of the state or market. In this discursive environment, cynics decry how architecture—or at least the architecture that we see on social media, which seems like the only architecture that counts nowadays—has become merely an image for promotional dissemination, or a container for speculative capital. In this scenario, we are only incidental inhabitants of a world of glittering office and apartment towers for investors to park their money in—no matter if those spaces are actually used or not—and of museums, libraries, and theaters, where the primary function seems to be neither cultural enrichment nor social benefit, but rather the raising of land values and the fulfillment of bureaucratic checklists.

There is, of course, more than a small amount of truth to this. But for line+ studio, like many Chinese architects, the current state of affairs represents not a hindrance to reconnecting architecture with more meaningful aims, but rather an opportunity to do so. Under Meng Fanhao and Zhu Peidong, line+ studio breaks from a long lineage of architectural ideas, fragmenting them long ago to frame architecture as a methodology and kit-of-parts that deploys those lineages on an as-needed basis.

In doing so, Meng and Zhu channel the forces of state and market power that fuel architectural production in China. They show a keen attention to detail, while taking on ever larger projects at ever bigger scales. Their oeuvre is equal parts site-specific and modular, small and large, user- and client-oriented, pragmatic and sublime, and rural and urban, though, as they would explain, the distinction is blurring. It is architecture that is both about and not about formal and dialectical agendas. In other words, it is the architecture of everything.

To be sure, the studio's projects are responsive to specificities—like site and landscape, as well as social, historical, cultural, and user contexts. Each project is different, whether it's a timber addition to a rammed-earth house or a prefabricated, solar-powered electric car charging station. Indeed, the studio seems as comfortable designing an intimately austere concrete museum in the countryside as it is building sparkling megacity office towers and sprawling tech campuses of glass and steel. Even in the context of hyper-speed China—or, perhaps more accurately, because of it—the pace at which the three-year-old firm has produced such a breadth and volume of work is remarkable. As Meng and Zhu describe their practice, line+ studio is a "creative factory."

It's an ethos that was instilled early on. In 2012, in a moment that would presage the establishment of line+ studio six years later, Zhu, who was then a 28-year-old recent arrival at the architecture firm gad, won the competition to design a campus for the newly established Zhejiang Conservatory of Music as one of the project principals. In order to meet the timeline for university accreditation, this massive commission in Hangzhou—for what would become the world's largest music academy—had to be completed in just three years. With the project's multiple technically challenging performance halls, soaring library and administration building, 700 music rooms, sculpted berms, lyrical 984-foot-long (300-meter-long) concrete sound barrier winding along the adjacent road, location near to an affiliated high school situated on the campus, and hotel and dormitories—all now spread across an idyllically landscaped site of 4,305,564 square feet (400,000 square meters)—one can imagine the mammoth challenge that suddenly confronted the young architect.

Zhu quickly assembled a team of 300 designers from gad alongside 200 consultants from more than ten external firms. His participation in the conservatory design competition had been self-initiated, and having already established some autonomy within gad, the stage was set for his and Meng's eventual establishment of line+ studio in 2018.

It's a novel arrangement that seems to give line+ studio the best of both worlds by granting it the advantages of being at once a small and large firm. It, in many ways, aptly describes the methodology of both efficiency and customization that Meng and Zhu have honed, by which form is not a polemic, but rather one of many tools.

There are some common threads, however, that one can discern throughout their work. As the studio's name implies, there is a skillful use of lines, especially horizontal ones, whether they're accentuating the topography of rural projects—as in their project Shilily Resorts in Jinjia Hill—or unifying the façades of their iFLYTEK AI Headquarters Campus. Lines, of course, extrude into planes, and the studio deftly layers the latter through clever screening devices. The horizontal curtain-wall bands on the façades of the iFLYTEK campus transform into balconies, just as perforated brick walls provide both privacy and visual variety in the Dongziguan Affordable Housing project, which Meng Fanhao led while at gad as the project principal.

With its forty-six houses iterated from four typologies, the Dongziguan project showcases the architects' use of permutation strategy to create a remarkable array of low-cost housing in a human-scaled configuration that, like their more recently completed brick-and-timber activity center in the village (Dongziguan Villagers' Activity Center), speaks to another of their strengths: composing aggregations of volumes in ways that equally emphasize the spaces in between.

Dongziguan Village—Dongziguan Affordable Housing project

"Green Valley" of the Zhejiang Conservatory of Music

It comes as no surprise then that when asked who their architectural influences are, Meng and Zhu struggle to answer with specifics. Like culture in general, architecture as a discipline has become too jumbled up. However, some architectural vocabularies are more appropriate than others in any given situation, and more than anywhere in the world, new architectural situations continue to abound in a dizzying array in China. When it comes to "architectural solutions"—to borrow market lingo—the demand is for new products in an already crowded field that requires differentiation, and line+ studio's "creative factory" responds by drawing from a repertoire of "best practices" in providing that.

That is no doubt what clients like to hear. But from an architectural standpoint, the studio nimbly navigates the contradictions between market and social needs, form and operability, and scale and specificity. It is simultaneously a boutique atelier and a corporate firm. At the same time, its versatility speaks of how architectural discourse has become both bankrupt and more important than ever. And perhaps, it is through this coexistence of contradictions—a condition that describes many things in China—that line+ studio points toward a new direction for architecture at large.

Context and Perception:

Commentary on the Architectural Works of line+ studio in the Urban-Rural Dialectics

Liu Yuyang

Founder and Principal, Atelier Liu Yuyang Architects
D. Kenneth Sargent Visiting Critic, School of Architecture, Syracuse University

Chengdu Luxelakes Blackstone Island

The recent rise of the highly acclaimed creative line+ studio, based in the historically significant and culturally rich city of Hangzhou, home of the West Lake, the Grand Canal, Lingying Temple, and Alibaba, might seem puzzling at first glance to those viewing from the outside. Headed by two relatively young partners, one in his mid-thirties and the other in his early forties, its prolific body of work includes boutique hotels and exquisite pavilions in the beautiful landscapes of the pastoral Zhejiang countryside, as well as in poor and remote villages in places as far as Yunnan and Shandong. Unlike many studios of their generation that may wish to maintain a more "pure" reputation, line+ studio didn't shy away from taking on large projects. Mega-scale built and current works in progress include corporate parks and luxury housing, as well as industrial compounds and college campuses. In fact, the two partners at line+ studio sought to publicize their large-scale works and to project even larger ambitions to the audience, often citing their works in the context of the urban-rural dialectics that have thus far defined economic growth and social development in contemporary China. It is remarkable to note—aside from all the built works and recent awards—that line+ studio was founded only seven years ago.

As the charismatic partner Meng Fanghao stated in his opening interview for the firm's newly compiled massive monograph, it is very much their explicit goal to become a "creative factory facing market demand" directly, and to defy what the previous generation of architects consider good architecture. On this, the cool-headed younger partner Zhu Peidong put it succinctly, explaining that it is not merely the traditional, ontological values of architecture—form, space, structure, and tectonics, just to name a few—which the previous generations held as the sacred standard to good architecture, though one can still see in the studio's works a level of maturity in that regard that is perhaps typical of the older design firms. Rather, it is in the notion of "space for empowerment" and "architecture as tool" that sets line+ studio apart from many of their contemporaries. This becomes especially evident when one goes from merely looking at those carefully selected images for publication to actually visiting their buildings first-hand and entering those "empowered spaces" in person.

Zhoushan Chaishan Island Elderly Care Home

In an intensely organized two-day trip in and around Hangzhou to visit projects undertaken by Meng and Zhu, we toured no less than six built projects of various programs and scales, as well as the line+ studio space which had recently been renovated to house an ongoing exhibition of their works. Of the numerous projects introduced, Meng and Zhu each presented a small, medium, and large project under their own creative direction. Despite their differences in site, scale, and style, what struck me was the unifying consistency in the way each project tackled its morphologically apparent urban or rural context, as well as its more subtle underlying cultural context. From the submerged path that leads to the entrance of Shuo • Gallery, to the way the horizontal concrete slabs of Teahouse in Jiuxing Village nestle with the adjacent picturesque hills, to how an existing working canal was incorporated into the planning of a mega corporate campus to form a significant urban strategy, contexts were never viewed as a static given, but rather a dynamic player in the architectural experience.

Hangzhou Qiantang River Museum

If contextual response is the more obvious choice of strategy in their works, perceptual quality, on the other hand, was a delightful surprise I discovered during the on-site visits. Several memorable moments can still be vividly recalled: the monumental approach to the front gateway of the Zhejiang Conservatory of Music, the meandering circulation paths within the line+ studio space, and the undulating pavilion and layered landscape within the central courtyard of Hangzhou Sunac • YonglinMansion luxury housing. The contextual, as well as perceptual approaches to design in the projects of line+ studio are testament to the great influence of the poetic urban landscape of Hangzhou and the picturesque rural landscape of Zhejiang Province. Like mountain streams that flow through a riverbed, picking up minerals along the way, the works of Meng and Zhu are clear products that pick up the most affable, as well as the most enduring characteristics, of everything they have gone through in their personal and professional lives.

Throughout the two days, it became increasingly intriguing to note the dynamics of Meng and Zhu, prompting one to wonder how the two partners collaborated or influenced each other during their time at gad—the large commercial office that still remains a part of their corporate identity through affiliation, and which also provides the essential backing for the technical aspects of their large projects by way of structure and HVAC. While line+ studio currently employs as many as eighty staff—over sixty of whom are architectural and interior designers with an average age of twenty-eight—it is by no means a small atelier in and of itself. gad, on the other hand, employs more than 500 multidisciplinary architects, designers, and engineers, projecting a sense of stability and technical competence. gad may not be the "mother" company of line+ studio in the legal sense of the word, but it is the DNA of the studio—given the organizational attributes of the company, a deep understanding of the market, and even the ability to handle large and complex projects under extreme pressure—that, in my mind, defines the uniquely creative genes of the two young partners of line+ studio; more so than any other predetermined vision or manifesto.

In fact, it is this seemingly lack of architectural agenda that makes their works resonate beyond the traditional audience of architecture, encompassing students, architects, and critics. Their small-scale works have gained a tremendous following in various social media platforms. Their housing projects and corporate campuses are favored by some of the top developers across China and they are even taking on overseas projects funded by Chinese developers. To top it off, their cultural projects are also gaining international recognition, leading them to be selected as a themed exhibitor in the 17th Venice Architecture Biennale, 2021. All of these, I believe, shed light on explaining how line+ studio achieves poetic qualities in their hugely varied categories of work, while maintaining a commercially successful practice. I would further argue that, in the foreseeable future increasingly dominated by artificial intelligence and robotics, it is the focus on cultural context and human perception that will continue to define the underlying trajectory of the works of line+ studio. And it is in this trajectory that I hope the relatively young energy of the firm will be further channeled to encourage a renewed idea of the craft of architecture and to empower more diversified programs that shape more unplanned events into their spaces.

Dialogue

Designing Between the Exploration of Local Culture and Rational Business Logic

Interview with Meng Fanhao

Interviewer: *Mo Wanli*
Date: *September 16, 2022*
Place: *line+ studio office, Hangzhou, Zhejiang Province, China*

Q

Could you begin by summarizing your practical experience? What was the catalyst that steered you and Zhu Peidong to co-found line+ studio?

Meng: Within the space of a few decades, China had undergone an extraordinary process of urbanization that took other countries an entire century to complete. This unique process has inevitably led to the formation of certain characteristics: for example, the scale and speed of construction have engendered a degree of carelessness and homogeneity. This, in turn, has meant that Chinese architects have had to learn how to strike a balance between quality and quantity.

After completing my master's degree, I began accumulating practical experience at one of China's top private design firms. You could say that, in doing so, I became part of the leading force behind China's urbanization. After a while, I wanted to break out of my comfort zone and, based on my experiences and ideas, explore different possibilities and take on new challenges. Zhu Peidong and I had collaborated on several projects by that point and naturally discovered certain commonalities, such as our open-mindedness. For example, neither of us would usually reject commercial projects. Instead, if we take them on, we approach them with the same degree of rigor and critical observation as we do any other project. This way, we developed a unique strategy for formulating designs based on balancing the exploration of local culture with rational business logic.

Q

Compared to the previous generation of Chinese architects who typically studied and worked abroad before returning to China to establish their own projects, or who worked for state-owned institutes for several years before finally launching their own studios, your trajectory is quite remarkable. How do you think this unique trajectory has benefited your practical work?

Meng: My educational background and professional trajectory have both had a hand in molding my current outlook as an architect. At a time when Chinese society was relatively closed to the world, architects from the previous generation, such as Yung Ho Chang and Zhang Lei, opened the eyes of the younger generation—especially those who hadn't yet had the opportunity to study abroad—to various possibilities in architectural education and design. Their avant-

1. Meng Fanhao and team meeting Rem Koolhaas in London
2. Meng Fanhao exhibiting at the Chinese Pavilion, 2023 Venice Architecture Biennale
3. Meng Fanhao being awarded the certificate of participation in RIBA "China Architects: Building Contemporary China" exhibition
4. Meng Fanhao presenting the Hangzhou Linyin Temple expansion scheme to Abbot Guangquan and Architect Wang Shu

garde works in China were a real source of enlightenment for my peers and me. Of course, as Chinese design evolved rapidly and the world became increasingly globalized, we gained more opportunities to go abroad for fellowships and study tours, and to have exchanges with foreign architects who had come to China for work. At the same time, the popularization of the internet has equalized access to information between China and the rest of the world, empowering us to approach our practical work with a more global mindset.

As for me, I didn't go abroad for my studies, but my work at a large private firm in China honed my skills in line with the needs of the domestic market, allowing me to accumulate experience in dealing with the complex realities of China's current development. I believe that this experience is still very valuable. Hustling at the forefront of the industry helped me to gain a more accurate understanding of how architectural projects are implemented in China today. It also taught me to adapt clients' ideas to make them architecturally viable. I often sit down with clients to discuss the effect they wish to achieve. Then, together, we explore what kind of design solution will be truly feasible in the Chinese context and how it can be implemented, be it in terms of form and scale, or construction budget. Therefore, I think that my past experiences contributed to a kind of pragmatic flexibility. Without sacrificing certain principles regarding the quality of our designs, we know how to adapt them to ensure their successful execution.

You completed your graduate studies at Nanjing University's (NJU) School of Architecture and Urban Planning, a school that played a vital role in the history of modern architectural studies in China. Although founded in the early 2000s, this school has significantly impacted contemporary Chinese architecture, and right from the start too, thanks to its distinctive educational principles and bold propositions. What kind of influence did NJU have on your architectural practice?

Meng: NJU's architectural education and several of its faculty members, like Zhang Lei, Zhao Chen, and Zhu Jingxiang, greatly influenced me. At the time, many architecture schools in China were still influenced by the Ecole nationale supérieure des beaux-arts de Lyon [France], and thus placed emphasis on formal artistic training—for instance, teaching composition in drawings. The teachers I mentioned were all educated at ETH in Zürich [Switzerland],

Meng Fanhao delivering a keynote speech at Churchill College, Cambridge University

Meng Fanhao and his master's degree supervisor, Zhang Lei

Meng Fanhao exhibiting at RIBA "China Architects: Building Contemporary China"

and hoped to use the NJU School of Architecture to adopt a more "boutique" research-oriented and construction-based approach to teaching architecture. This was entirely at odds with my undergrad studies and revolutionized my understanding of the discipline. In response to your question, as I once said to Zhao Chen and Li Hua: "NJU's notion of 'basic architecture,' as well as their emphasis on analytical methods and the composition of different materials, had a decisive and fundamental impact on my design practices."

After I graduated and joined the workforce, my first project was a residential community composed of English-style villas. Perhaps some people would find such a project very boring, but I quickly noticed that it contained certain elements that were interesting from a typological standpoint. I believe the education I received at NJU allowed me to develop this unique perspective, thanks to which I could grasp the underlying significance of a seemingly banal residential project. Once the project was completed, I even compiled a booklet summarizing my observations. In this way, a commercial real estate project served as the inspiration for academic research. The NJU School of Architecture's method of training students' critical thinking skills is of tremendous significance even in the context of China's large-scale commercial construction initiatives. Of course, my experiences are also linked to the state of Hangzhou's real estate market at the time. It's precisely because of the emphasis that Hangzhou's local developers, led by Greentown, placed on quality that we had room to discuss matters like typology, space, materials, and structure, while working on a residential development project, and in doing so, exert an influence on contemporary Chinese residential design.

i

Compared to other architects of your generation, your practical experience and background are probably at the forefront of the ongoing urbanization process in China. How do you interpret the influence that this large-scale and rapid city-building movement has had on current Chinese architectural practices? And specifically, those of line+ studio?

Meng: In a certain sense, I believe that Chinese architects, especially the ones belonging to the younger generation, are very lucky. For me, launching my practical career amid China's large-scale, rapid urbanization was a formidable opportunity that served to hone my

Meng Fanhao at a meeting with villagers from Dongziguan Village, Fuyang District, Hangzhou, China—Dongziguan Affordable Housing project

Dongziguan Villagers' Activity Center

skills. When we speak to foreign architects who are about the same age as us, they tend to express surprise, often startled by the scale and speed of our projects. In our opinion, the Chinese architects taking part in this urbanization process that is changing the face of the earth and shaping urban skylines need to understand their place in history, and have a strong sense of responsibility to continually reflect on their behavior and its consequences.

Compared with independent architects, our attitude is perhaps not one of "resistance," but we still hope to make positive changes by upholding principles in our designs. This is why we hope that line+ studio can maintain a certain scale rather than be continuously expanding. This *modus operandi* gives us more selectivity in terms of clients and projects. It means that we can focus on things that are more aligned with our values.

In 2021, you were the only architect from the Chinese mainland who was invited to participate in the 17th Venice Architecture Biennale themed *How Will We Live Together?* at the Arsenale in Venice, Italy. There, you presented an installation titled *Rural Nostalgia and Urban Dream*. This title of the installation reflects two parallel trajectories in the studio's work: rural and urban. Is there a dialogue between these two trajectories that informs their design strategies and concepts?

Meng: Because there are usually specialized developers, suppliers, and supporting teams in the city, our role in the city is often limited to that of just architects, in the traditional sense of the term. But it's completely different in the countryside: from the client to the construction team, the people we deal with often aren't professionals. Under these circumstances, architects have to play an organizing role and even deploy their own social resources to ensure a project's smooth development, and to boost its influence.

Rural revitalization has provided many opportunities for younger architects to carry out independent initiatives. As for me, because I've already gained experience with and developed insights into rural design, I'm more concerned with exploring original practices and testing their scalability—that is, whether or not a successful experience in a specific village can serve as a template to be applied throughout rural China. I hope that in the future, we can publish works

iFLYTEK AI Headquarters Campus

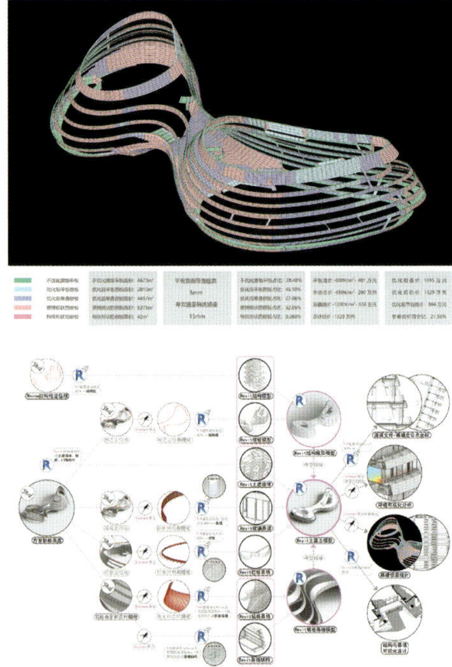

Digital design tool developed for iFLYTEK AI Headquarters Campus

that summarize these experiments, which can then serve as references for the revitalization and development of China's vast countryside.

In addition to your work in the countryside, line+ studio is also designing business parks and company headquarters for several of China's leading high-tech and manufacturing companies. In these projects, how do you combine architectural design with technology and the future of work?

Meng: To an extent, these different types of projects demonstrate line+ studio's open-mindedness. As for the business parks of high-tech and manufacturing companies, we were fortunate to gain some relevant experience in this field, such as with iFLYTEK global headquarters. In this type of project, we always ask ourselves how people will probably work and live in the future. Based on our reflections, we think a business park should be wholly integrated into the city, present a comprehensive vision of the future, and embody a company's spirit. Specifically, our future-oriented design comprises the fusion of artificial and natural elements, as well as ecological considerations, such as energy efficiency, greenery, and the reduction of emissions. Of course, these projects' specific form and systematic design have pushed us to try and streamline our workflow. Last year, line+ studio founded its own technical research center, which is devoted to researching the design and construction of complex architectural forms and low-carbon and prefabricated buildings. We've also tried to create a lateral industrial chain by collaborating with suppliers, even striving to incorporate prefabs into our rural practice. Though, in China, this type of exploration is more common for large state-owned institutions, it's virtually unheard of from a medium-sized private studio like ours.

We've also continually strived to explore new materials and building techniques in our daily operations. We maintain close contact with suppliers and construction firms and invite them to deliver presentations on the latest industry developments.

Wienerberger Brick Installation at Xuhui Binjiang, Shanghai

Rural Nostalgia and Urban Dream exhibition at the Venice Architecture Biennale, 2021

As the level of urbanization in China approaches that of developed countries, Chinese construction is beginning to slow down. In your opinion, what challenges will Chinese architecture face in the future? And what kind of prospects do you envisage for line+ studio?

Meng: China has made massive accomplishments in terms of construction and infrastructure, becoming a global leader in this regard. By comparison, Chinese design has yet to attain a sufficiently powerful global influence. Crafting an architectural language that is at once contemporary and distinctly Chinese is one of the focal concerns for our generation of architects.

Since the founding of line+ studio, we've been "crossing the river by touching the stones" and, slowly but surely, we've formed our own unique position. Within the Chinese context, it would be difficult to find another firm with the same practical approach as us. Given the currently slowing urbanization process in China, the challenge for the future will perhaps be in redefining this position of ours based on emerging trends. We are still contemplating how to continue our development as the paradigm shifts from creating new assets to the continued extraction of value from existing ones. Ultimately, this sense of insecurity will push us to continue experimenting, adjust our methods, and take on new challenges.

In the past few years, in addition to taking part in the 17th Venice Architecture Biennale, line+ studio has also participated in a number of projects overseas. Does the studio intend to develop a more globalized approach in the future?

Meng: I think you'd be hard-pressed to find a Chinese architect who doesn't want to obtain the approval of the international community and expand their practice overseas. But in my opinion, it's perhaps more important to remain level-headed. We'll continue to hone our professionalism and design skills through our work in China, but if the opportunity presents itself, we'll also consider furthering our development overseas.

Dialogue

Building for a Diversity of Lifestyles

Interview with Zhu Peidong

Interviewer: *Mo Wanli*
Date: *August 12, 2022*
Place: *line+ studio office, Hangzhou, Zhejiang Province, China*

Could you begin by summarizing your practical experience? What was the catalyst that steered you and Meng Fanhao to co-found line+ studio?

Zhu: After finishing my bachelor's and master's at Zhejiang University, I took on a teaching role at Zhejiang A & F University. A year later, I began pursuing a PhD in Architecture at Tongji University in Shanghai. During my doctoral studies, I was invited to join gad, and to form my own design team. It was at that point that I started my practical career as an architect. I met my business partner Meng Fanhao during the design for the Zhejiang Conservatory of Music, where I served as one of the project principals at gad. I invited Professors Joan Busquets and Yang Dingliang, who both taught courses for the Harvard Graduate School of Design's (GSD) [United States] major program in Urban Design, to visit Hangzhou and teach a class using the Dongziguan project as a case study. This initiative, as well as our subsequent return visit to GSD, gave Meng and me the chance to get to know one another and discover similarities in our conceptions of architecture, which eventually inspired us to collaborate.

Compared to the previous generation of Chinese architects who typically studied and worked abroad before returning to China to establish their own projects, or who worked for state-owned institutes for several years before finally launching their own studios, your trajectory is quite remarkable. How do you think this unique trajectory has benefited your practical work?

Zhu: Locality and *caogen* are the two terms that sum up my work. Though *caogen* literally means grassroots, I use it as a kind of pun. For me, it means being as tenacious as wild grass, but it also sounds like *caogen*, a term used in the field of architecture that means taking part in design initiatives as a freelancer. My studies coincided with the most rapid phase in China's urbanization and economic growth. From 2007 to 2012, I participated in approximately fifty design competitions; around half of my designs won bids. Maintaining such a high level of productivity trained me to rapidly identify the central requirements of a specific project and to fully incorporate them into a design while considering different practical limitations. It also honed my collaborative and organizational skills.

Bird's-eye view of the Zhejiang Conservatory of Music

Dormitory of the Zhejiang Conservatory of Music

Theater of the Zhejiang Conservatory of Music

While my experiences at this stage were largely conceptual, the more hands-on work I did later with gad trained me to deal with the complicated realities of implementing architectural projects in China. One breakthrough moment in this learning process was the design of the Zhejiang Conservatory of Music. This project was very ambitious and pushed us far outside of our comfort zone. Although gad didn't have much experience with this type of project, after the competition was announced, I nonetheless decided to formulate a design with the aid of five interns. Throughout this process, I coordinated all the work, from the master plan to the building dimensions, and from floor plans to elevation drawings, even cost estimates. To everyone's surprise, our plan won first prize. But winning the competition was just the beginning, for after came the real challenge—elaborating on and implementing the design. Although gad didn't have experience with large-scale campus designs, they were hugely supportive when it came to deploying human resources. I led a team of around 400 members from different fields—architecture, structural engineering, electromechanics, and landscaping—and oversaw the project's progress to ensure it would be completed on time. Throughout the project's construction, I would spend literally half of every workday resolving different problems on site.

Compared to other architects of your generation, your practical experience and background are probably at the forefront of the ongoing urbanization process in China. How do you interpret the influence that this large-scale, rapid city-building movement has had on current Chinese architectural practices? And specifically, those of line+ studio?

Zhu: Again, I refer to the Zhejiang Conservatory of Music. Perhaps it's only in the context of China's rapid urbanization that a young architect could have obtained such an opportunity to hone his or her skills. Although the total built-up area of the campus is around 3,767,400 square feet (350,000 square meters)—close to that of a large exhibition venue—there are far more problems that require resolving and coordinating on a campus project than there is on a single building. First, campuses include various building types, such as libraries, student dormitories, teaching buildings, and theaters. Second, given that the conservatory was to be designated a "top-level" institution, we had to ensure that the design of the concert hall and theater conformed to the highest standards. Finally, as the campus is flanked on one side by Xiang Mountain, its design had to consider

VR density perception experiment by Zhu Peidong

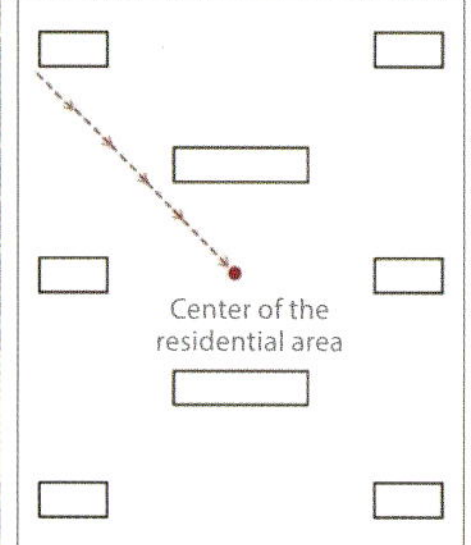

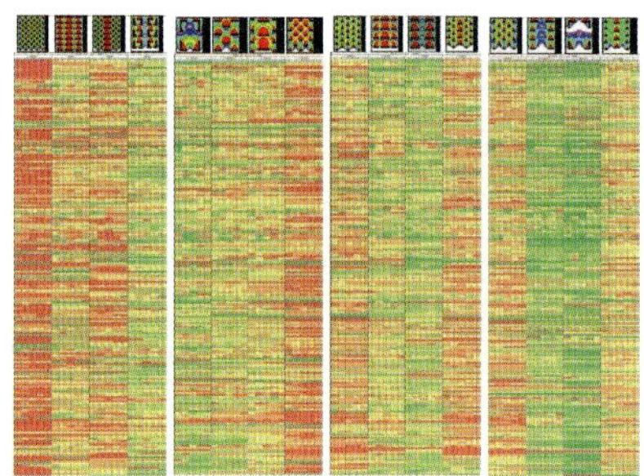

Evaluation results of perceived density under different layouts

Competition for public housing design of Jiangong Community in Shenzhen

Section diagram

the surrounding natural elements, such as the mountain and the adjacent natural river. The second phase in this project—beginning with our design winning the competition in 2012 and ending with the campus opening in 2015—significantly improved my abilities as an architect. The process of turning two-dimensional drawings into three-dimensional buildings not only honed my design skills, more importantly, it taught me to identify problems, deal with complex circumstances, and allocate resources.

As a result, line+ studio's practical work mainly consists of finding solutions to the design problems created by China's complex realities rather than maintaining a singular focus on a specific architectural subject or formal language.

What was your subject of research during your doctoral studies at Tongji University? And what impact did that research have on your design practice?

Zhu: My thesis topic was related to the perception of density. Although we can't see density, as a kind of data, it can reflect the changes in the state and scale of a space, and ultimately exert an influence on people's perceptions. I wanted to see if qualifying and measuring this influence would help determine better design strategies. Overall, my research placed an emphasis on rational data analysis. With the aid of virtual 3D modeling and holographic glasses, we simulated different spatial experiences. We then invited respondents to complete a questionnaire in which they evaluated their psychological state based on their behavior as potential users. Thanks to this scientific approach, we were able to explore the relationship between abstract spatial density and people's genuine experiences.

FOREST Community, San Francisco, United States

Deep Blue project, Hangzhou

That's a fascinating topic that coincides with how Rem Koolhaas describes "density," "bigness," and "speed" as the problems that typically plague contemporary architecture and urban planning. Given how heavily involved you are in the ongoing urbanization process, these problems of "density" or "quantity" must be a central concern for line+ studio. What is the relation between this research and the studio's practice?

Zhu: The primary purpose of my PhD research was to establish a predominantly human perspective. When we discuss architecture, we all too often focus on "things" to the detriment of "people." My study used a psychological assessment to determine how people perceive and respond to the things we architects create, as well as the relation between different environments. This data then served as the basis for a series of design techniques that take into consideration density and users' feelings. Unconsciously, we've applied these techniques in some of line+ studio's projects. For example, I proposed the concept "intensity of natural lighting"—meaning that, even in highly dense built-up environments, spaces can still provide pleasant experiences, so long as they offer a reasonable amount of sunlight. This notion was applied in the Deep Blue project in Hangzhou, and the competition for public housing design of Jiangong Community in Shenzhen.

China's urban and architectural design currently relies upon data regarding the building itself—such as its surface area—to control density, rather than employ a more human-centered approach. When designing FOREST Community in San Francisco [United States], we were introduced to the American method of calculating density according to persons per unit. Why do they apply this method? Because this determines the overall urban planning, supporting facilities, and the allocation of public resources. I consider this way of representing density, which revolves around humans' needs, feelings, and experiences, and which considers the project's place in the community and city, to be an invaluable reference for our work.

Inventronics Tonglu Production Factory (Phase 1), Hangzhou

Inventronics Electric Vehicle Charging Station, Hangzhou

❶

Other than density, scale is another important dimension to consider in urban architectural design. This is particularly evident in your industrial projects.

Zhu: Indeed. In these projects, I attempted to explore the impact of design and environments on users under relatively extreme circumstances. For the Inventronics LED Driver Production Base project in Tonglu, Zhejiang Province, we designed an urban façade spanning 0.6 miles (1 kilometer) in length. This element of the project primarily served to address the factory's functional needs. Each of its six assembly lines is 150 meters long. Of course, we could have divided the building and spread it out over a larger area, but given its location along National Highway 320, we felt that we had been given a novel opportunity to experiment with length. For this extremely long façade, we created a relief in the style of Huang Gongwang's painting *Dwelling in the Fuchun Mountains,* using specially made clay bricks placed on different angles and arranged into different motifs. Similar to traditional Chinese paintings, the façade can be enjoyed from a distance, at mid-range, and up close, providing different visual experiences. Its grandiose scale is on par with that of the highway and also contributes to noise reduction. However, when it came to the choice of building materials, we still opted for red clay bricks to reflect the factory's rural setting.

One of our campus designs also included us experimenting with scale. Currently, when it comes to designing sprawling campuses for China's "super schools," planners often prefer to divide buildings into smaller ones. However, for the Hangzhou International School campus, we adopted the opposite approach, which was a more concentrated layout, where the same buildings simultaneously serve a multitude of functions. At this school, all student year-groups share a central hub. This doesn't mean that the spaced-out "village" approach is unviable. It just means that we need to explore which circumstances it would be the most appropriate for and which ones it wouldn't—where it would be better to turn the school into an organic whole, thus inspiring more uses and opportunities for exchange.

Although conventional architectural education currently emphasizes different forms of continuity between buildings and their urban settings, there are times when either Meng Fanhao or I will adopt strategies to isolate the project from the "bigness" of the city, as in the case of iFLYTEK AI Headquarters Campus, which has just won a construction bid. Our judgment in this regard is based on whether we believe that "bigness" can, in a specific context, benefit the users by contributing to the project's readability or diversity of functions. By "users," I'm referring to not only the people who'll frequent the building as part of their daily routine, but also our clients.

Woven Passage to Cloudy Peaks, Xiayanbei Rural Scenic Area

Twelve Tents Beyond Clouds, Xiayanbei Rural Scenic Area

Rural revitalization currently represents the forefront of architectural practice in China and constitutes one of the main categories of line+ studio's work. How do you interpret rural revitalization, as well as the role that buildings and their architects play throughout this process?

Zhu: Compared to Meng, I have a tad less experience with rural projects, though I have a few in the works that will be finished between the end of this year and the beginning of next. The most significant difference between these projects and urban projects is construction conditions. Rural projects have significantly smaller budgets, with architects taking responsibility for coordinating most of the work. Meng and I both believe that we need to break free of certain stereotypes concerning rural architecture and complete design projects without any preconceptions. In doing so, we've come to realize that when it comes to the design process, the difference between a rural project and an urban one is actually not that great. With rural projects, we face budgetary limitations, unprofessional labor, and a higher risk of unprofessional clients, but our task as architects is to use design to overcome these problems, to realize the full potential of the architecture. Therefore, in these projects, I often opt for more innovative materials with an industrial feel, in the hope that the building will act as a vector of change in the village.

Regarding materials and technology, your current project, Qiantang River Museum, in Hangzhou, is a good example.

Zhu: In Qiantang River Museum, we've attempted to use material and technical innovation as a means of expressing additional layers of cultural significance. Other than that, we're also trying to gradually develop our own workflow. During the unregulated phase of China's rapid urbanization, our work was a lot more flexible and variable. However, as a more professionalized market has currently been taking shape and the rate of development slows, we have been attempting to create a regular workflow: from carrying out investigations to formulating a design; to creating drawings and plans; and finally, to producing different-scaled models and mock-ups. Due to its complexity and scale, Qiantang River Museum allowed us to put this workflow to the test.

Hangzhou Qiantang River Museum under construction

Zhu Peidong at the mock-up site of the Qiantang River Museum

Hangzhou Qiantang River Museum

Judging from your work in recent years, line+ studio seems to be going down an increasingly globalized path. Is this in keeping with your expectations for the studio's future development? What is the greatest challenge when it comes to implementing architectural projects in different cultural contexts? And is the experience the studio has accumulated—courtesy of the insights brought on by China's urbanization—contributed to your projects abroad, like the ones in the US, such as Universal Studios in Los Angeles and FOREST Community in San Francisco?

Zhu: When working in unfamiliar cultural contexts, people tend to be at once excited and afraid. I think that the trend of globalized development is an opportunity for this generation of Chinese architects to lead a transition from "Chinese products" to "Chinese designs." Relating to a specific cultural context requires an open, tolerant mind, as well as a general understanding of foreign cultures. I feel that when an opportunity arises, we need to embrace it. The project's owner in San Francisco had collaborated with us in the past, and it's because he approved of our design skills that he invited us to participate in the design competition for FOREST Community. By that time, several major American design firms had already been hard at work on their submission for the competition. We only had around twenty days to the deadline. However, by completely redefining the project around the concept of a "park," we were able to win the client's approval. Another reason why our design was chosen was because it took into consideration the impact of the pandemic on the construction supply chain. I think that both our redefinition of the project and our global vision of the supply chain were the fruit of our experiences in China. Of course, the first time we worked on a project abroad, we encountered several legal and organizational challenges, which required us to become more familiar with our collaborative partners and the local design codes.

When you say "insights"—that is perhaps not the right word—we feel that there are three differences between Chinese and American architects. The first is that the latter tend to be more focused on their field of expertise, while the former—perhaps due to exposure—on more complex problems; they demonstrate greater lateral thinking and assume larger roles in the implementation. The second is efficiency. Even though we consciously slowed down the pace of our work, our collaborative partners were still struck by our team's speed and progress. The final difference is mental dexterity. In the US, because there's an abundance of well-established, professional agencies to collaborate with, architects can leave details such as curtain-walls, structures, or lighting in the reliable hands of these partners, while they focus on the building itself. The fact that Chinese architects are less specialized than their American counterparts, perhaps, helps us to think outside the box.

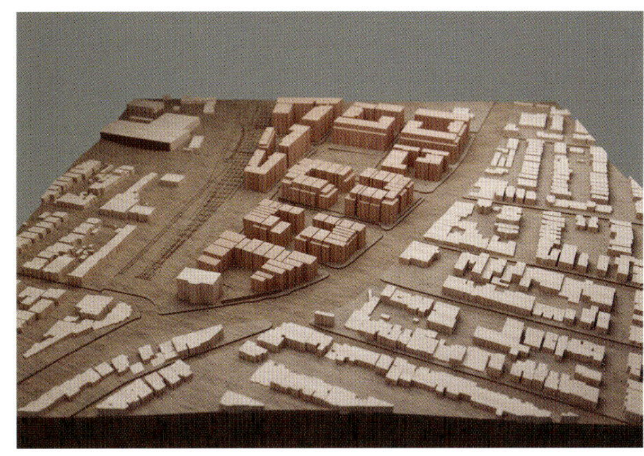

Model of FOREST Community, San Francisco

Rendering of FOREST Community

Rendering of FOREST Community

As the level of urbanization in China approaches that of developed countries, Chinese construction is beginning to slow down. In your opinion, what challenges will Chinese architecture face in the future? And what kind of prospects do you envisage for line+ studio?

Zhu: When we founded line+ studio, Meng and I agreed that, in the context of China's lightning-speed urbanization, it was important to strike a balance between quality and quantity. As construction slows as we move into the future, I believe that we'll move from a period of large-scale construction to one that places a greater emphasis on diversity and personality. In my opinion, cities should be highly diverse, like rainforests. On many occasions in the past, urban planners sought uniformity above all else—perhaps a necessity of large-scale construction. But in the future, we believe that buildings can't just be constructed *en masse*; they must be the result of a proper design process that serves to maintain a diversity of lifestyles.

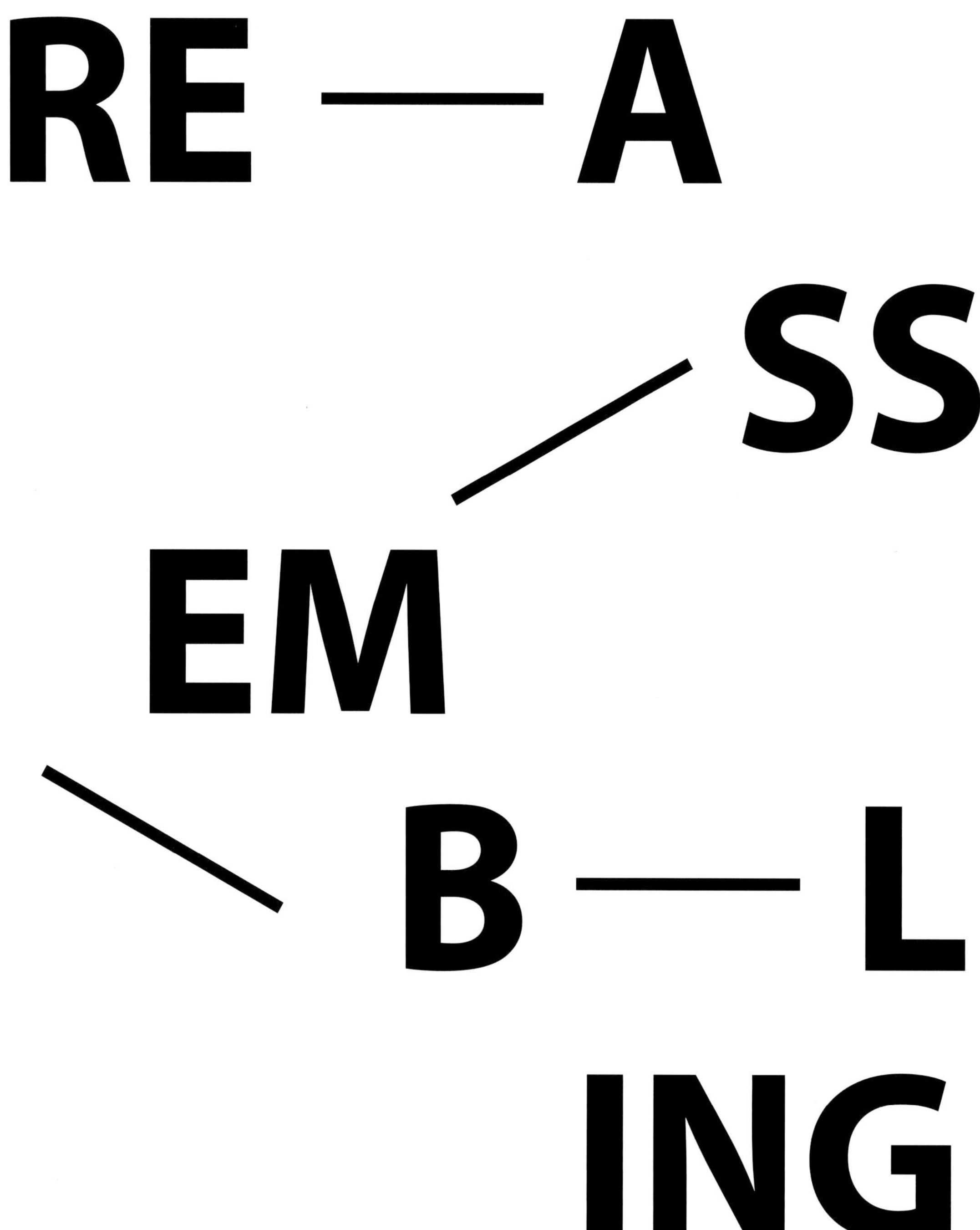
RE — A
SS
EM
B — L
ING

Empowering the Countryside

The world's population today lives in urban areas. This figure is expected to increase to 66 percent by 2050. Yet, these numbers blur the fact that the other half of the population is still living in the countryside. While we are busy focusing on the challenges and opportunities brought on by rapid urbanization and developing metropolitan areas, we should not overlook the tremendous changes taking over countrysides on a global scale.

China is no exception. Along with the rapid urbanization of the country following the reform and opening up policy, the countryside became increasingly dysfunctional. The imbalance between urban and rural development has prevented the revitalization of rural resources and the accelerated population movement between urban and rural areas has hollowed out villages one after another. Changes in production and lifestyle have also resulted in the gradual disappearing of the rural landscape of the past. Confronted with these massive and diverse challenges, what role can architecture play to stimulate changes?

In 2017, the 19th CPC (Communist Part of China) National Congress report put forth a rural revitalization strategy, which makes rural development an issue of concern for the whole society on the policy level. line+ studio believes that in the face of the many challenges of rural development, architecture is no longer an autonomous object; it needs to be regarded as a medium in its social relationship network. It is not just about the creation of a unique space, it is about searching for a way to activate existing resources and introducing new opportunities through the empowering role of space. Of the five projects included in this chapter, some constitute "acupuncture points" to stimulate the village economy by providing unique spatial experiences; some achieve the rebirth of traditional dwellings through newly added structures; and some explore new spatial patterns that are integrated with the rural landscape. However, *all* are committed to creating new cultural, economic, and social values for the countryside.

01

Re-assembling

Tai'an Dongximen Village Revitalization

Architecture as Agent

The revitalization of Dongximen Village brought about a reorganization of resources through architecture, in which demands from different stakeholders had to be met.

Location: Dongximen Village, Tai'an, Shandong Province, China
Design firm: line+ studio
Principal architect: Meng Fanhao
Architecture design team: Tao Tao, Zhu Min, Xu Hao, Zhang Erjia, Huang Guangwei, Yuan Dong, Li Sanjian, Xie Yuting, Hao Jun, Xu Tianqu, Tu Dan
Interior design team: Zhu Jun, Jin Xin, Deng Hao, Zhang Sisi, Qiu Limin, Hu Jinwei, Zhou Xinyi, Zhang Ning, Wang Lijie
Landscape design team: Li Shangyang, Jin Jianbo, Chi Xiaomei, Su Chenjuan
Area: renovation—32,545 square feet (3,023 square meters); study and amenity—6,135 square feet (570 square meters)
Design period: February 2019–August 2019
Construction period: May 2019–September 2020
Client: Lushang Pusu (Tai'an) Cultural Tourism Development Co. Ltd
Photography: zystudio, Pan Jie, Jin Xiaowen
Model photography: Sun Lei

Site plan

Rural Revitalization in the Age of New Media

Mount Tai, one the Five Great Mountains of China, has carried great cultural significance since historical times. "Leaning against a cliff, I overlook all eight directions. All my eyes can see is calmness." In the words of the famous Chinese poet Li Bai, Mount Tai exhales the breath of the world and offers the most beautiful scenery on earth. Located at the foot of the Peak of the Nine Maidens, or Jiunüfeng in Chinese (Jiunvfeng), Dongximen Village is surrounded by mountains on all sides. Adjacent to the Shenlong Canyon, this village administrated by Tai'an City (Shandong Province) offers panoramic views of the gorge and the mountain peaks in the distance. Ironically, this magnificent natural scenery also hampered the development of Dongximen Village. Its isolation and the barrenness of the land caused the village to gradually lose touch with general economic progress. The young people of the village had left to work in the city, and only the elderly remained, resulting in a "hollowing-out" rural community—a growing phenomenon that China faces. This "hollowing-out" further aggravated the village's decay. There are dozens of villages in the Jiunvfeng area that share the same fate, but Dongximen Village was the most remotely located; and it also faced the greatest challenges to its development.

In recent years, the countryside has become the focal point for Chinese architectural practice. In 2017, the government's rural rejuvenation strategy had proposed in the 19th CPC National Congress report that rural development had become an issue of concern for all of society, starting with the top levels of government. That same year, a housing project in Dongziguan, Zhejiang Province—Dongziguan Affordable Housing—led by Meng Fanhao during his time at gad as the project principals, had gained popularity fast and achieved more than 1 billion clicks on social media platforms Wechat and Xiaohongshu as word spread online. The white-walled courtyard-style farmhouses evoked memories of a typical Jiangnan village, and the sustained media attention quickly turned Dongziguan Village into a popular destination. It not only prompted a return of young people who had previously left the village, but also attracted new inhabitants seeking to start businesses. The moment the abandoned village had been revived through the power of construction/buildings, line+ studio realized that in the Digital Age, architecture could act as a catalyst for the creation of value beyond its proper space.

In October 2018, the Shandong Lushang group had come to Zhejiang to inspect a series of other rural projects of line+ studio in Hangzhou, Songyang, and Moganshan. After, they commissioned the studio for a rural rejuvenation project in Tai'an, Shandong Province. One month later, the team arrived in Tai'an to inspect the site. The nineteen villages at the foot of Jiunvfeng were linked

Aerial view of Jiunvfeng Study and Jinuvfeng Bubble Pool

only by a winding, rugged mountain road. These villages were not only severely hollowed out, but also scattered. Faced with these challenges, line+ studio fast realized the importance of the project and determined how to best navigate it, guided by lessons from their past experiences. Based on their suggestion, the most remote village, Dongximen Village, eventually became the focal point for the overall rejuvenation of the villages.

Dongximen Village was a typical mountain village with dense vegetation and a small river running through it. If you were to climb to the nearby peak, you would be treated to spectacular views, and can even see Mount Tai in the distance. The project site was located in an abandoned area of the village—sixteen dilapidated stone houses, some remaining stone walls, and a few farm buildings that had formerly been used as pigpens formed the initial context for the project. Due to the constraints of the land-use plan, the village didn't allow for an extension of the construction area, so the design scope was limited to the sites of the existing houses, prompting the questions: How can the remaining architectural structure stimulate the renewal of the village? And how can we deliver new growth potential for the sustainable development of the village?

To get around the many challenges of the project, line+ studio proposed a two-pronged design strategy. The first was through needle-like renovations: while maintaining the boundaries of the existing lots, the revitalization of the old village was achieved by taking the spatial stimulation of the surviving buildings and the ecological restoration of the environment as entry points. Second, visually expressive architecture was used as a medium to create media interest that could draw in visitors. This two-pronged strategy would jointly drive the overall development of Dongximen Village through the promotion of tourism.

Location has often been a constraint on rural development in the past, however, the dissemination prowess of the internet has opened up the possibility of overcoming this limitation. Despite its benefits, this new trend prompts the fraternity to question how architecture and architects should respond to it. In the Dongximen Village renewal project, line+ studio sought to go beyond traditional architectural design—combining it with the specific social environment and policies; integrating resources from all levels; establishing a workflow from planning and design to construction, operation, and communication; and developing a model of innovation with design as the motor. In this way, architects become the node and link between various sectors, and evolve from "creators of space" to "enablers of space."

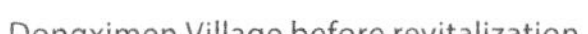

Dongximen Village before revitalization

Abandoned houses in the village

The Renewal of the Village

With regards to the remaining stone houses and walls in Dongximen Village, line+ studio first carefully mapped and sorted through them, identifying and preserving the better maintained parts, while the walls that could not be retained were dismantled and reused as building materials. Just as the stones had undergone changes over time, they became an important foundation for "anchoring" the new buildings.

Stone buildings tend to have heavy walls and good insulation, but they also have the disadvantages of being costly, less waterproof, and less resistant to earthquakes. Therefore it became a priority for line+ studio to design stone buildings that met the needs of contemporary life based on the original materials and building form. Adding blockwork on the inside of the rubble walls, with insulation, waterproofing, and protective layers between them enabled the traditional local stone wall masonry to finally satisfy contemporary usage requirements. This new structure has been inserted into the old rubble wall in the form of a steel frame. After considering the on-site construction conditions, line+ studio opted for the most commonly used I-beams as the decidedly appropriate material. The beams and columns are made of 7.9-by-7.9-inch (200-by-200-millimeter) I-beams, while the purlins are made of 39-by-5.8-inch (100-by-148-millimeter) I-beams. Rigid joints which provide greater structural strength are used in between the main frames and the purlins are lap-jointed to the main frames. This facilitated construction while paying homage to traditional Chinese wood frames.

This frame system is flexible enough to respond to the complex site characteristics of the old houses by applying linear, L-shaped and U-shaped layouts as needed. The small-scale frames form the corridors, while the large-scale frames became rooms. In a sense, this way of generating units from basic frames, and then expanding those units into a whole, is analogous to the way traditional settlements are composed.

Ground-floor plan

1. Pavilion
2. Reception/café
3. Restaurant
4. Multifunction room
5. Guestroom with a children's space
6. Guestroom
7. Bridge
8. Parking lot
9. Jiunvfeng Study
10. Jiunvfeng Bubble Pool

Ground-floor plan of courtyards No. 1 to No. 12
(stone walls that were retained are highlighted in red)

Courtyards No. 1, 2 and 4:
The existing structures were newly built stone houses. The design preserves part of their rubble walls and organized the relationship between the buildings and the site. Courtyard No. 1 is formed around a tree, while courtyards No. 2 and No. 4 form an L-shape.

Courtyard No. 3:
On the site stood a few small auxiliary stone houses which were used for storage and production in the past. The design utilizes the existing rubble masses and connects them with glass boxes. Each of the stone boxes hosts a bathroom, bedroom, and other facilities, while the glass box serves as a shared space for children to play in.

Courtyard No. 5:
The existing building had two parts arranged parallel to each other, running north to south. The south side hosted a new elongated stone house built by the farmers, but it was too long. The design breaks up the existing volume and divides it into two parts. The building on the west side retains its original linear layout, forming two guestrooms. On the east side, a vertical volume was inserted in line with the topography, to create a public space on the ground floor that serves the guestrooms. Additionally, large steps were set up inside according to the terrain, to form a multilayered and multifunctional interior space.

Courtyard No. 6:
The plot is located close to the main road leading up the hill, so it was decided that it would function as a gathering space. Considering its different purpose, and based on metal plates as the main material, the design concept of "folding" was adopted to form a continuous entity of walls, roofs, and railings. It has also been blended with the steps to resolve the height difference of the site, giving the whole building exterior a light origami look.

Courtyard No.12

Courtyards No. 7, 8 and 9:

The existing buildings were all old residential houses with an enclosed layout. The new buildings follow their architectural texture and spatial form, enclosing a central courtyard by adding and subtracting volumes from the original spatial logic. These courtyard spaces integrate indoor and outdoor areas and changes in elevation. The ancient trees on the site of courtyard No. 8 were also left untouched. The structural framework has been flexibly expanded around it, thus creating a courtyard under the shade of a tree, and a multifunctional internal space.

Courtyard No. 10:

The existing building had an L-shaped layout. The design follows the original spatial pattern and adopts an L-shape similar to that of courtyard No. 5 to envelop a courtyard. The entrance ascends along with the terrain, forming an outdoor platform rising above the slope, forming a dialogue with the distant mountains.

Courtyard No. 11:

The existing buildings were constructed in recent years, with a north–south alignment and a 10-foot (3-meter) height difference between the front and back rows. The design preserves the spatial layout of the original buildings and resolves the height difference between the front and rear buildings. The partial enlargement of the roof provides a new, shared public space and roof terrace.

Courtyard No. 12:

The plot is located in the westernmost area of the project site. Given its relative isolation, the design turned it into a standalone guesthouse. The existing structure was an old residential building that had fallen into a state of disrepair. The new building retains the old rubble walls and inserts a two-story steel structure with a gable roof. The sloping roof is covered with simple, flat cement tiles. Courtyard No. 12 presents itself as a lighter structure with a large L-shaped gray space overhanging the second floor, which blends in with the surrounding native trees to converse with nature.

Courtyard No. 6

Courtyard No. 1

Entrance of courtyard No. 3

Courtyard No. 8

Restaurant

1. Abandoned houses before renovation
2. Abandoned houses after renovation

In addition to this sequence of mainly residential courtyard-centered spaces, line+ studio also renovated and updated the old pigpen and three private houses, inserting new architectural functions one by one—a reception area, café, and a restaurant.

The abandoned pigpen is separated from the planned parking lot by a stream, and provides good accessibility, thus serving as a reception area for the new buildings. Based on the site, the light steel structure gives life to a new space, with a large-scale pitched roof and a permeable spatial interface, which also emphasize the invisibility of the building volume among the natural environment, and the fluidity between the indoor and outdoor spaces. Environmentally friendly and natural burnt cedar shingles have been elegantly arranged on the roof, echoing the surrounding lush vegetation. The other two residential buildings situated in the middle of the hill are backed by mountains and provide a panoramic view. A prefabricated light steel structure transforms them into a restaurant. The rubble walls and glass curtain-walls open up to different views of the landscape, dissolving the building into the mountain scenery to provide an immersive dining experience.

Between the courtyards and the new buildings, a meandering walkway and landscape experience has been created. line+ studio aimed to incorporate the rich and varied natural environment into the design of the footpaths, enhancing the perception of the settlement and the environment through the motion of the body. Coming from the outside, visitors walk through scattered forests along wooden bridges and stone steps; they climb, look up, turn, and finally ascend to the top, to catch a glimpse of the natural wilderness to the north, forming a narrative experience from the beginning to the end; from low to high, and high to low. A large number of stones showing traces of the old village have been reused to pave stone paths, steps, and low walls, continuing to chronicle the growth of the new village. When it came to plant selection, the integrity of the forest and a diversity of plants were achieved by replanting Chinese hackberry, Chinese photinia, and Chinese fountain grass, to complement the large native trees on the site.

View toward the reception/café

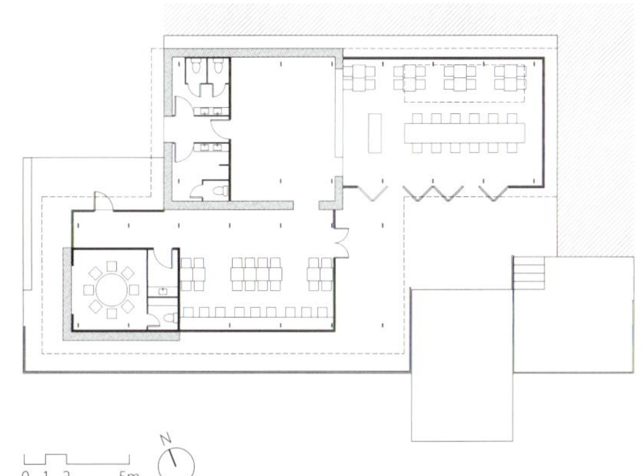

Restaurant—ground-floor plan

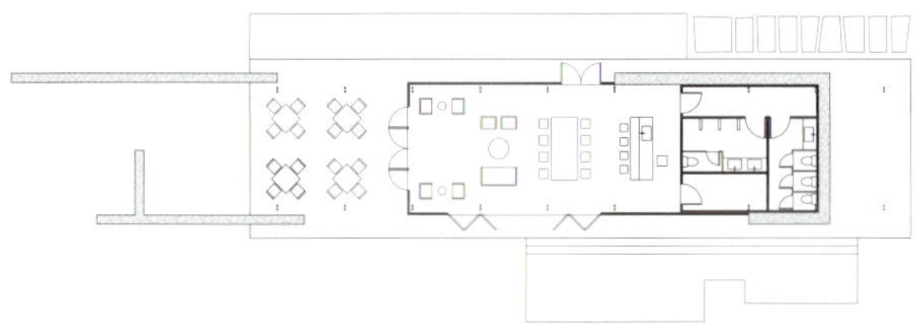

Reception/café—ground-floor plan

1. The abandoned pigpen before renovation
2. The pigpen after renovation

Aerial view of Jiunvfeng Study

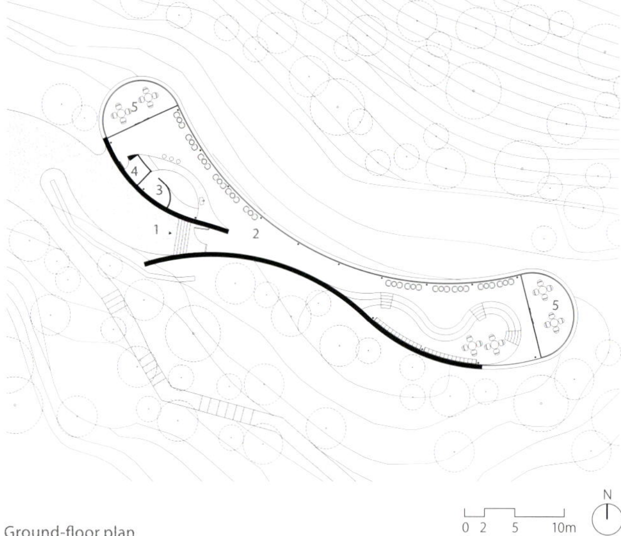

Ground-floor plan

1. Entrance
2. Book bar
3. Counter
4. Restroom
5. Balcony

Jiunvfeng Study

As a building designed to attract media attention, Jiunvfeng Study on Mount Tai is located on the top of a scenic mountain ridge. It can be easily spotted on the drive up the sloping mountain road, with the mountains to its east and the village to its rear. The main idea for the design of the Jiunvfeng Study was to create a highly distinctive "white space" that sits on the top of the exposed rugged mountain ridge in the north.

The building's structure is divided into three parts from top to bottom: a white "cloud," a transparent glass center, and a heavy rubble-wall base. To the north, it overlooks a permeable interface of canyons and peaks. The long and narrow path at the entrance connects the café and reading areas at either end of the building, blurring the boundary between the structure and the natural landscape to give visitors the illusion of being on top of a mountain forest. A structural system of light steel and membranes was chosen for the main building, allowing the design to follow the profile of the mountain range, acquiring a seemingly weightless shape.

The entrance of the building lies on the south side, toward the village. Its walls are made of local rubble that is heavy and solid, seemingly merging with the mountain; the curved interface guides visitors inside. As they turn, panoramic views of the canyon and the mountains become visible through glass panes that seem to extend limitlessly, in a space formed by a series of arched, light steel joists of gradually changing dimensions. The entrance is placed in such a way as to indicate the general orientation of the building in relation to the site. The transparent glass interface not only allows the external landscape to enter the space, but it also conceals the physical structure hoisting the roof. From afar, Jiunvfeng Study appears like a cloud resting gently on top of the mountain rocks.

Curved glass curtain-wall toward the mountains

Entrance to the Jiunvfeng Study

Jiunvfeng Study interior

The construction of the study began in April 2019 and was completed in September 2019. During the construction process, the precise and fast assembly of the prefabricated light steel construction modules ensured a timely completion.

Foundation:
In order to achieve the desired floating effect, the foundation was raised slightly higher than the surrounding ground. After surveying the terrain, lighting conditions, and landscape features at the site, it was found that the height and density of the canopy of the surrounding vegetation directly affected the positioning of the foundation and the viewing height of the building. Therefore, the foundation height was readjusted to 15.7 inches (400 millimeters).

Main structure:
The prefabricated modular components guaranteed the accuracy of construction. Steel columns that are 5.9 inches (150 millimeters) thick support a curved girder, on top of which twenty-eight pairs of arched double joists have been erected. This sequence of gradually changing, densely arranged arched joists allows for the smooth application of the interior and exterior membranes.

Interior and exterior membranes:
Wire mesh is attached in between the twenty-eight pairs of arched joists, on top of which evenly laid out tin foil reflects the light from LED strips, while encapsulated insulation is laid and fixed above the tin foil. Fixed to the lower side of the joists, the inner membrane is made of a translucent fabric, which is carefully suspended and tensioned with metal clasps.

Rubble walls:
The south entrance and wall façade are built with local rubble and tied together with small steel columns. For this, the team selected appropriately sized colored stones from the site and guided the local construction team in completing the masonry work.

Lighting and interior design:
LED light strips are arranged longitudinally above the lower joists. In order to achieve a uniform lighting effect on a large area of the interior membrane, several experiments with different arrangements and illumination levels, as well as different intervals of the LED light strips, were carried out on-site.

Exploded axonometric diagram

1. Outer membrane surface: Valmex Mehgies 1,050 g/m^2

2. Outer keel: 80x80x2.5mm square tube frame
   Insulation cotton encapsulation
   Stretched steel wire mesh
   Tin foil padding

3. Inner keel: 80x80x2.5mm square tube frame
   LED light strip

4. White frosted lightbox membrane
   Silver strip for lightbox membrane

5. 60mm cast-in-site terrazzo floor
   40mm floor heating layer
   30mm insulation layer
   Waterproof layer
   20mm cement mortar leveling layer
   Steel-mixed structure layer

6. Local ashlar masonry
   Steel column
   30mm insulation layer
   Half-brick wall
   Leveling layer
   White texture painting

7. 12+12mm curved surface ultra-white laminated glass
   D100 steel column sprayed with white fluorocarbon

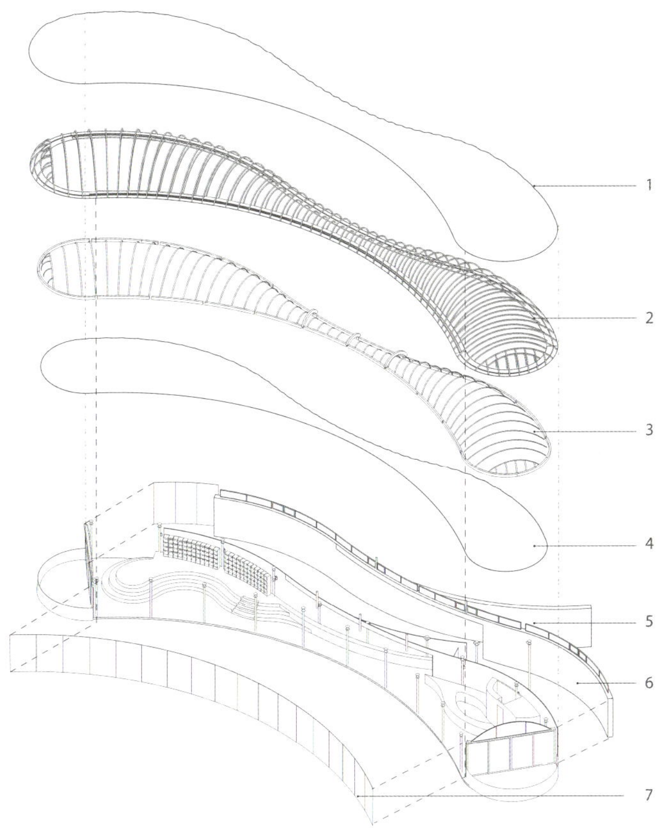

Membrane roof

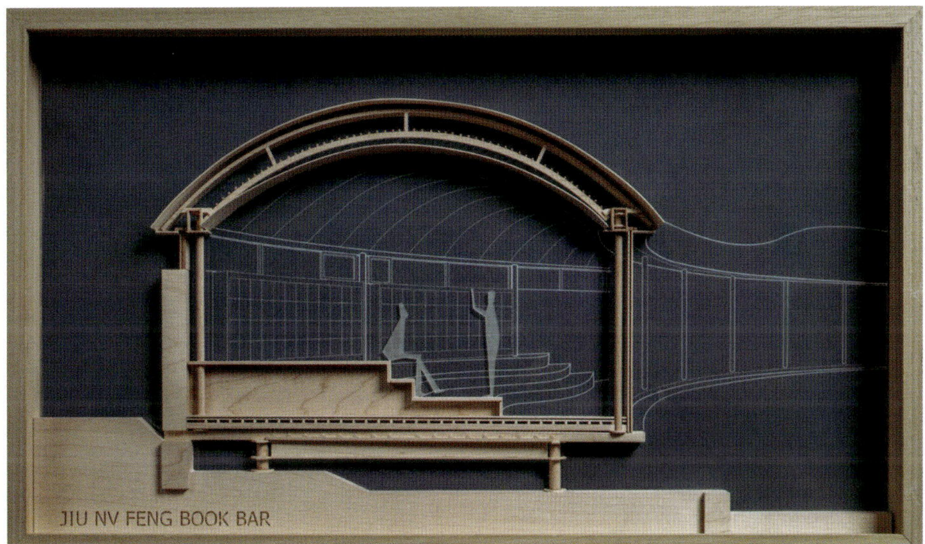

Section model

Aerial view of Jiunvfeng Bubble Pool

Jiunvfeng Bubble Pool

Like Jiunvfeng Study, Jinuvfeng Bubble Pool also serves to attract visitors. If the study is a "cloud" located at the top of the mountain, then the Bubble Pool and its supporting facilities are like shells scattered on the hillside of the village, echoing the vast and magnificent forest scenery. As one walks through the entrance of the village, past the guesthouses arranged along the hillside, and up the path made of local stones, the pure white Bubble Pool slowly emerges from the mountain's vegetation.

The Bubble Pool and its supporting facilities are divided into three areas: dressing rooms, sea-bathing section, and a fitness area, which make up three building volumes. To the west sits the semi-outdoor sea-bath. To ensure the flow and permeability of the pool building, it was essential to create an unspoiled space without pillars and visual obstructions. The pure white roof thus rises from the ground in an open and airy shape with a height of 32.8 feet (10 meters), and protrudes toward the distant mountains. Sheltering the pool area within, it displays a "rising" posture to maximize the landscape views for visitors relaxing in the water. On the east side lies the indoor area serving the pool, characterized by a smaller, more restrained arch shape. It hosts the reception, dressing rooms, showers, and a small sauna. To the south, in the third volume, is the fitness studio, which faces the village and the foot of the mountain; enclosed in the shell, yet still partially visible because of its design character, it draws curious gazes and invites people to enter to discover what lies within. From a distance, Jiunvfeng Bubble Pool looks like precious shells lost in Mount Tai's sea of clouds. The spaces enclosed by the three curved surfaces incorporate the local landscape and follow the topography of the mountain, establishing a balanced connection between nature and the village.

Shell-like space

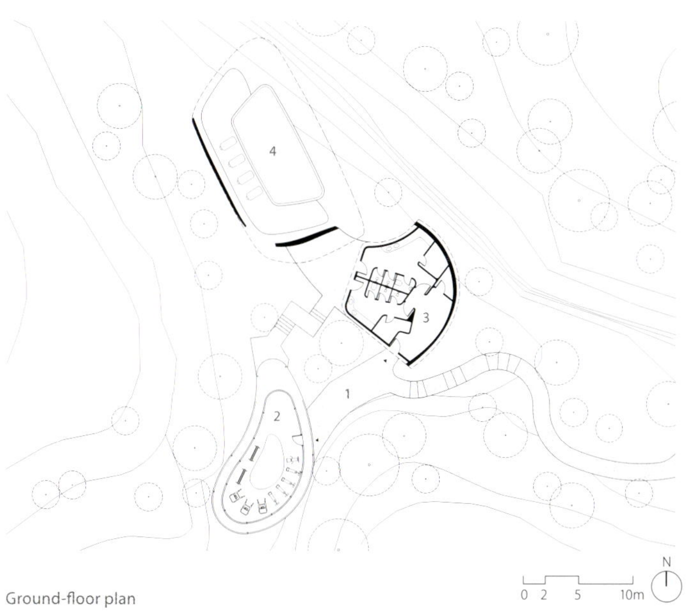

Ground-floor plan

1. Entrance
2. Gym
3. Dressing room
4. Pool

Entrance to the gym

View toward the mountains

The construction of the Bubble Pool took into account the purity and simplicity of the space, balancing the relationship between the building, the landscape, and the interior, while simplifying the structure and materials as much as possible.

Frame:
Overhanging the pool by 32.8 feet (10 meters), the roof is made of prefabricated curved steel joists. With the help of precise modeling and calculation, the vertical and horizontal joists meet high in the air, while being firmly fixed on the foundation, making the structure durable and easy to install.

Surface:
After the main frame of the building made of steel joists was built, an external insulation layer was added and then covered with a stainless-steel surface, combining high plasticity, toughness, and mechanical strength. Through highly accurate joints and meticulous polishing, a smooth and seamless appearance is achieved, providing the basis for the free-flowing form.

Finishing:
A coherent metallic-white spray paint for the interior and exterior of the building ensures the integrity of the building. Combined with large floor-to-ceiling glass walls and highly reflective glass, a pure and transparent look and feel is created.

Pool

Structure detail

1. Diagonal brace PD89mm×4mm

2. I-beam steel
148mm×100mm×6mm×9mm

3. Square tube frame
250mm×250mm×16mm

4. Steel structure foundation + embedded parts

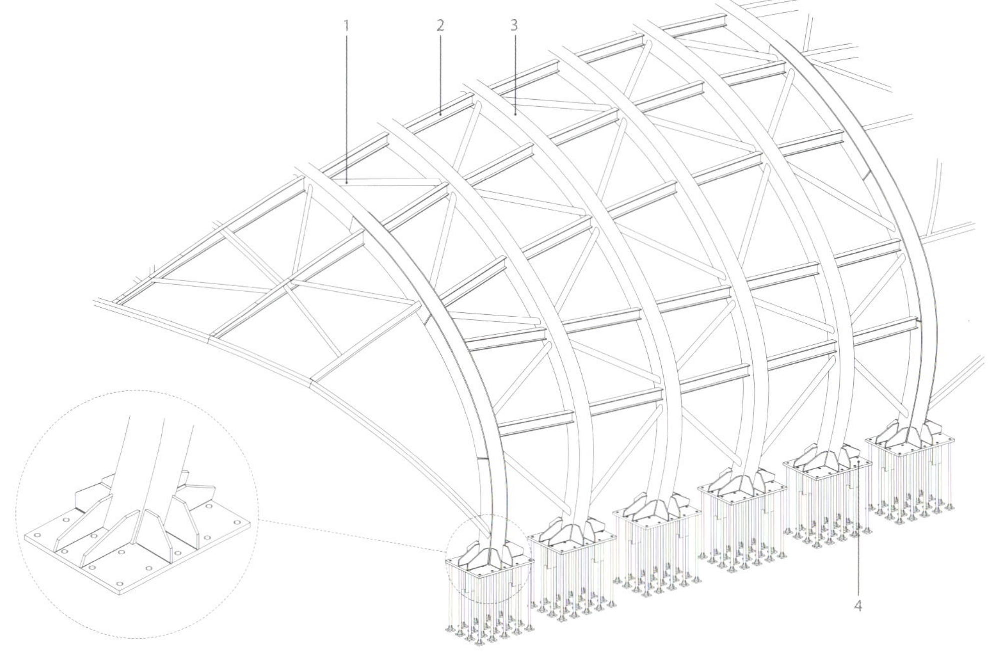

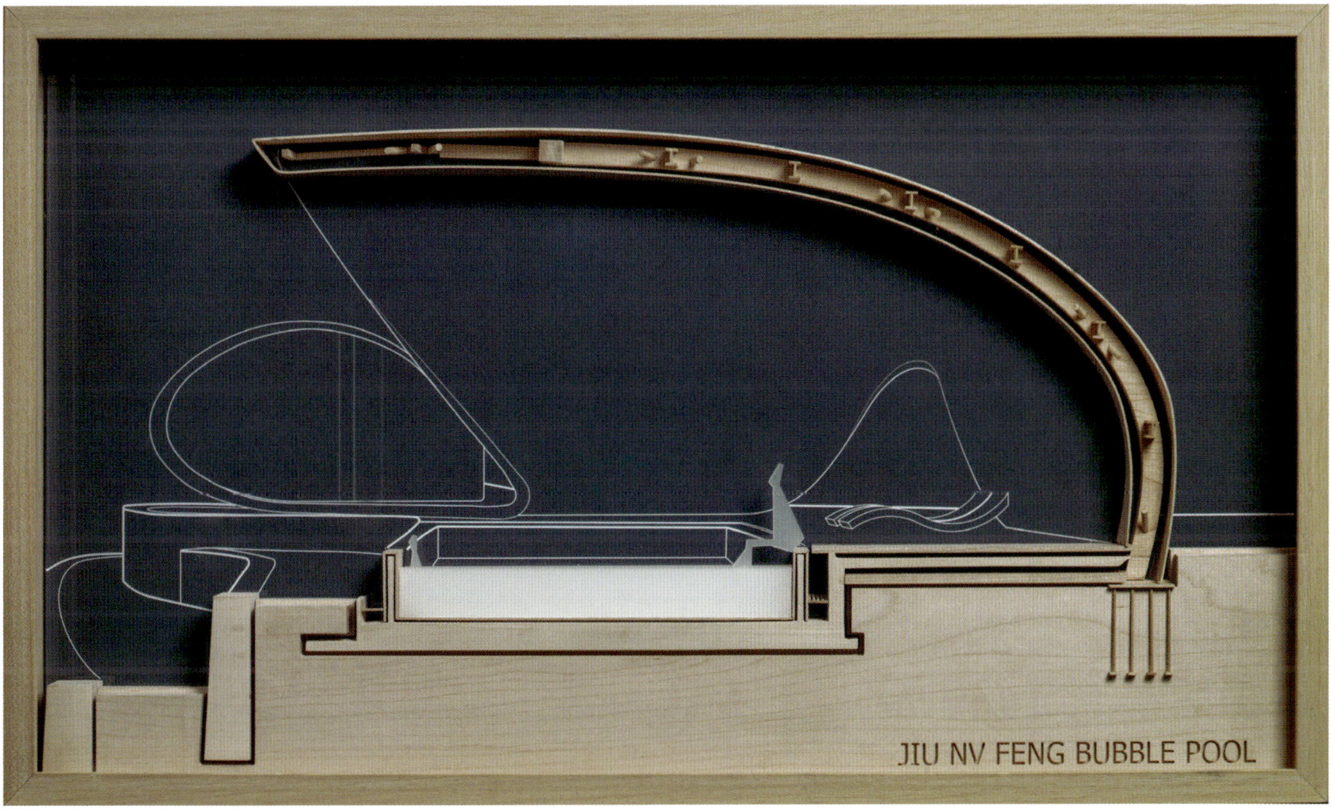

JIU NV FENG BUBBLE POOL

Section model

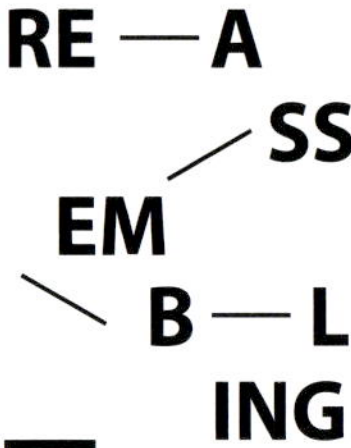

Architecture as Agent

When the whole project went into operation in October 2020, the Jiunvfeng Study and Bubble Pool quickly became a popular photo destination, thanks to the internet, just as the team had envisioned. During the Chinese autumn holiday season, the project as a whole generated a revenue of more than 1 million yuan (US$153,000), which indirectly benefited local businesses as tourists flocked to the area. As a typical rural rejuvenation project, in which a focal point drives the overall development—while being jointly supported by the local government and state-level funds—the revitalization and modernization of Dongximen Village achieved a reorganization of resources through architecture. In this process, demands from different stakeholders had to be met: the government sought to explore a model for rural rejuvenation, the financiers sought to maximize the return on their investment, and the villagers sought to improve their quality of life and increase their income. In turn, the architects not only had to focus on their own disciplinary expertise, such as village types and construction techniques, but also acted as mediators to maximize the allocation of resources and benefit all parties involved.

学习强国
xuexi.cn
中共中央宣传部主管
梦想从学习开始，
事业从实践起步。
学习强国 >> 微视频类
九女峰的故事
CGTN
FARMERS' HARVEST FESTIVAL
Fields of Hope
Integrated model of culture, tourism, green development boost rural vitalization
CCTV 13
山东泰安
深山书房 让乡村有了“诗和远方”

Songyang Stray Birds Art Hotel

Updating the Rural

The ultimate purpose of protecting traditional, historical, and cultural villages lies in improving the chance for development. Therefore the development of villages can't only rely on the natural environment and traditional culture. It also requires the introduction of a range of outside resources.

The structure preserves the original architectural style

Strategies in Response to Constraints

The existing houses are a typical example of the mountain dwellings in southern Zhejiang Province—built with rammed-earth on three sides and incorporating a rough-stone retaining wall on the mountain-facing side, while its roof sits on a traditional timber framework. The structure that was to be converted into a guesthouse had lost its original function as a private residence and became one of the town's construction projects, but the shape of the building still needed to reflect the traditional culture of Chenjiapu. To line+ studio, the challenges in retaining yet transforming this traditional house were in incorporating modern standards as well as making it suitable for modern lifestyles.

To address this challenge, line+ studio began by thoroughly researching the construction systems of local vernacular settlements. This research focused on material ratios, construction techniques, plot creation, and adaptations to the local environment and climate. The team visited local artisans to learn traditional techniques, studied the characteristics of materials, and consulted experts in modern rammed-earth techniques to optimize material properties and improve technical processes. By synthesizing this information, the team established a solid understanding of the local materials and methods, which became the foundation for renovation designs that maintained the village's characteristics.

Another challenge that came up during the project was materials transportation. Vehicles could only reach the entrance of Chenjiapu Village, which meant that large machines could not be used during construction. Although the project site was just a 984-foot (300-meter) walk away from the entrance, the village road was winding and the stone steps were rugged; plus, at the narrowest point of the path, only one person could pass at a time. In order to tackle the severe construction conditions, the design adopted a new prefabricated light steel structure system, which was suited to the transportation constraints of the site.

The structural beams are modular posts with a cross-section of 7.9 by 3.5 inches (200 by 90 millimeters), made of two C-shaped bars with a wall thickness of 0.1 inch (2.5 millimeters), which are formed through cold rolling. These bars were bolted together without welding. Reducing the size of the structural units solved the transportation problem, while the high degree of prefabrication and the joining methods of different elements facilitated on-site construction and installation.

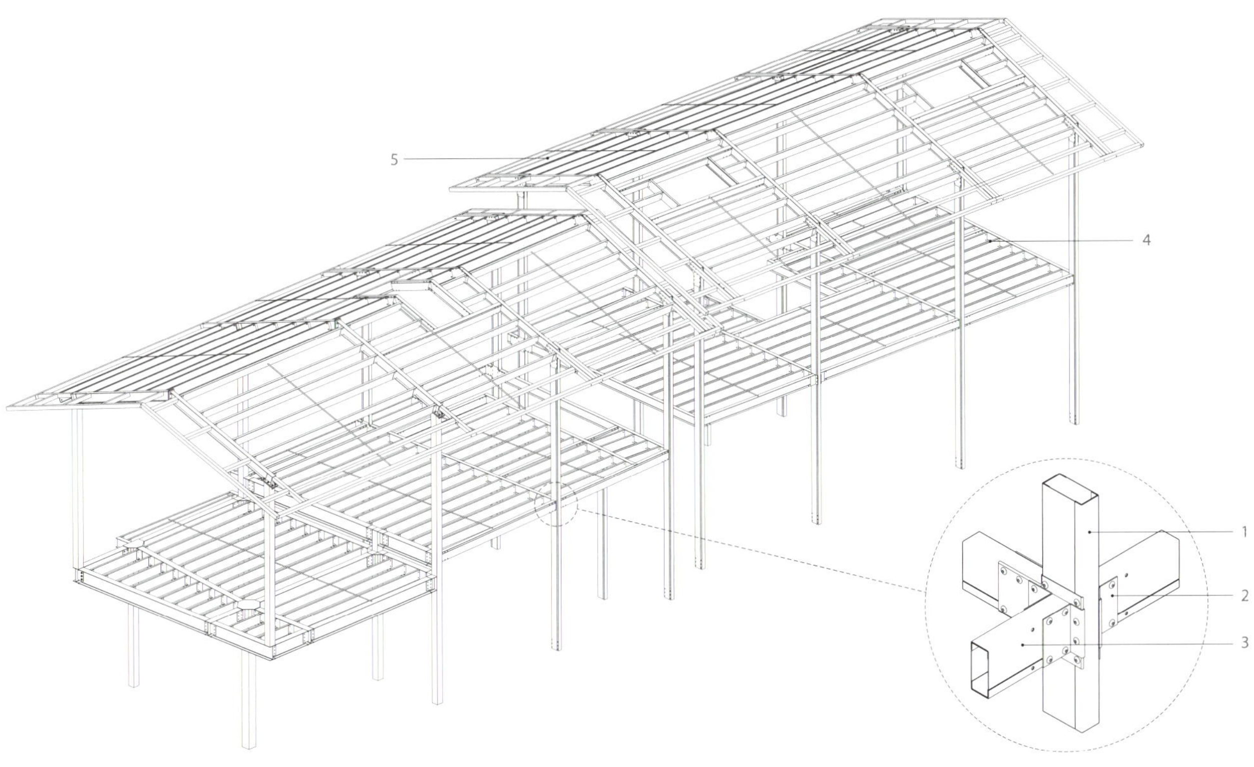

Structural system axonometric diagram

1. 200mm×90mm×35mm steel columns
2. Connectors
3. 200mm×90mm×35mm steel beam
4. 200mm×45mm×15mm floor C-shaped purlin
5. 200mm×45mm×15mm roof C-shaped purlin

Building with local villagers

External view of the project after renovation

Night view of Stray Birds Art Hotel

Following Natural Contours and Shaping a Harmonious Form

Stray Birds Art Hotel is designed as a complete homestay complex that provides accommodation, catering, and cultural experiences. The complexity of the design lies not only in the adaptive reuse of individual buildings but also in the understanding of the settlement's relationship with its natural environment.

To reach the village entrance, one must pass through a winding path, with the view obscured by the dense mountain settlement until the site is reached. The experience is one of gradual unfolding, where the path opens up to reveal a panoramic view of the canyon landscape.

The site itself stretches horizontally from east to west, with elevation changes from north to south. Stone steps and paths weave through the village, connecting various levels and offering access to different parts of the site.

line+ studio conducted on-site surveys of the existing homesteads, preserving several rammed-earth walls, stone walls, and other usable structures. The functional layout was adjusted to maintain the original spatial pattern. Three residential buildings were selected for conversion into public spaces, including the hotel lobby, restaurant,

Ground-floor plan

1. Check-in area
2. Courtyard
3. Restaurant
4. Tea room
5. Café
6. Guestroom

and cliff café. The remaining cliff dwellings were converted into guestrooms, with elevation differences cleverly managed by using the original east–west corridor.

Adaptive renovation was carried out with respect to the village's texture and style. Local materials were used for repairs, and some collapsed buildings were rebuilt within their original contours. Floating transparent glass boxes were incorporated at key locations to create a dialogue between the old and the new, balancing tradition with modernity.

The cantilevered glass volume

Traditional and Modern Integration in the Guestrooms

The interior space of the rammed-earth houses was originally quite cramped, so after dismantling the dilapidated wooden frames, line+ studio introduced a new type of lightweight steel structure, raised the roof as a whole, reasonably allocated the space between the two floors, and reserved space for equipment installation. The exterior rammed-earth wall façades were repaired or rebuilt, respecting the original traditional style, retaining decorative elements such as wood veneer and waist eaves while enlarging the openings of doors and windows or adding new glass volumes according to the landscape orientation to create better viewing conditions. Some spaces under eaves were designed as viewing balconies, and the roofs were re-laid with old tiles, integrating a sense of history with modernity.

For severely collapsed rammed-earth houses, line+ studio used local rubble stones as the exterior wall material, unifying the volume of new buildings to compensate for the missing texture of the village with local materials, maintaining its local characteristics and architectural coherence.

The interior design of the guestrooms, based on the principle of respecting the allocation of ancestral land, were designed with various floor plans according to the characteristics of different homesteads, adapting to the complex natural environment of the mountainous area. The living area of each guest room is adjacent to the road, while the bedroom and bathtub face the scenery, ensuring privacy while maximizing the best view.

Guestroom with mountain view

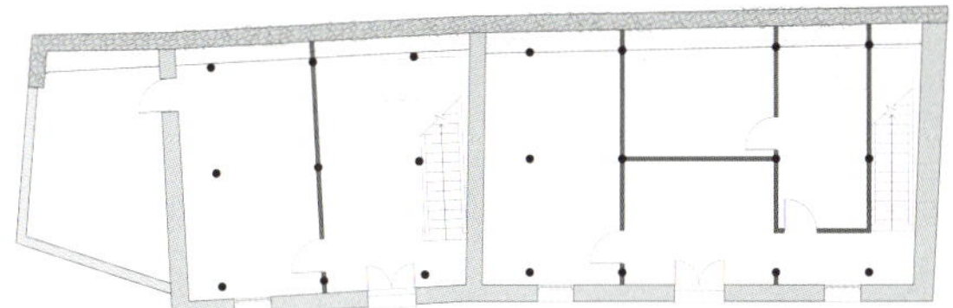
Ground-floor plan before renovation

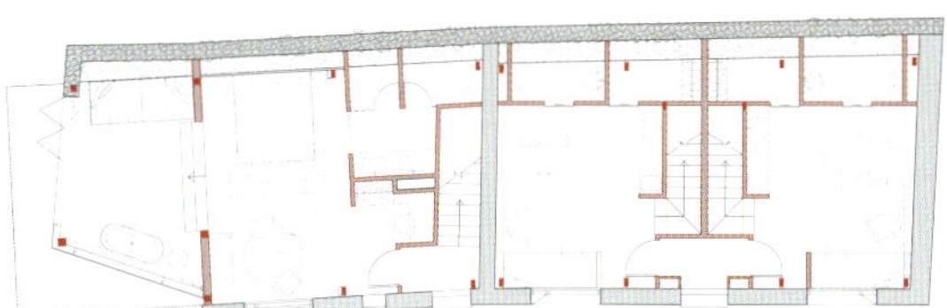
Ground-floor plan after renovation

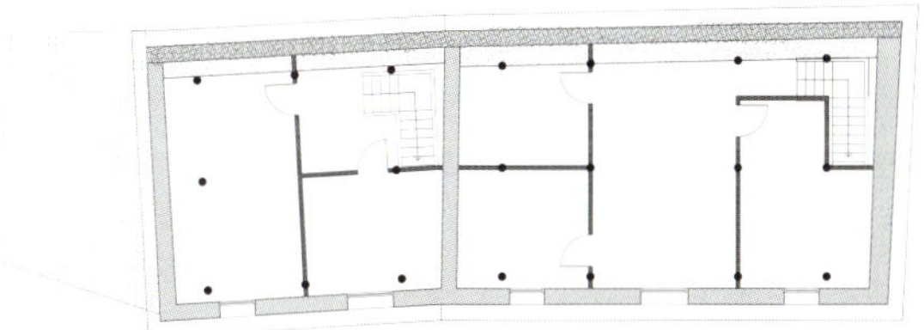
Second-floor plan before renovation

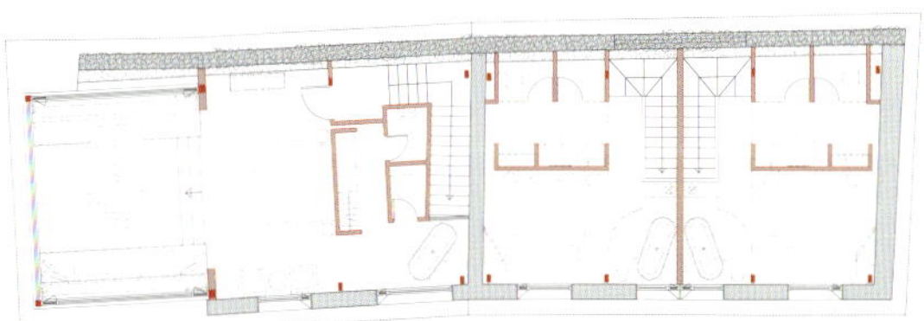
Second-floor plan after renovation

Guestroom interior

Bathroom

Construction in harmony with the terrain

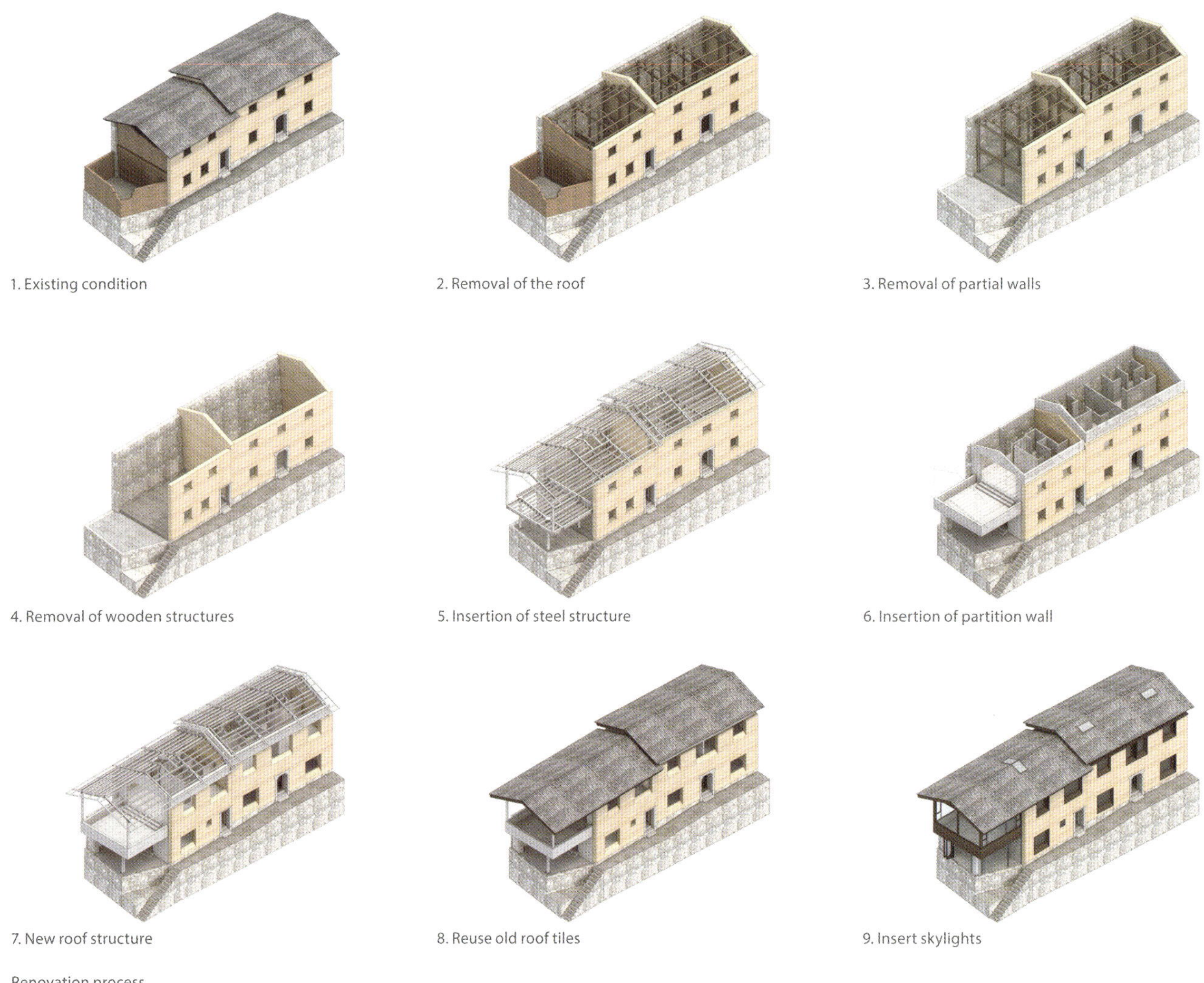

1. Existing condition
2. Removal of the roof
3. Removal of partial walls
4. Removal of wooden structures
5. Insertion of steel structure
6. Insertion of partition wall
7. New roof structure
8. Reuse old roof tiles
9. Insert skylights

Renovation process

Assembly and Construction Process

Demolition and protection:
A comprehensive building quality assessment of the existing rammed-earth farmhouses was conducted, identifying and removing parts that posed potential safety hazards. Structures with good architectural quality were preserved and renovated, while materials from the demolished sections—such as wood, gray tiles, bricks, and stones—were recycled and reused wherever possible.

Foundation flooring:
The original building foundation dimensions were carefully checked to ensure that the newly constructed structure remained within the original site boundaries and that the foundation soil layer was stable. A slab foundation was used, with structural reinforcement provided in the column foot area. A safe distance was maintained between the foundation and the earth wall to ensure stability and allow space for construction. Integrated pipelines were pre-buried, and floor heating was installed as part of the design.

Main structure:
The structural units were prefabricated and processed in a factory. These were then packaged and transported to the site as complete units. On-site, the workers assembled these structural units based on precisely pre-drilled bolt holes, allowing the main structure to be completed in as little as one day.

1. Demolition and protection
2. Foundation
3. Main structure
4. Partition walls
5. Preservation of the existing rammed-earth walls
6. Stone retaining walls
7. Roof with old gray tiles

Roofs and interior partitions:

The renovation plan adopts an integrated design and construction approach for both the architecture and the interior. As a result, interior partition walls, stairs, and pre-buried pipelines were all prefabricated in the factory and assembled on-site to ensure construction accuracy. The indoor walls use C-shaped light steel as the keel, with metal mesh serving as the formwork. These walls are filled with EPS foamed concrete, resulting in lightweight walls with excellent thermal insulation and soundproofing properties, while allowing for convenient and efficient construction.

Model

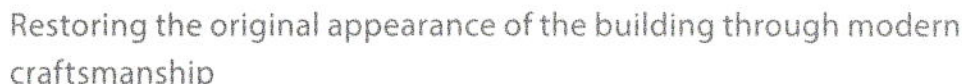

Restoring the original appearance of the building through modern craftsmanship

Exterior after renovation

Restoration Techniques for the Dwellings' External Envelope

Preservation and restoration of earth walls:
The roof was elevated, and new exterior walls beneath the eaves were suspended as curtain-walls, supported by the main steel structure. Local artisans meticulously restored the earth walls using traditional techniques, while protective coatings were applied to the interior walls. The original doorways and stone frames were preserved, maintaining the buildings' historical integrity.

Enclosing with retaining walls:
The rural dwellings were built in harmony with the mountain terrain. Most houses are backed by the mountains, with their enclosing exterior walls constructed from rubble masonry, serving as slope protection. The new design preserves this structure, reflecting the regional construction characteristics. To ensure stability, the stone walls with structural issues were repaired and reinforced. Given the high moisture content in the mountain soil, water seepage was a concern for the stone walls. During the foundation construction, drainage pipes were pre-installed to manage water flow. The interior of the stone walls was treated with grouting to fill gaps, while a waterproof coating was applied, ensuring a comfortable indoor living environment.

Update of door and window systems:
Traditional dwellings often feature small window openings, which don't meet the requirements for lighting, ventilation, or scenic views. To enhance the lighting environment and improve views, the design enlarged the original door and window openings and installed modern door and window systems. This not only improved thermal insulation and sealed the exterior but also enhanced the aesthetic appeal. Specially designed aluminum perforated window frames were installed, which provide ventilation while maintaining a clean and unified façade.

Preservation of the gray tiled roof:
A light steel keel roof was installed, filled with EPS foamed concrete, and waterproof rolls were laid on top. The design incorporates small gray tiles reclaimed from old buildings, responding to regional culture and reflecting sustainable ecological principles.

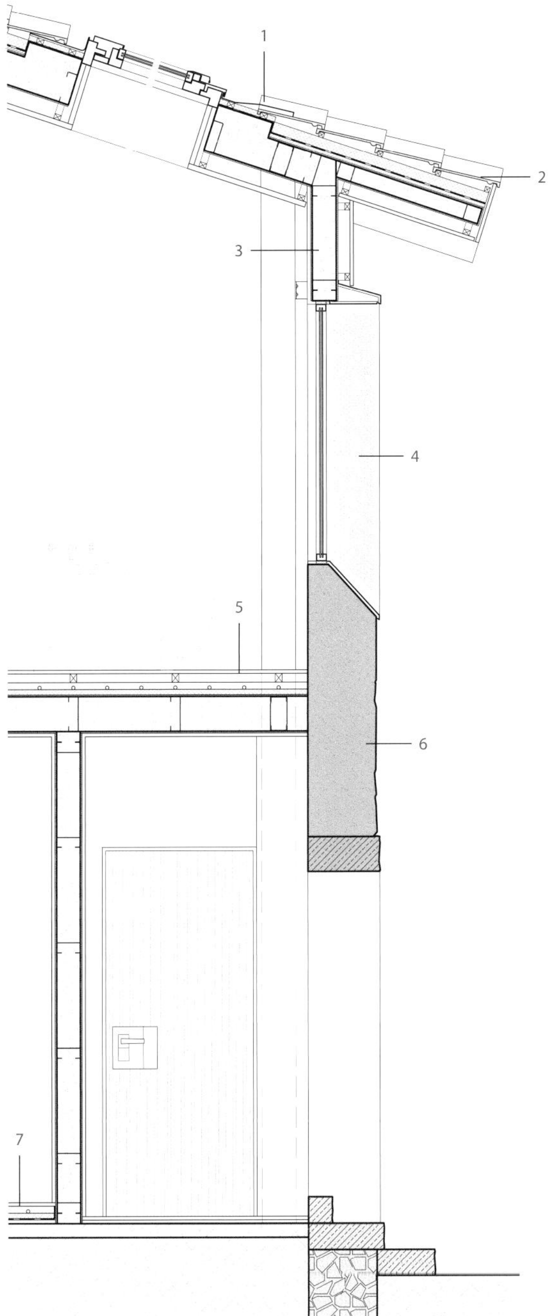

Wall section details

1. Roof
   - Blue tiles (retained from original building)
   - SBS waterproof layer
   - 12mm OSB board underlayment
   - 200mm light steel keel roof
   - Ceiling interior finish

2. Eaves
   - Blue tiles (retained from original building)
   - SBS waterproof layer
   - 12mm OSB board underlayment
   - 100mm light steel keel roof
   - Black bamboo wood exterior cladding
   - Black decorative purlins

3. Exterior Wall
   - Interior finish
   - 140mm light steel keel wall
   - Black bamboo wood exterior cladding

4. Windows
   - Double-glazed insulated windows
   - Black prefabricated metal window frames

5. Flooring
   - Indoor wooden flooring
   - 40mm underfloor heating layer
   - 30mm thermal insulation layer
   - 200mm light steel keel floor slab
   - Ceiling interior finish

6. Exterior Wall (retained from original building)
   - Rammed-earth wall
   - Stone door frames
   - Bluestone steps
   - Rubble stone wall base

7. Floor Slab
   - Indoor floor tiles
   - 40mm underfloor heating layer
   - 30mm thermal insulation layer
   - SBS waterproof layer
   - 20mm cement mortar leveling
   - 150mm reinforced concrete layer
   - Unpaved rammed-earth base

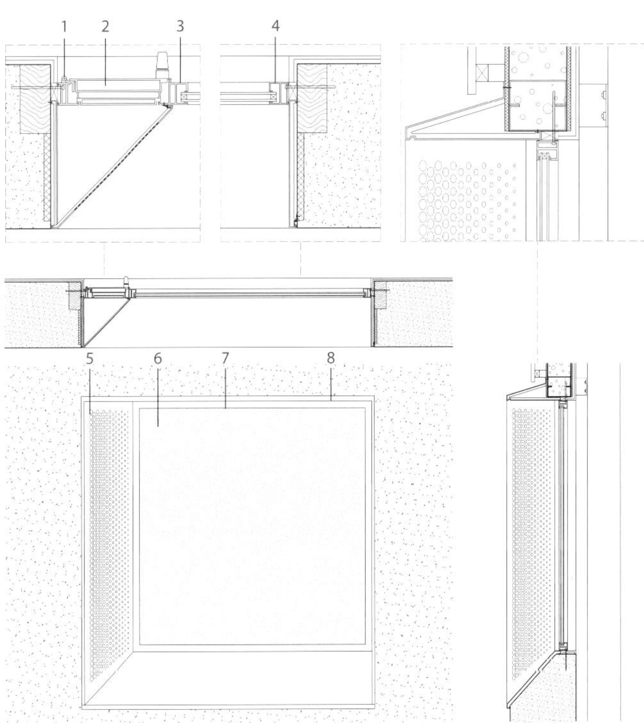

Window system junction

1. Window hinge
2. Aluminum alloy inward-opening window (wood grain exterior, dark gray interior)
3. Aluminum alloy middle post (wood grain exterior, dark gray interior)
4. Aluminum alloy window frame (wood grain exterior, dark gray interior)
5. 1.5mm stainless-steel perforated panel (anti-rust color)
6. 6mm + 12mmA + 6mm insulated double tempered glass
7. Aluminum alloy window frame (wood grain exterior, dark gray interior)
8. 1.5mm stainless-steel sheet (anti-rust color)

RE — A
SS
EM
B — L
ING

Re-organizing the Village

The Stray Birds Art Hotel project represents a practice of assembling that involves two dimensions. The first dimension concerns the reorganization of physical materials and melding the local artisanal skills and talents of Chenjiapu Village with modern building techniques during the construction process. The building not only echoes the regional culture, but also provides the old house with the spatial quality of a modern construction. The second dimension is the reorganization of external social resources to develop a historical and cultural village economically and socially. The ultimate purpose of protecting such villages is so that the rich traditions and cultural perspectives and practices that have been passed down for generations can be better protected and preserved without losing their authenticity. Therefore, the development of villages can't rely only on the natural environment and traditional culture; it also requires the introduction of resources from different external organizations of society. This doesn't only refer to tourists and businesses, but also to an industrialized construction system as a resource in itself. Hence, this design project responds to its isolated yet beautiful context by simultaneously attracting more economic resources to Chenjiapu Village, while renewing and integrating local construction techniques, behaviors, and ways of thinking.

村：有小布达拉宫的美名，还有家位800米的先锋书店

山傍海的大省，在山中藏有特别多的古村庄和古村落，有些村子由于地处交通相对来说并不是那么方便，但同时也使得这些村子被保存得十分完好开发过的浓厚商业感，到今天也还有着它们最原始最开始的模样。

有这么一个村落，说上一句是浙江最美丽的古村落也不过分。它就是位于阳县的陈家铺村，距今有600多年的历史，是崖居式古村落的典型代表之一，村子背靠着平均海拔均为800多米以上的高山岩石及悬崖，

浙江省丽水市松阳县：唤醒沉睡古村落 打造新"归园田居"

人民日报社主管 CCN中国城市报

坐落在浙江省丽水市松阳县四都乡的传统古村落陈家铺村。

新华网

2024新质生产力发展案例征集

04/07 2022

依托古村落资源 弘扬传统文化精髓

学习强国 xuexi.cn

梦想从学习开始，事业从实践起步。 习近平

浙江松阳：景致原生态 旅游新业态

2024 新质生产力发展 案例征集

学习强国 xuexi.cn 中共中央宣传部主管

梦想从学习开始，事业从实践起步。 习近平

二十大时间 习近平文汇 学习理论 红色中国 学习科学 五个一工程 学习电视台 学习电台 强军兴军 学习文化

家铺村：传统乡村吸引八方游客

中国丽水

秀山丽水 丽水资讯 党务公开 政务公开 政务服务 政民互动

昔日下山脱贫，如今上山致富，松阳陈家铺村不断探索山区共同富裕发展密码——"空心村"逆袭变身"网红村"

三联生活周刊

民宿，远方亦故乡

陈家铺蝶变 从"三无村"到

陈家铺蝶变 从"三无村"到"网红村"

为破解城乡发展问题提供"中国式方案"

"千万工程"让乡村走向复兴

2003年6月，浙江省启动"千村示范、万村整治"工程。这是一项从农村人居环境整治入手，统筹生产、生活、生态三者关系，全面推进乡村振兴和城乡融合发展，实现共同富裕的重大实践。

精品民宿飞茑(niao)集是白云藏在陈家铺村的一个海拔800余米的山谷民宿

浙江在线

深山古村换新颜

1月30日，住宿在陈家铺村一家民宿的露台上晒太阳。

游走好县｜"最后的江南秘境"松阳：民宿之外，被"拯救"的如何留住游客脚步？

秘境 拥抱美好｜松阳：藏匿在悬崖之的云间屋舍

江松阳地处浙西南，距今已有1800多年历史，被誉为"最后的江南秘境"，是留的"古典中国"县域样板，拥有78个国家级传统村落，目标打造"中国古村民宿

民晚报推出"重逢秘境 拥抱美好"专题，一起走进这里的传统村落和秘境民宿，山云巅，或隐深坳谷间，或卧清溪水畔，或藏竹海山林，每一处都是人们向往桃源。

期，走进一家藏匿在悬崖之上的云间屋舍。

CCTV 节目官网

《我的美丽乡村》20230511 探秘悬崖上的古村落

视频简介

栏目介绍

Twelve Tents Beyond Clouds, Xiayanbei Rural Scenic Area

Modern Ruralism

"The lights of Twelve Tents at night not only guide travelers on their way, but also mark the homeward path for villagers."

—Zhu Peidong

Location: Xiayanbei Village, Xinchang, Zhejiang Province, China
Design firm: line+ studio
Principal architect: Zhu Peidong
Architecture design team: Wu Haiwen, Du Mengying, Zhou Yang
Interior design team: Zhu Jun, Deng Hao, Ge Zhenliang, Fan Xiaoxiao, He Yukuan, Yang Li, Zhang Sisi, Lv Siqi, He Zhiyi
Landscape design team: Li Shangyang, Rao Feier, Jin Jianbo, Zhang Wenjie
Area: 28,013 square feet (2,603 square meters)
Design period: February 2022–September 2022
Construction period: September 2022–May 2023
Client: Xinchang Nineteen Peak Scenic Area Development Co., Ltd
Photography: Arch-Exist Photography, line+ studio
Model photography: line+ studio

Site plan

A Differentiated Rural Scenic Area

Xiayanbei Village, perched on the ridge of Eastern Zhejiang at over 300 meters above sea level, has evolved significantly over the years. Initially part of a provincial land improvement and rural tourism initiative, the village revitalized unused land and rural housing to create a "tea culture experience tour" and a "rural slow-life experience zone." This transformation turned it into a tourism model for Xinchang County. Recently, the rise in popularity of outdoor activities like hiking and camping has drawn visitors to Xiayanbei, attracted by its high elevation and panoramic views of the sea of clouds. As the demand for rural tourism grows, the local government is investing in infrastructure upgrades, diversifying business activities, and exploring new avenues for rural development and shared prosperity.

In recent years, many Chinese villages have successfully transformed into tourism destinations, creating income for local residents. For instance, Anji was named one of the "World's Best Tourism Villages" by the United Nations in 2021. Unlike urban areas where the industry system is well-established, rural construction faces various challenges, such as insufficient construction funding and limited land availability for new developments. In Xiayanbei, enhancing the village's infrastructure while creating a distinctive tourism appeal was one of line+ studio's key challenges.

Surrounding site environment

Existing site

Distant view of the Nineteen Peaks

The design of Twelve Tents Beyond Clouds addresses these challenges through the adaptive reuse of underutilized land, introducing new functions like a community center , visitor center, dining and shopping options and boutique accommodation. The site, previously a large tea-processing factory, had an imposing scale that disrupted the surrounding village's harmony. Moreover, the factory blocked access to the best viewpoints for the sea of clouds and Nineteen Peaks. After the tea factory's relocation, the area became available for the renovation of public spaces, unlocking new potential for tourism and community use.

Twelve units volume

Main entrance

Adjusting Scale and Redefining Space

The site is located near the village entrance and adjacent to a cliffside walking trail. It previously featured a massive, boxy white factory and unevenly arranged viewing platforms. The design approach focused on two strategies: first, breaking down the factory's overwhelming size by transforming its structure of 178.81-by-159.45-by-27.33 feet (54.5-by-48.6-by-8.33 meters) into smaller, more human-scaled volumes that blended with the surrounding village fabric. This transformation opened up the previously enclosed space, creating a continuous flow from the parking lot through Twelve Tents Beyond Clouds to the viewing platforms and trail. The second strategy was to take advantage of the natural slope; the design introduced a series of cascading platforms starting from the second floor of the original factory. These platforms extend to the existing cliffside viewpoint, offering unobstructed views of the sea of clouds and Nineteen Peaks, while hosting various functions like guesthouses, restaurants, cafés, and retail spaces for both visitors and villagers.

The twelve architectural units, inspired by outdoor camping tents, feature a simple geometric design. Their sculptural forms, varying in height, evoke the distant Nineteen Peaks, creating a visual harmony with the landscape. The modular steel structures are linked by platforms of varying heights, offering flexible spaces for commercial activities. Two platforms near the cliff, once popular camping sites, have been preserved as public viewing areas, with a pedestrian route passing beneath the upper platform to connect visitors directly to the viewpoint and walking trail.

Second-floor space

Aerial view

Viewing platform

Model photo

Modular Layout and Diverse Spaces

The floor plan adopts a scattered settlement approach, emphasizing permeability and blending interior and exterior spaces. The twelve units on the ground floor are grouped unevenly, with openings facing the central courtyard, creating a unified exterior while offering dynamic display areas and inward-facing views. Overlapping roof panels above the courtyard function like a ceiling, creating skylight-like openings that allow ample light and ventilation to reach both the courtyard and the upper-level atrium. These flexible "gray spaces" can accommodate a variety of activities, from outdoor dining to village gatherings, tourist flows, markets, and exhibitions.

The second-level walkways connect the spaces, acting as passageways and multi-directional viewing platforms that foster free-flowing, three-dimensional social spaces. This vertical circulation creates a unique experience for visitors, allowing them to wander between the sculptural units and under the overlapping roof panels, akin to walking through clouds.

View from the street

Second-floor space

Ground-floor space

Dusk view

Differentiated Forms and Industrialized Construction

The choice of materials was influenced by its irregular form, environmental resilience, and ease of construction. The structures feature a steel frame covered with semi-transparent PTFE material, creating a sculptural, soft matte finish. Beneath the PTFE membrane, LED light strips are evenly distributed, making the building glow at night and transforming it into a luminous landmark in the otherwise quiet rural landscape.

The large roof is clad in carbonized pinewood, adding warmth and texture. The roof structure incorporates metal elements and green roof modules, offering a visual link to the meadow-like vistas above the clouds while reducing the overall load. These sustainable materials not only contribute to the building's aesthetic but also ensure durability and functionality.

Self-illuminating film material

Façade details

Section wall details

1. 60mm gypsum perlite hollow slab
   Light gray galvanized steel keel
   Rock wool insulation
   LED light strips
   ETFE membrane

2. 30mm gravel

3. Ceramic foam board planting module
   Ventilated noise reduction wire mesh
   Waterproof breathable membrane
   Galvanized steel leveling layer
   HV-900 type pressed galvanized steel base plate
   Main steel structure/purlins
   Fire-retardant treated substrate board
   Finished wood veneer panel

4. Silver stainless-steel handrail
   Diameter steel cable
   Stainless-steel woven mesh rope barrier
   Honed granite slab surface layer
   Steel plate
   30mm gravel

1. Guestrooms
2. Viewing platform
3. Guestrooms

Embedded Landscape and Integrated Design

The lower viewing platform extends outward, forming new architectural volumes as it drops from the roof into a series of flat, cascading platforms. The guesthouse buildings adopt a material language distinct from that of Cloud Peaks, primarily using locally sourced rough stone and dark charred timber. This design seamlessly integrates the structures into the mountain, making them almost invisible within the natural landscape.

Inside, the design maximizes the connection to the outdoors, using colors and materials inspired by the local green hills and misty clouds. The harmonious relationship between the built environment and nature is emphasized through understated colors and soft furnishings, creating a tranquil atmosphere that aligns with the rural landscape. As the saying goes, "The clouds pass unnoticed, and the trees stand still as the wind fades. At the end of the path, it is the perfect time to enjoy the view."

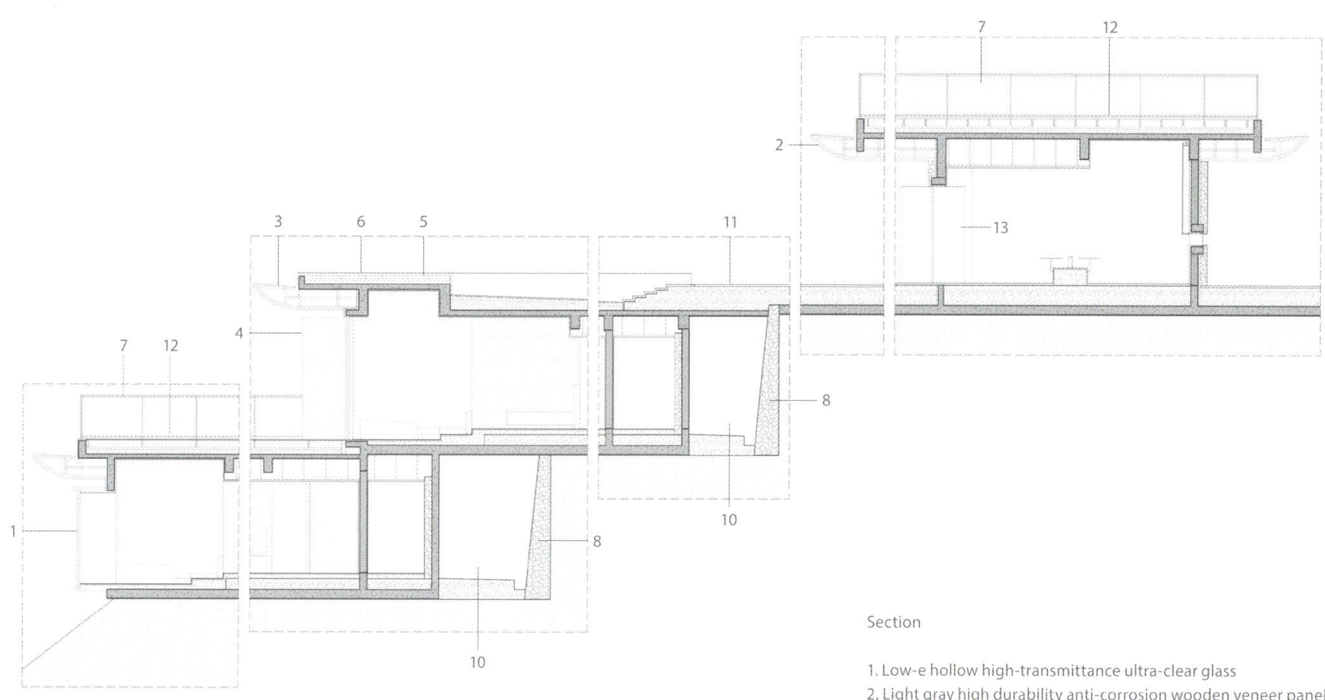

Section

1. Low-e hollow high-transmittance ultra-clear glass
2. Light gray high durability anti-corrosion wooden veneer panel
3. Light gray aluminum veneer panel
4. Natural rough stone
5. Black polished granite slab
6. Landscape water surface
7. Silver stainless-steel wire mesh railing
8. Black aluminum alloy profiles
9. Permanent support
10. Cavity
11. Natural rough-finished granite
12. High durability anti-corrosion wooden panels
13. Gray fluorocarbon coated steel plate

Accommodation interiors

The site in daily use

Distant view of the Nineteen Peaks

RE — A
SS
EM
B — L
ING

Night view

Revitalizing Rural Identity

As rural areas gain traction in the tourism industry for their unique landscapes, architects must consider the gap between the distinct lifestyles of local villagers and tourists. The Twelve Tents project creates a shared space for both, integrating flexibility and adaptability to bridge this divide. Its modern form stands out in the rural landscape, becoming a new landmark that not only attracts attention but also shapes the future of rural commerce, blending the traditional with the contemporary to redefine the village's identity.

Woven Passage to Cloudy Peaks & Sky Ring

Rooted and Elevated

"The activation and development of rural scenic areas require a deep connection to local history and natural landscapes, while also embracing future possibilities with imaginative and vibrant interventions."

—Zhu Peidong

Aerial view of the environment

Ecological restoration and sustainable design:
Previously, a road was built between the two villages, splitting the natural hillside and causing vegetation to wither, exposing bare soil. After frequent rain, the road would become blocked. In 2018–2019, a simple concrete retaining wall was erected to prevent soil erosion, but the exposed yellow earth continued to erode. Thus, the new passage not only served as a wayfinding element but also contributed to ecological restoration, replacing the crude retaining wall with a more sustainable solution. The design ensured that the passage aligned with the natural landscape, following the contour of the hill, and utilized sustainable construction techniques.

Inspiration from traditional craft:
The passage's design is rooted in the rich tradition of bamboo weaving from the Xinchang region, recognized as part of the local intangible cultural heritage. While the primary structural material is eco-friendly natural wood for its sustainability, the design integrates elements of the bamboo weaving craft, blending local cultural heritage with modern construction techniques. The passage's external cladding was made from locally sourced dark slate, allowing the structure to blend seamlessly with the surrounding environment.

Hidden in the environment

Design concept

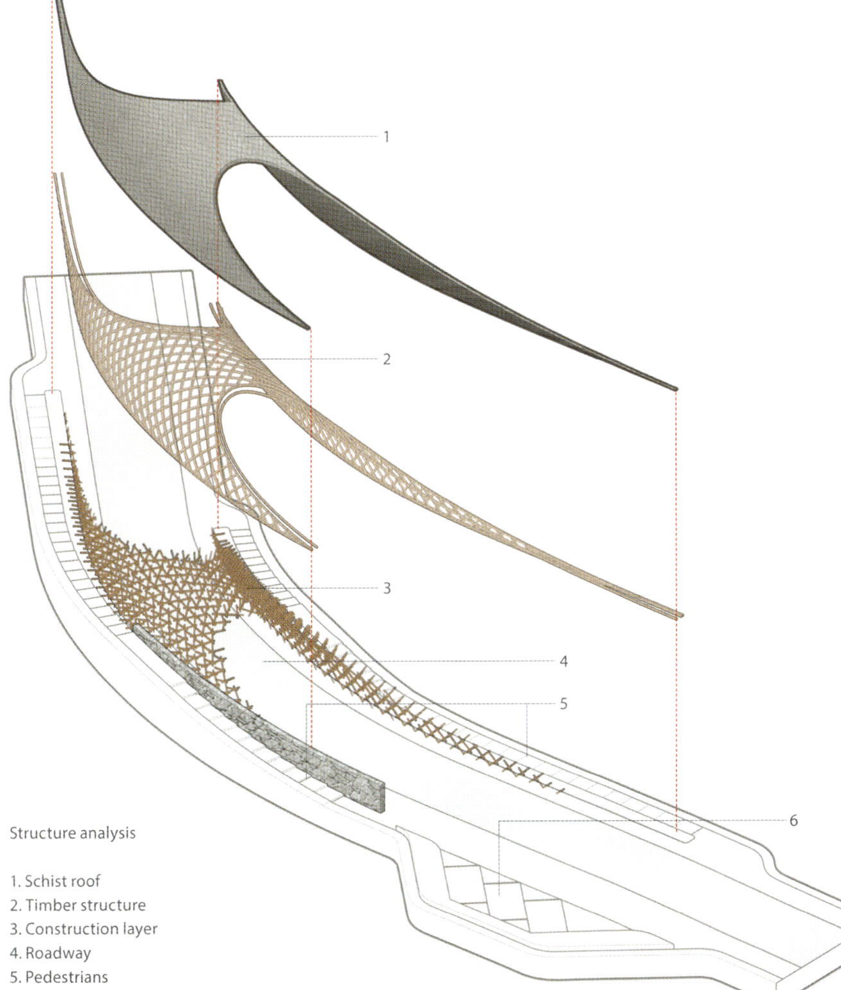

Structure analysis

1. Schist roof
2. Timber structure
3. Construction layer
4. Roadway
5. Pedestrians
6. Temporary parking

Entrance

Internal structural tension

New rural landscape

Nature-inspired materials

Nature-inspired materials

Complex curved structural integration:
The design challenge of the hyperbolic wooden structure involved the geometric relationships between shape and material stresses. Collaborating with structural engineers, line+ studio developed a series of tests to ensure the strength and stability of the structure, addressing potential weak points to ensure the tunnel's success in both form and function.

Efficient and precise prefabricated construction:
From design to site, selecting processes and organizing construction were key. Architects, engineers, and manufacturers employed Rhino-Revit parametric design to model the hyperbolic beams and each joint, determining the curvature and position of each component for fabrication. The most suitable 13mm Douglas fir was chosen based on bending radius and thickness.

Components were first defined in the model, unfolded to produce the floor plan, and then milled into shape. CNC programming was used for template cutting and prefabrication, followed by transport and assembly on site. After the wooden frame was built, stainless-steel mesh was applied to the surface, fixed with galvanized steel ribs, while irregular stone slabs were secured with metal wire. Local artisanship adds a distinctive, natural texture to the otherwise precise prefabricated structure.

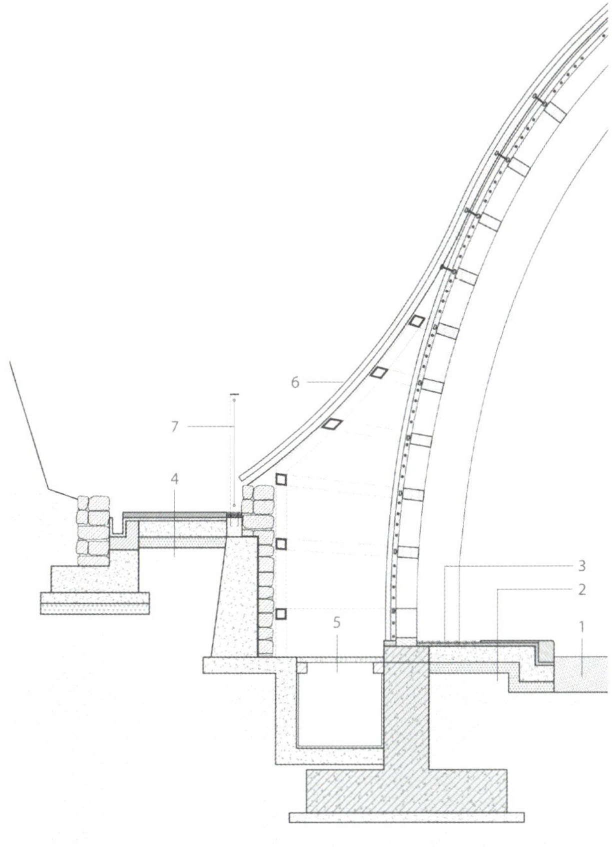

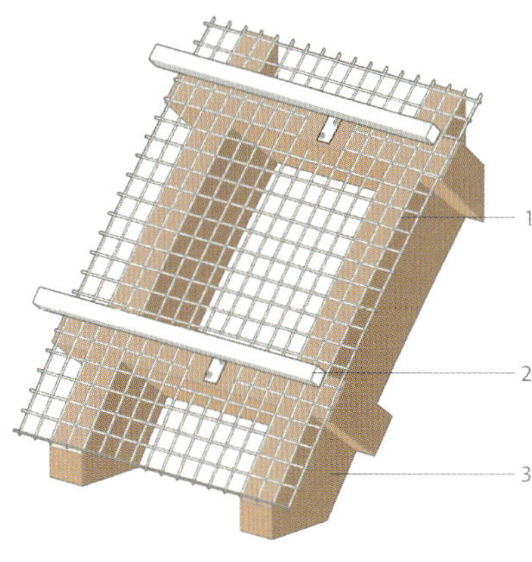

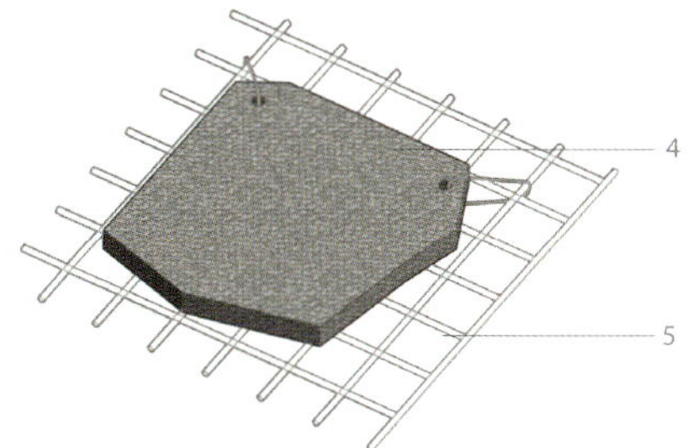

Section wall details

1. Existing asphalt pavement

2. Sesame black flamed granite
   Cement mortar leveling layer
   Concrete cushion layer
   Crushed stone cushion layer
   Compacted subgrade soil

3. Fine stone concrete with embedded cobblestones

4. Bluestone slab
   Cement mortar leveling layer
   Concrete cushion layer
   Crushed stone cushion layer
   Compacted subgrade soil

5. Reinforced concrete drainage channel

6. Natural fractured rock slab
   304 stainless-steel wire mesh
   Galvanized steel plate
   Galvanized square steel joist
   Natural fractured rock slab
   Stainless-steel wire mesh
   Wooden structure framework

7. Stainless-steel wire rope mesh guardrail

Joint connection

1. 304 stainless-steel wire mesh
2. Galvanized square steel joist
3. Spatial framework with wooden structure
4. Natural fractured rock slab
5. 304 stainless-steel wire mesh

Construction process

Distant views

Modernized Signage: Sky Ring

The weather heavily influences the activities of Xiayanbei Village, which include cloud viewing, camping, hiking, and farming. The Sky Ring is both an iconic installation and a functional piece of meteorological equipment. Aside from its stunning visual impact, it monitors weather conditions using balloon-like equipment and gives weather forecasts to both visitors and inhabitants. Additionally, the meteorological ring is intended to become a new icon of public space in Xiayanbei. When airborne, its projection on the ground creates a communal area for people to gather and enjoy.

Air retention device:

After numerous design iterations, line+ studio chose a ring-shaped helium balloon for the structure, which offers both aerodynamic efficiency and the flexibility to differentiate itself from traditional spherical weather balloons. The meteorological ring is 30 meters in diameter and features multiple integrated systems to manage its operation and safety. When the wind speed is below 8 meters per second, the meteorological ring is tethered at 25 meters, supported by sixteen ropes. If the wind exceeds 8 m/s or in adverse weather conditions like rain, snow, or storms, the outer ropes activate, alerting the management team. The winch retracts the ring, and the remaining ropes secure it to the ground, improving its wind resistance.

Sky Ring in the rural landscape

Anchored to the site

Suspended in the air

RE — A
SS
EM
B — L
ING

Rooted in Memory, Shaped for the Future

With the rise of modernity and urbanization, China's built environment faces criticism for losing unique cultural characteristics and becoming disconnecting from traditional construction methods, particularly in rural areas. In the Woven Passage to Cloudy Peaks & Sky Ring project, the relationship between local memory and future growth is seen as complementary rather than contradictory. The project respects the architectural context while addressing emerging needs. By merging traditional memory with modern technology, it offers visitors a rich visual experience. The design revitalizes the village's identity, blending seamlessly into the landscape and conveying the countryside's unique character through modern architecture, setting Xiayanbei apart from increasingly standardized rural tourist destinations.

New rural landscape

Dali Erhai Lake Ecological Rest Station

Micro-topography

"The fusion of architecture with climate, ecology, and public activity was the core design intention. This landscape-driven approach integrates the artificial and the natural in form, experience, and construction, allowing the modern rest station to grow from the earth, offering shelter to all who pass through."

—Meng Fanhao

Location: Dali, Yunnan Province, China
Design firm: line+ studio
Principal architect: Meng Fanhao
Project Architects: Xu Hao, He Yaliang
Architecture design team: Xu Yifan, Zhang Jinyue (Intern), Fang Sitao (Intern), Lin Nijun (Intern), Yu Qizheng (Intern) , Qiao Ziyang(Intern)
Interior design team: Zhu Jun, He Yukuan, Deng Hao
Landscape design team: Li Shangyang, Jin Jianbo, Zhang Wenjie
Area: 1,615 square feet (150 square meters)
Design period: July 2020–July 2021
Construction period: July 2021–October 2022
Client: Dali Cang'er Investment Co., Ltd
Photography: Wang Ce
Model photography: line+ studio

Site plan

Erhai Lake, located in the northwest of Dali City, Yunnan Province, is one of China's largest and most ecologically significant lakes. Nestled between the Cangshan mountain range to the west and wetlands to the east, the lake sits at an altitude of 6,470 feet (1,972 meters). Cangshan stretches 29.83 miles (48 kilometers) in length, with peaks rising over 2.55 miles (4,100 meters). Since 1988, the lake has been a focal point for conservation, preserving its rich biodiversity and scenic beauty.

The Dali Erhai Ecological Corridor aims to create a sustainable land-water buffer zone that enhances the interaction between local residents, tourists, and the lake. This 80.2-mile (129-kilometer) ring corridor will feature multiple service stations designed to serve both ecological and social functions.

Conventional service stations are typically isolated and lockable, but line+ studio reimagined the typology with a focus on integration into the landscape. The stations are open and integrated into the landscape, encouraging a deeper connection with the natural environment. Rather than being mere infrastructure, these spaces serve as platforms for engagement, allowing both visitors and locals to interact freely with the landscape, fostering a more dynamic and immersive experience.

Traditional rest stations by Erhai Lake

Building volume embedded into the landscape

Site environment

Viewing the project at distance

A New Topography

The project site is located along the southwestern edge of the Erhai Lake Scenic Corridor, near Xiaoyi Village. The terrain is flat, bordered by the lakeside bike path and ecological wetlands to the east, with Cangshan to the west. Upon visiting the site, line+ studio moved away from the idea of an isolated building, opting instead for a deeper, more harmonious relationship with the surrounding landscape.

The design carefully avoids disrupting the existing trees, integrates the paths, and aligns with the dual orientation of Cangshan to the west and Erhai Lake to the east. The building unfolds from south to north, gently rising from a "crack" in the earth, creating a platform for sweeping views and a sheltered space for rest. This approach recalls ancient human experiences of living in balance with nature.

Climate considerations were paramount. With abundant wind and sunlight, the design opens the space beneath the folded concrete roof to facilitate natural airflow and a seamless visual connection to the landscape. This allows air to circulate freely between the interior and the exterior, creating a space that feels alive and "breathing."

Connected to the road

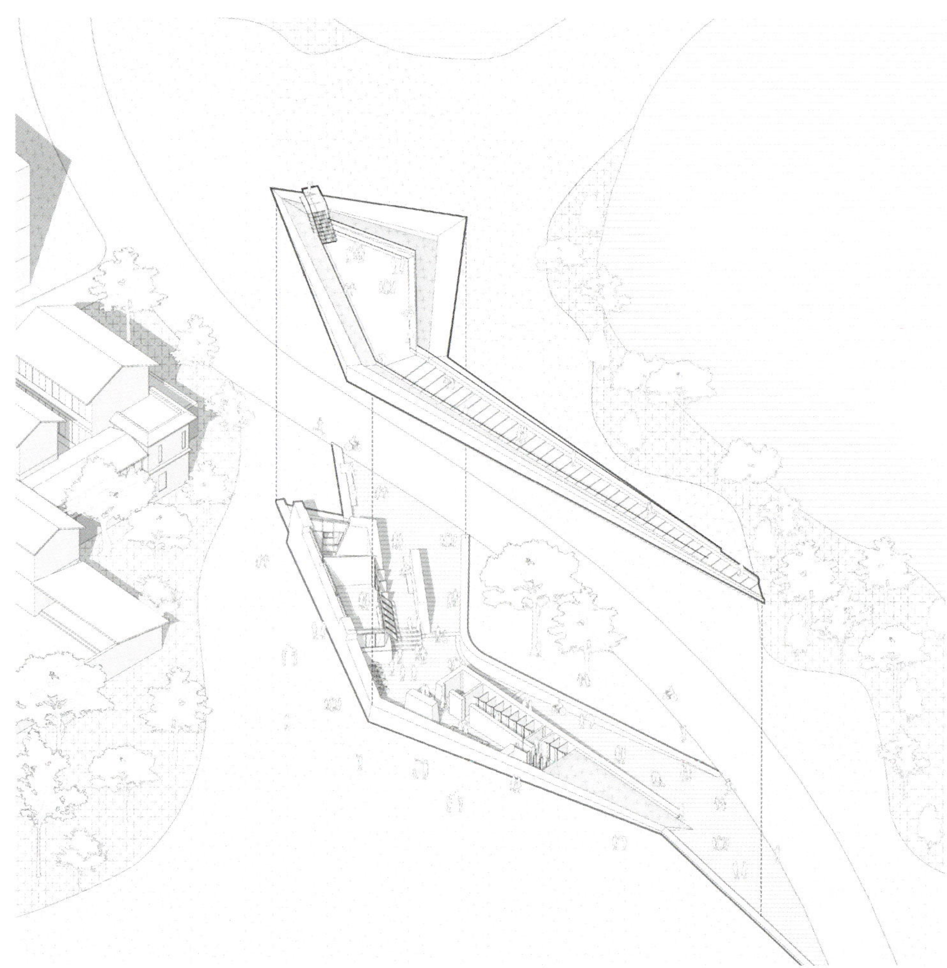

Concealed public service facilities

Concealed public service facilities

Dialogue between the large roof and the rubble stone wall

The base space under the roof

1	2	3	
4	5	6	7
	8	9	10

Construction process

1. Concrete formwork sample
2. Formwork construction
3. Placement of reinforcement
4. Roof concreting
5. Stripping formwork
6. Finishing of concrete
7. Stone wall construction
8. Installation of wash basin
9. Wooden doors and windows
10. Final inspection

Low-tech and Low-carbon

The material strategy focused on responding to the regional vernacular. Key material characteristics were extracted and reinterpreted with three primary materials: rough stone, concrete, and wood. These materials, requiring minimal maintenance and capable of "growing" over time, contribute to the sustainability of the public building, while reinforcing the relationship between the local context and contemporary architecture.

Folded plate roof:
The folded concrete roof, designed using parametric structural calculations, spans a large area and cantilevers outward. The color and texture of the exposed concrete were carefully controlled through experimental simulations and on-site mock-ups, achieving a natural, unembellished effect with stable physical properties.

The primary formwork material used for the textured finish is pinewood, chosen for its natural grain and tactile qualities. Constructing the large cantilever roof involved careful attention to load-bearing capacity, with a monolithic box structure poured in one go and a secondary pour for the roof slab to ensure structural integrity and waterproofing.

To achieve the black concrete finish, two key measures were implemented: natural mineral pigments were added during the pouring phase to achieve the desired dark color and material strength. After demolding and curing, a semi-transparent colorant was applied to enhance the texture and deepen the hue.

Limestone wall base:
The base of the building utilized local limestone, which was sourced on-site and cut into 0.5-1.5 feet (150-450 millimeters) pieces, matching the scale of the building. To avoid visible joints, galvanized angle steel was embedded within the concrete or walls and welded to the rebar in the stone masonry.

The drainage system of the roof departs from conventional vertical downspouts. Instead, a UHPC (Ultra High Performance Concrete) panel design incorporated open seams that direct rainwater to cavities below the finished surface, which then flow through garden supports and into nearby drains.

The floating relationship between the building roof and the land

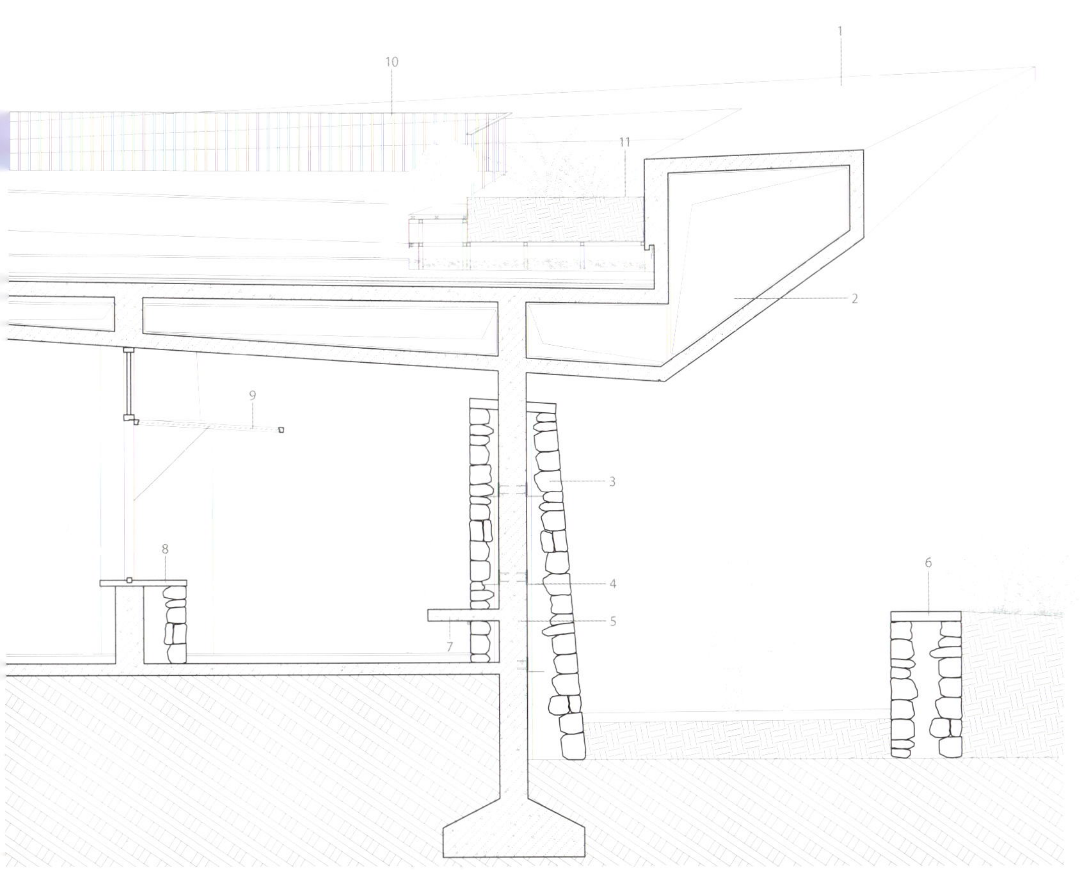

Wall section details

1. Black wood formwork concrete
2. Box structure cavity
3. Masonry rubble stones
4. Steel joists
5. Concrete wall
6. Stone roof pressing
7. Cast-in-place black concrete seats
8. Solid wood countertops
9. Solid wood-framed glass windows
10. Steel bars
11. Green roof

1	2
3	4
5	6

Material strategy

1. Local limestone feature wall
2. Base made of local limestone
3. Cangshan black marble rock wall
4. Black wooden formwork concrete
5. Solid wood window shutters of traditional Bai ethnic residences
6. Oak window frame

Interactive concession window

Wooden door and window system:
The design of doors and windows emphasizes practicality and ecological climate considerations. The toilet door features a solid wood dwarf door, while the high windows are equipped with wooden blinds, ensuring natural ventilation and privacy in the toilet. Oak wood, chosen for its resistance to decay and durability, is used for its high hardness. The retail store features sliding and fully openable wooden doors, enhancing interaction between the indoor and outdoor spaces.

Sustainable use of metal materials:
After the completion of the main structure, a considerable amount of leftover industrial materials such as rebar and steel plates remained at the construction site. Upholding sustainable and eco-friendly principles, through secondary processing these materials were repurposed for components such as railings, handrails, staircase treads, and flower beds. This integration transforms them into a vital part of the building's life, experiencing renewed growth.

The restroom

Details

The station in daily use

Roof platform used by tourists and residents

Aerial view

RE — A
SS
EM
B — L
ING

Open to All

In the post-pandemic era, Dali has become a popular destination for digital nomads and travelers, attracted by its natural beauty and serene lifestyle. The rest station, more than just a viewpoint or rest stop, becomes a platform for urban public life within the rural context. The design focuses on re-assembling the relationship between modernity and rural life, creating a space that welcomes all with a sense of ordinary inclusivity.

Though understated and silent, the structure embodies a powerful energy, sprawling organically between Cangshan and Erhai Lake. It serves as a bridge between humans and nature, inviting visitors to engage physically and perceptually with the space, reconnecting with the surrounding landscape. By seamlessly integrating with the natural environment, the rest station evolves into a dynamic "living landscape" that reflects the tranquil rhythms of rural life, while accommodating the new demands of contemporary visitors.

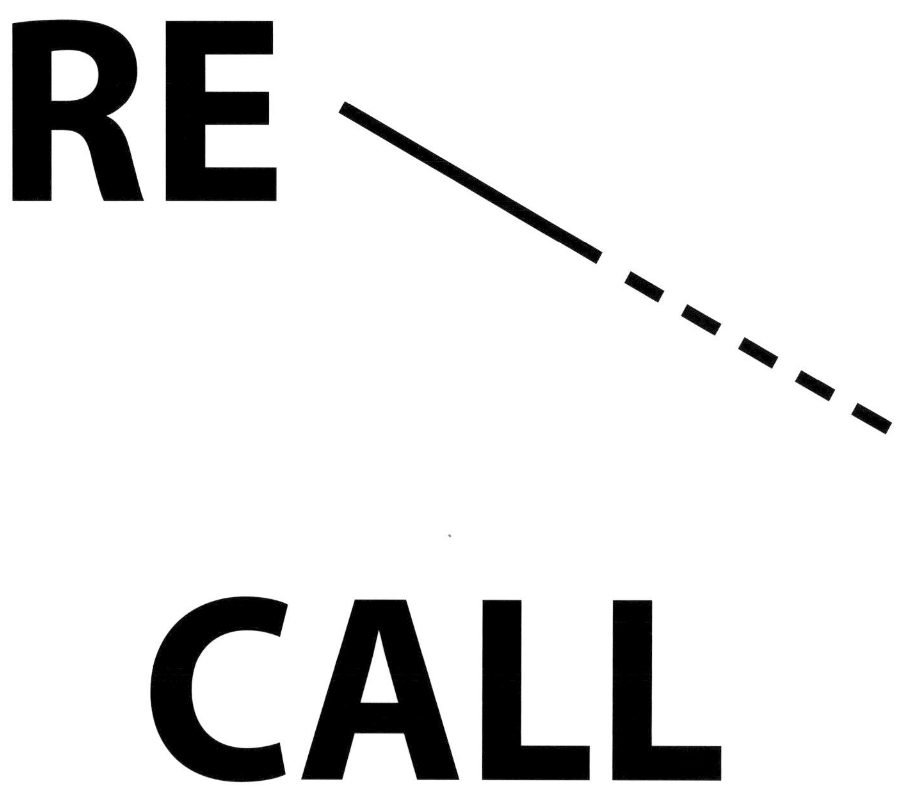
RE
CALL

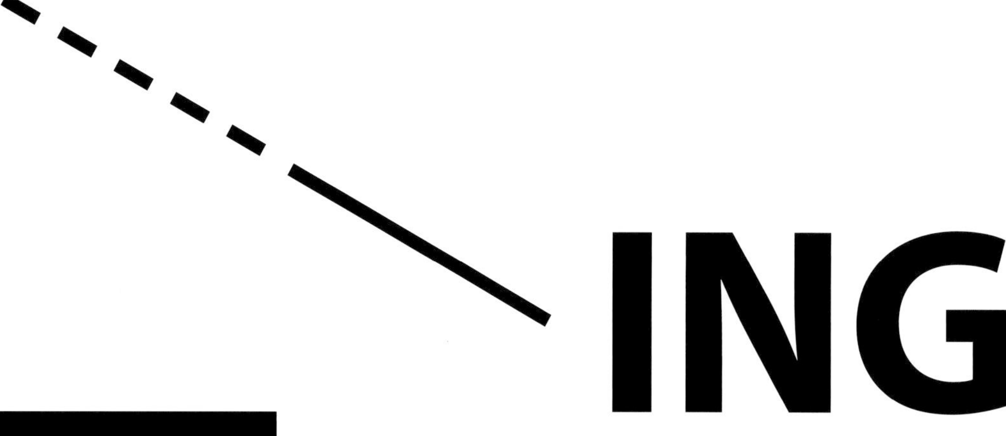
ING

Sheltering spirits

Modern-day consumerism and high consumer demands have created many powerful empires in the Fast Moving Consumer Goods (FMCG) industry. FMCG refer mainly to consumer goods that have a short lifespan, and which sell quickly. FMCG include food, personal hygiene products, alcoholic beverages, sodas and soft drinks, and products that consumers use in their daily life. The high production and purchase frequency, low price, and rapid consumption of these products make them place their value in aspects like packaging and branding, and their recognition and recollection among the masses. In today's era of unprecedented internet reach and media permeability, the term FMCG is slowly but surely expanding to include items that extend beyond just daily commodities. In this current-day era of FMCG, products compete for high market shares, the consumer is often at the mercy of persuasive advertisements, out-of-this-world assertions, claims about product benefits, and even third-party suggestions—courtesy of social media influencers who are making good use of the current pervasiveness of the internet and social media to tout certain products as "cool" or fashionable, giving these items high social value. This constant smothering of the consumer has cut people's lives from connections with things that have a deeper and unchanging meaning. Whether it is a spiritual force or a primitive connection with nature, the absence of these connections often leaves people in the modern world in a state of loneliness and disconnection.

Architecture has always offered shelter in the sense of its physical form, as well as its spiritual essence. Through spatial order, it implies a sense of a higher power to people. Through light and the framing of views, it allows people to feel closer to nature and its changes. Through spatial scenes, it shapes and evokes individual and collective memories. Through materials and crafts, it provides a tactile and bodily perception.

The five projects included in this chapter—although different in scale and program—are all dedicated to helping people reclaim memory and the source of spirit in the noisy modern-day era of FMCG. Whether it is the ritualized spatial organization or the play of light; whether it is learning from natural forms or the integration of space with nature, they *re-call* something more profound and unchanging. And by doing so, architecture gains its power as a spiritual space.

02

Re-calling

Yunnan Dongfengyun Art Center

Blending into Nature

Resembling red stones, Yunnan Dongfengyun Art Center is not only a physical space, it also strives to be the spatial symbol of the town's future. Seemingly forgotten by this world, it not only provides a rich spatial and material experience for the people who come here, but also inspires future users through its visually distinctive spatial imagery.

Model

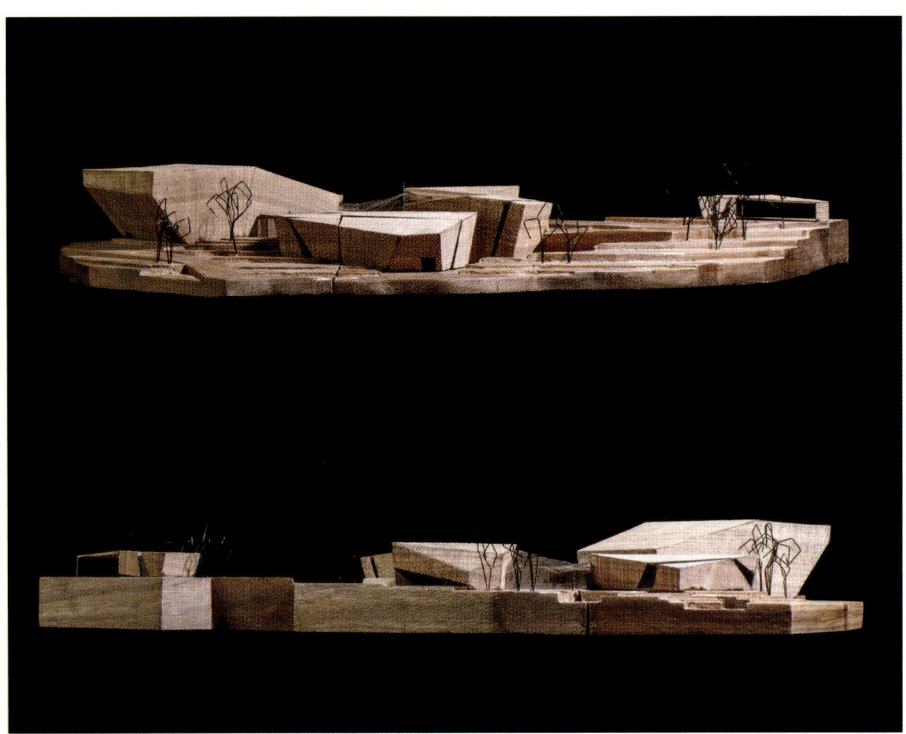

Model

"Stones" in the field

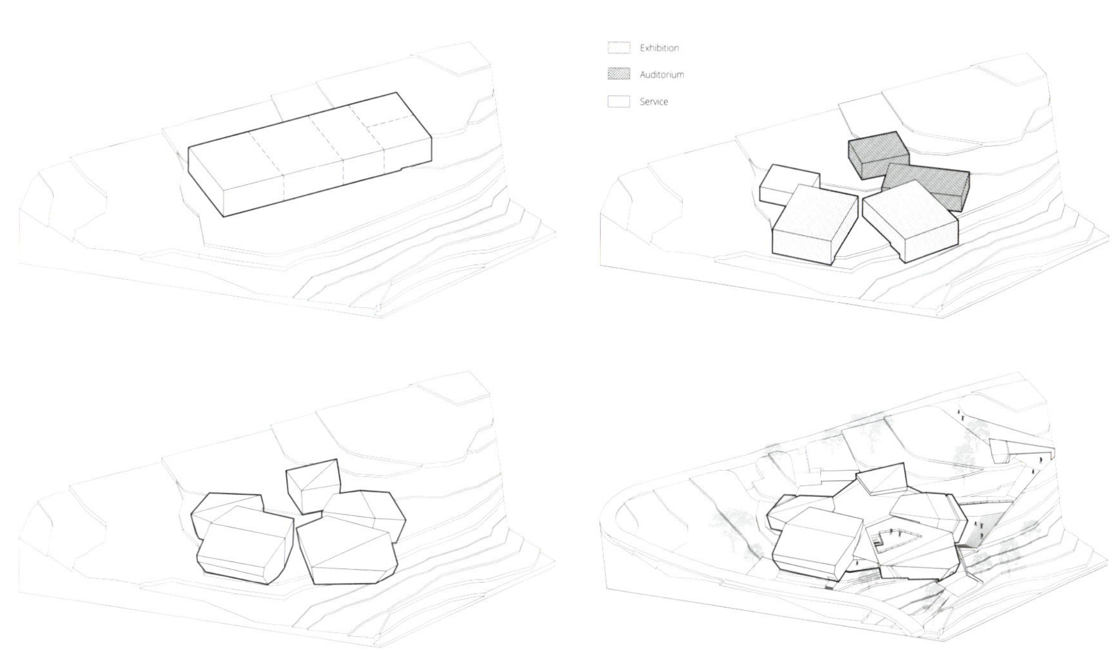

1 | 2
3 | 4

1. Programmatic volumes
2. Repositioning
3. Cutting
4. Atrium and plaza

Generation diagram

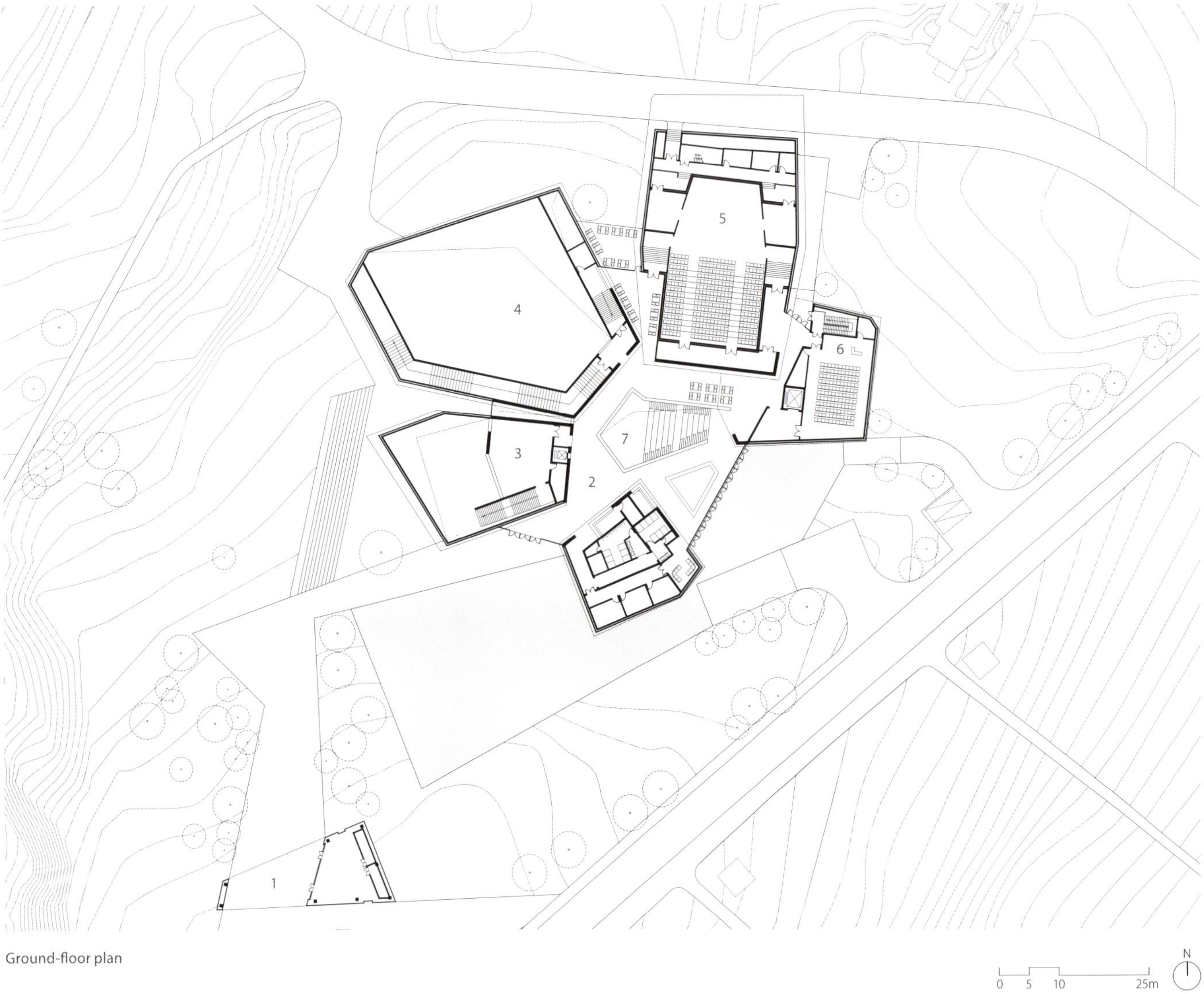

Ground-floor plan

1. Security office
2. Main entrance
3. Small gallery
4. Main gallery
5. Main auditorium
6. Small auditorium
7. Terraced atrium

"Stones" in the field

Entrance hall

Terraced atrium

Section through the atrium

Main gallery

Small gallery

Main gallery

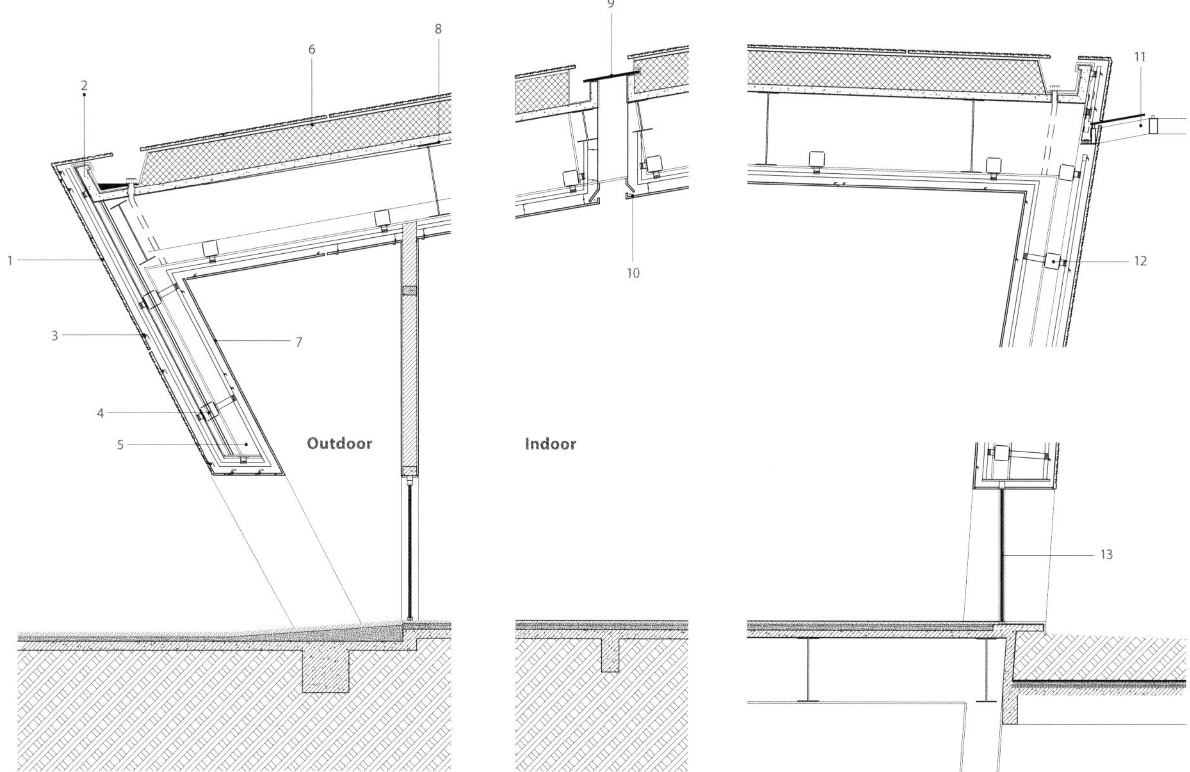

Wall detail

1. 50mm textured red concrete panels
2. Reinforced concrete parapet
3. 120×5mm steel L-profiles
4. 250×250mm steel box profile
5. 800×800mm steel column
6. External wall (roof) concrete panels
7. 30mm cement board interior finish
8. Concrete supporting structure
9. Skylight comprising aluminum profiles and 8/12/8mm glazing unit
10. LED lights
11. Glazed atrium roof comprising 8/12/8mm glazing unit
12. 250×250mm steel box profile
13. Low-e insulating glass

Materials and Construction

The main body of the building is composed of a steel structure, with a façade made of red concrete cladding, which creates a texture and feel similar to red stone. In order to achieve this, line+ studio conducted several material tests and mock-ups, finally settling on a red concrete cladding with a horizontal texture, combining two to three standardized prefabricated cladding panels according to specific principles. The irregularly chiseled concrete texture lends a certain depth to the surface of the building and creates different shades in the sunlight.

By installing the industrially fabricated cladding with metal clasps, the construction cycle was shortened while guaranteeing a high level of precision. Using red concrete cladding panels also helped the design overcome the limitations of the smaller red sandstone panels common in Yunnan Province, resulting in a rugged texture that fits the scale of the building. Exploring and experimenting with prefabricated construction materials, as well as techniques at high altitudes and under mountainous conditions, also provided the studio with valuable experience that will serve well for future developments with industrialized construction in the city of Mile.

Canyon-like walls

Model detail

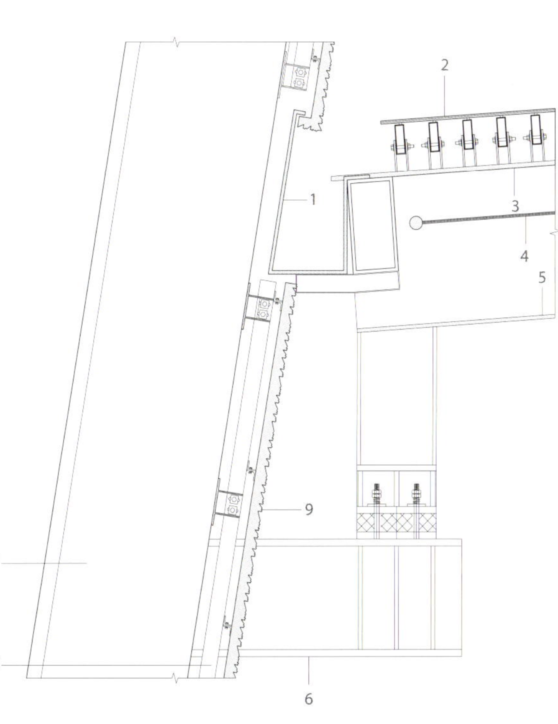

Atrium detail

1. Metal gutter
2. Tempered laminated white glass
3. Tempered glass
4. Motorized sunshade
5. Steel beam
6. Steel corbel
7. Steel column
8. Scaffolding
9. Red concrete wall panel

Façade detail

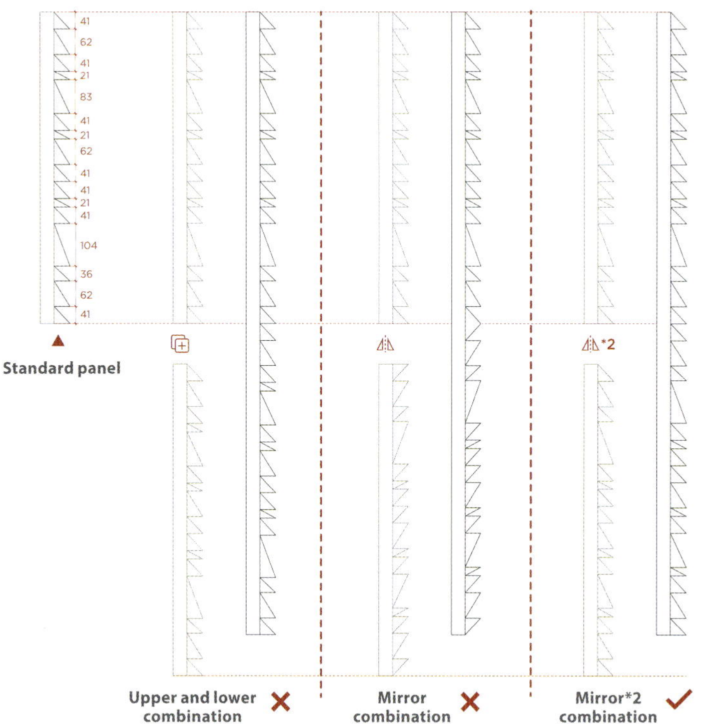

Panel combination study

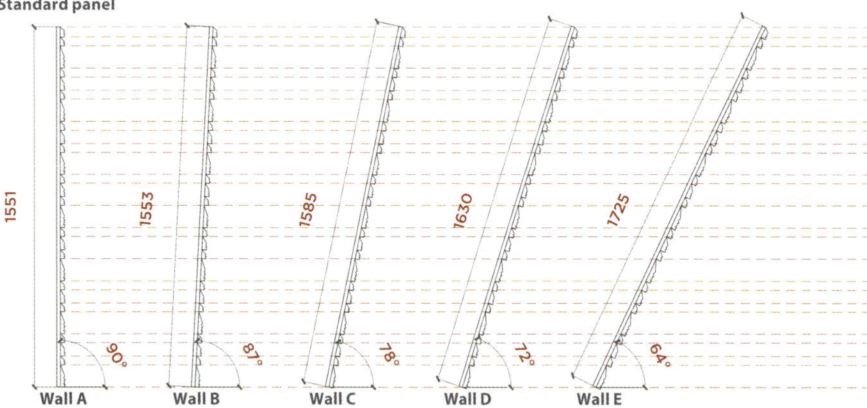

Slope effect study

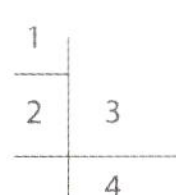

1. Construction process
2. Prefabricated cladding panels
3 & 4. Façade texture

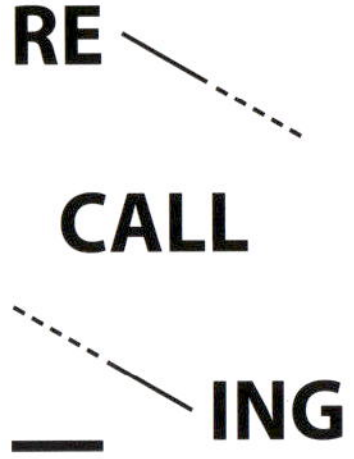

Back to Nature

Dongfengyun Art Center sits facing a vast stretch of land that has a rich, deep history, and manifests its multiple identities as a recorder and commemorator of the passage of time. Its raw and bold architectural form evokes the millions of years of changes that have taken place here on the land. It is not only a physical space; its red stone formation will also be a spatial symbol of the town's future. Seemingly forgotten by this world, it will not only provide a rich spatial and material experience for the people who visit, but also inspire future users through its visually distinctive spatial imagery. Ultimately, it will serve as a precursor to the future development of the town.

Embedded in the natural surroundings

View toward the Dongfengyun Art Center

Zhejiang Lishui Guyanhuaxiang Art Center

Large-Scale, Daily Interaction

"Rather than designing a purely austere and minimalist art center, I envisioned the Guyanhuaxiang Art Center as a vibrant and multifunctional space. By day, it serves as a venue for exhibitions, and by evening, it becomes a place for strolling, socializing, and dancing. The iconic suspended structure offers visual prominence, while the smaller, scattered volumes at ground level foster a lively atmosphere. Art and everyday life coexist, enriching one another in a symbiotic relationship, creating a shared space that seamlessly blends cultural and daily activities."

—Meng Fanhao

Location: Lishui, Zhejiang Province, China
Design firm: line+ studio
Principal architect: Meng Fanhao
Project architect: Li Xinguang
Architecture design team: Hao Jun, He Yaliang, Xu Hao, Wan Yuncheng
Interior design team: Zhu Jun, Jin Yuting, Yang Li, Liang Guoqing, Zhang Sisi, Lv Siqi, Deng Hao, Ge Zhenliang, Qiu Limin, Chen Wen
VI designer: Liu Xinhui
EPC manager: Ding Yibo
Area: 217,459 square feet (20,203 square meters)
Design period: January 2020–October 2021
Construction period: October 2021–March 2024
Client: Lishui Liandu Tourism Investment Development Co., Ltd
Photography: schranimage, DONG Image, line+ studio
Model photography: line+ studio

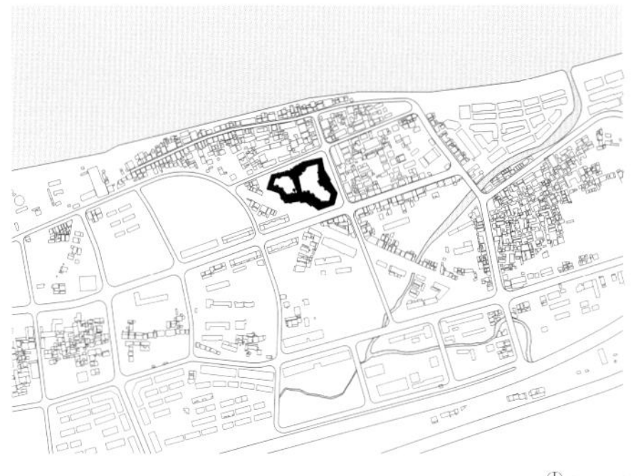

Site plan

Nestled between the waters of Tongji Weir and the serene landscapes of Bi Hu, Guyan Huaxiang has long been a place where art and nature converge. Steeped in a history of over 1,500 years, this charming town has become a canvas for artistic souls seeking inspiration from both its rich heritage and its natural beauty. Since it became a National 4A Scenic Area in 2014, Guyan Huaxiang has drawn artists from all corners of China, each eager to capture its essence on canvas.

In response to the growing influx of creative minds, the local community, alongside the government, envisioned an artist village to provide both a sanctuary and a platform for the arts. By the end of 2018, a 717,691-square-foot (66,667-square-meter) art park blossomed, offering free studios, galleries, and spaces where over 120 artists could live and work, their creations weaving the town into a living, breathing art gallery. The park's vibrant presence has since fueled an oil-painting industry that now generates over 160 million yuan (USD$22.4 million) annually, while attracting more than 1.7 million visitors each year.

To continue nurturing this cultural renaissance, the Guyanhuaxiang Art Center is the next chapter in the town's story. This art center not only meets the growing demand for exhibition space and educational programs but also serves as a beacon for artistic exchange. It amplifies the town's already resonant artistic pulse, expanding its influence beyond the local and into the global stage, inviting all who visit to witness the marriage of history, creativity, and community.

Street view

The old town of Guyan Huaxiang

Overlooking the art center

Abstract Art and Vivid Daily Life

The art center is located within a densely populated residential area, adjacent to the town's ancient streets, with views of the Ou River to the north and surrounded by mountains. The site radiates the energy of local life.

In the early design stages, line+ studio recognized that the traditional role of art buildings as isolated, self-contained institutions would not be sustainable here. While art centers are often viewed as "stages" for exhibitions, these buildings tend to operate in isolation from the surrounding community. In this case, the town's existing artistic foundation was not sufficient to support such a large-scale cultural facility in the long term. Therefore, line+ studio sought to create a space where the art center and the town's daily life could coexist and support one another, blurring the boundaries between cultural space and public life.

To achieve this, line+ studio worked closely with the client to develop a proactive operational model. The design brief aimed to ensure the center would function as a dynamic, multiuse public space. By integrating the rhythms of daily life, the design envisioned the center hosting a variety of activities—including commerce, culture, entertainment, leisure, education, and curatorial programs—that enhanced the center's vibrancy and relevance.

The design positions the art center with two primary functions: as a space for contemporary art exhibitions and as a venue for the everyday activities of the town. The architecture is intended to juxtapose abstract art with the lively energy of daily town life.

Street corner scene

Northwest corner elevated entrance

Art center inner courtyard

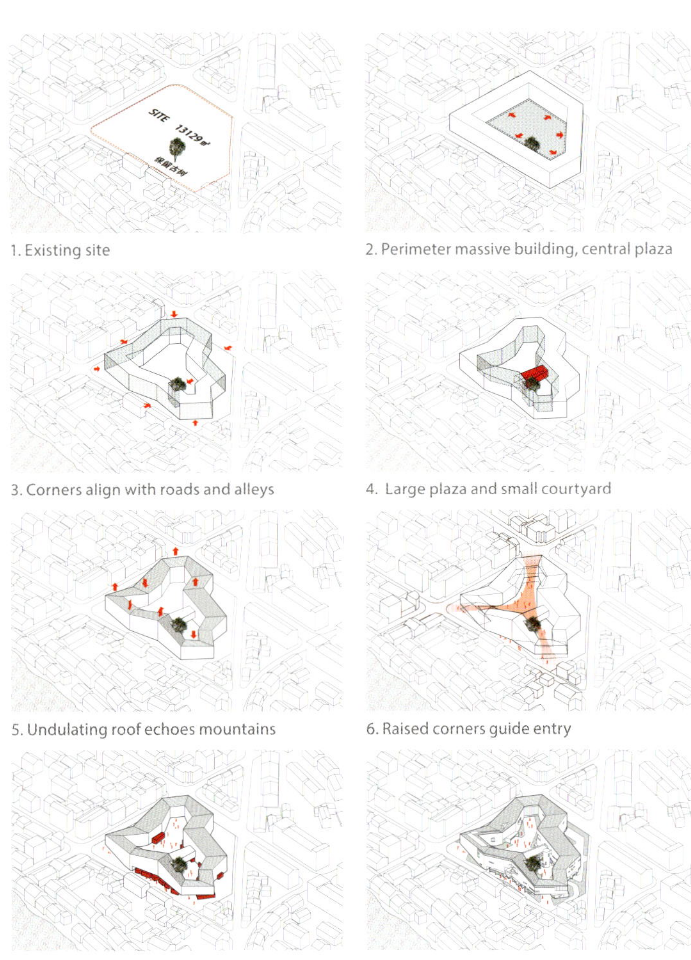

1. Existing site

2. Perimeter massive building, central plaza

3. Corners align with roads and alleys

4. Large plaza and small courtyard

5. Undulating roof echoes mountains

6. Raised corners guide entry

7. Ground-floor box spaces for commerce

7. Blend public use with artistic institutions

Generation diagram

Model

Resolving Site Contradictions through Scaled Design

This project addresses the dual challenge of ensuring public accessibility while respecting the surrounding residential and natural environments. The site spans 141,330 square feet (13,130 square meters), with a floor area ratio of 1.05. The design strikes a balance between large-scale institutional functions and smaller, more intimate public spaces.

The building is situated near the site's red line boundary, seamlessly integrating with the local context and preserving the continuity of surrounding streets and alleys. Two courtyards—one large, one small—are enclosed within the site. The building adopts an open form with setbacks and elevated corners, inviting interaction with the surrounding public space.

The upper section of the building houses the exhibition spaces, expressed through a dramatic suspended structure that evokes the distant mountains. Below, the building is aligned with the residential scale, with staggered small box-like volumes housing retail and leisure functions. This vertical division effectively balances the institutional and public aspects of the art center.

Aerial view

Northwest corner elevated entrance

Public Engagement

The public nature of the art center is enhanced not only by its open design but also by its seamless integration into the daily life of the town. The building actively invites the community to engage, transforming it into a space for collective participation. This approach is shaped by three key strategies:

Street corner plazas:
Three large-scale plazas are created by pulling back the building's boundaries and elevating the corners. These plazas serve as welcoming entry points, drawing people from the streets into the space.

Ground-floor integration:
The ground floor is designed to blend with the surrounding streets and alleys, breaking down the building into smaller, more approachable volumes. Commercial spaces are arranged to echo the town's historic small-scale fabric, reinforcing the art center's public character.

Inner courtyards:
The second floor features elevated walkways that enrich the spatial experience. Various courtyards offer different public experiences. The large plaza serves as a venue for town gatherings, while smaller courtyards, centered around centuries-old trees, continue the town's tradition of communal spaces.

Small courtyard

Art center inner square

Spatial flow

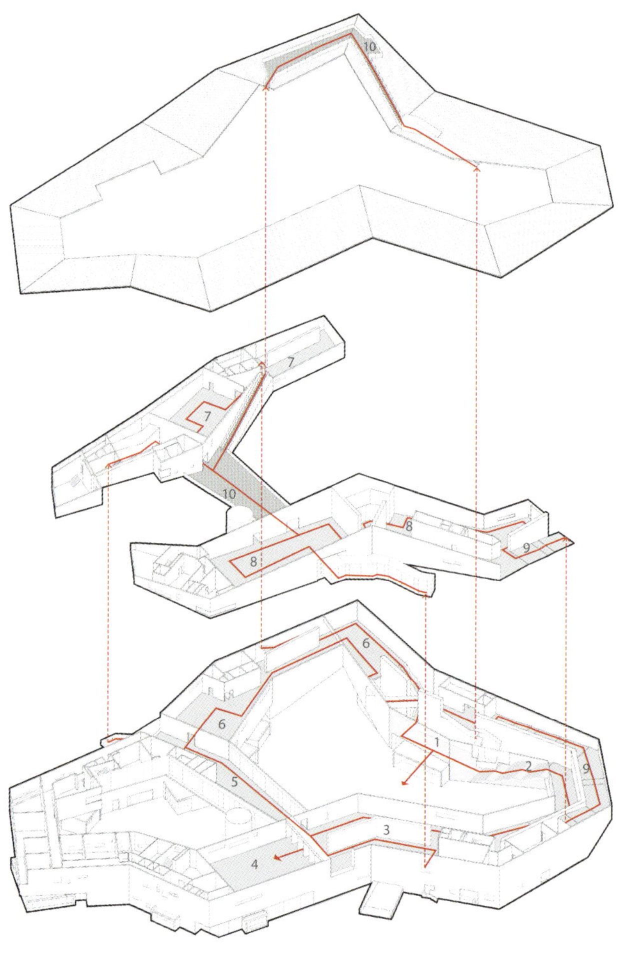

Exhibition circulation

1. Art center lobby
2. Staircase gallery
3. South gallery 1
4. Multifunctional hall
5. Café
6. North gallery 1
7. North gallery 2
8. South gallery 2
9. Ramp gallery
10. Observation deck

Three-dimensional Exhibition Narrative

The exhibition spaces are elevated above the town, connected by a series of galleries and corridors that guide visitors through a carefully curated narrative. The spatial flow takes visitors on a journey, with architectural transitions leading from exposition to climax, offering a unique perspective for both curators and visitors.

Visitors enter the exhibition spaces from the plaza, ascending through a sequence of steps, ramps, and suspended bridges that lead to the rooftop. Transparent and translucent materials facilitate dynamic interactions between the exhibition areas and the surrounding town, creating moments of surprise and contrast between art and everyday life.

Inside, the predominantly monochromatic exhibition spaces are punctuated by a striking red rusted metal staircase that resonates with the building's architectural language. This design breaks away from the conventional "white box" format, inviting a more fluid integration of interior and exterior spaces.

Ground-floor plan

1. Elevated entrance
2. Lobby
3. Cultural and creative reading area
4. Mother and baby room
5. Commercial area
6. Logistics area
7. Exhibition preparation room
8. Storage room
9. Square
10. Ancient tree

0 5 10 20m

N

Section

Exhibition space

Three-dimensional foyer space

Exhibition space

Exhibition space

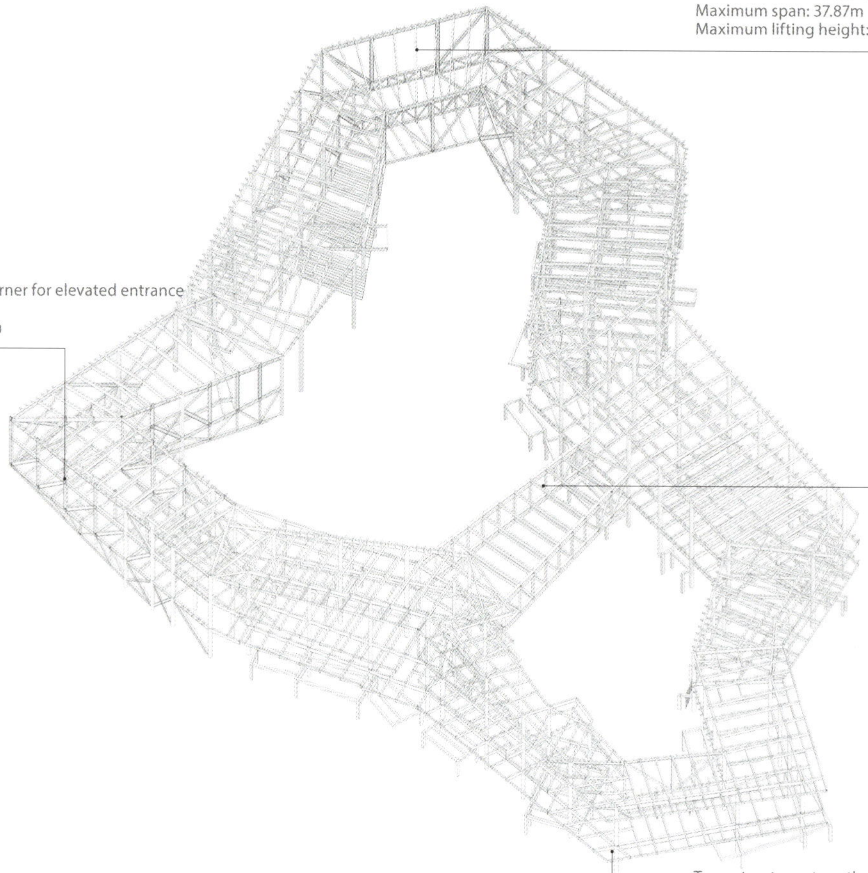

Truss structure at southeast corner for elevated entrance
Maximum span: 37.87m
Maximum lifting height: 7.15m

Truss structure at northeast corner for elevated entrance
Maximum span: 24.42m
Maximum lifting height: 5.23m

Vierendeel truss structure
Maximum span: 32m
Maximum lifting height: 4.93m

Truss structure at northwest corner for elevated entrance
Maximum span: 20.84m
Maximum lifting height: 5.33m

Steel structure

Structure and Materials

The architectural challenge lies in the large-scale cantilevered forms, while the material challenge focuses on balancing structural integrity with the need for varied spatial experiences.

Steel structure:
The cantilevered sections of the building were constructed using a steel framework, chosen for its structural feasibility and cost-effectiveness. Trusses were incorporated in areas requiring large spans and elevated spaces. Skybridges, suspended from the roof, connect different sections of the building, imparting a sense of lightness and fluidity.

Courtyard

Rooftop platform

Ground box area

Truss structure at northeast corner for elevated entrance

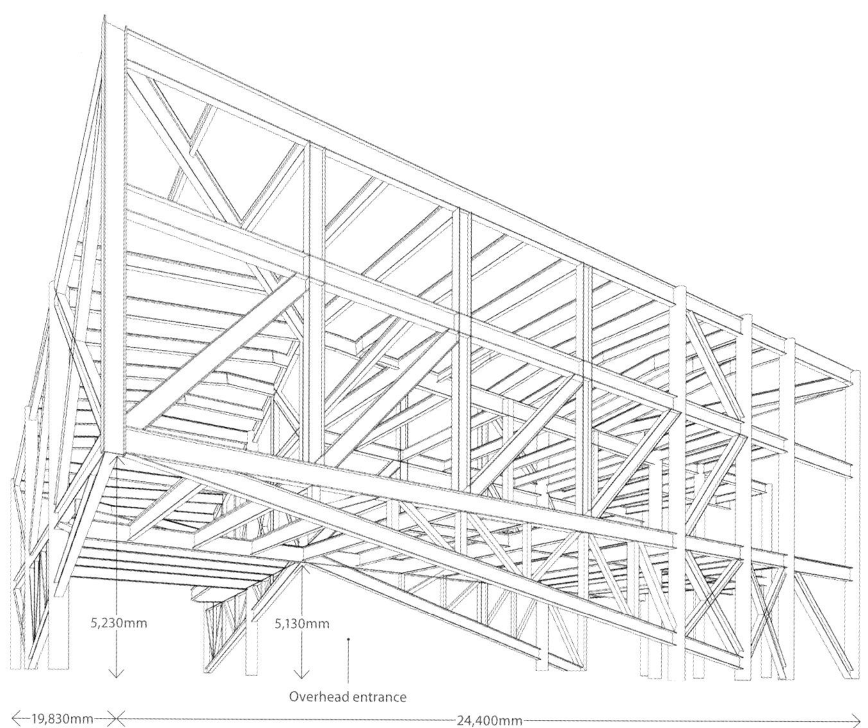

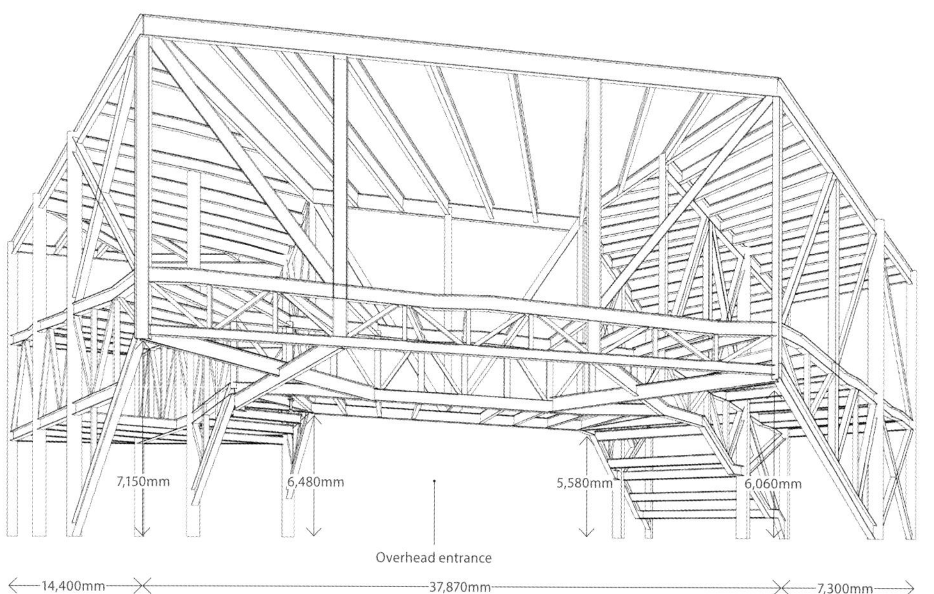

Truss structure at southeast corner for elevated entrance

Elevated entrance at northeast corner

Elevated entrance at southeast corner

Aerial view of the art center

Residents' activity space under the elevated entrance

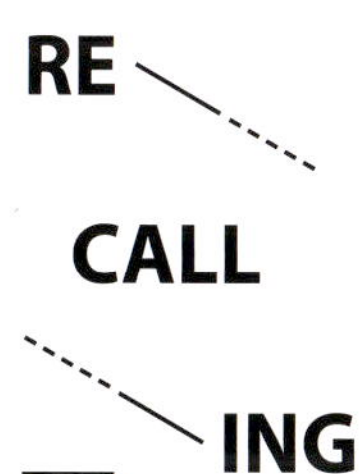

The center blends with the town's landscape

Reclaiming Community

Building an art center for the town is not just about creating a space for art exhibitions; it's about reconnecting the community with its roots and traditions in a world filled with fleeting modern distractions. Rather than catering exclusively to a niche group of professionals, the Guyanhuaxiang Art Center serves the broader community, integrating daily life into the traditional concept of a closed-off art space. By transforming it into an organic hub, it also generates deeper values, accommodating commerce, culture, training, and education. In doing so, it fosters a space that empowers life in the town while recalling the essence of community and tradition.

Hangzhou Qiantang River Museum

Convergence of Time and Place

With its open, shared, and inclusive attitude, Hangzhou Qiantang River Museum has created a new urban public gathering place.

Location: Hangzhou, Zhejiang Province, China
Design firm: line+ studio
Principal architect: Zhu Peidong
Architecture design team: Sun Xiaoyu, Li Binmiao, Hong Yang, Zhang Qiqi, Du Mengying
Construction drawing: Zhejiang Baoye Construction Group Co. Ltd
Area: 124,216 square feet (11,540 square meters)
Design period: July 2018–May 2019
Construction period: December 2019–2024
Client: Hangzhou Qianjiang New City Management Committee, Hangzhou Qiantang River Museum
Photography: Chen Xi Studio, line+ studio
Model photography: Chen Xi Studio

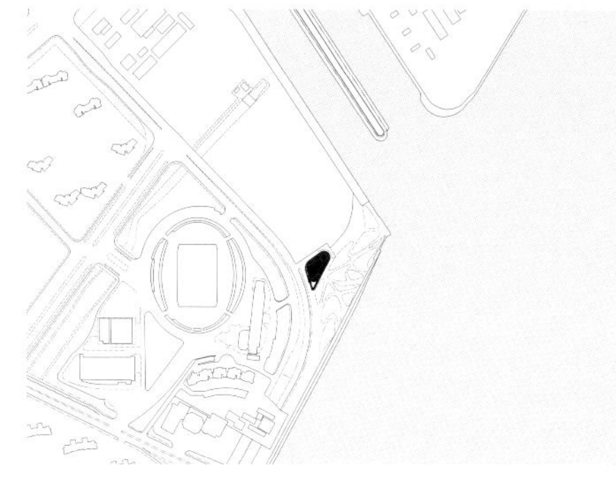

Site plan

Time and Place Meet

Urban development has changed with the times in the capital of Zhejiang Province, an important, centrally located city in the Yangtze River Delta, and the second-largest city in Hangzhou, east China. In ancient times, the location of the city was determined by the Qiantang River, the Grand Canal and the Wu Mountain. In the last century, Hangzhou's urban development was centered only on the West Lake area. However, at the start of the twenty-first century its urban construction began moving southward along its canal system, as a multicentered, networked, and clustered urban structure took shape. The city defined its overall development direction as "urban expansion to the east, tourism to the west, and development along and across the river." Hangzhou is today officially moving toward a new "Qiantang River era," as a next step after the "West Lake Era" that lasted for a thousand years. The energetic rise on both sides of the Qiantang River adds a new spiritual core to the culture of Hangzhou, while the shift of the center showcases the city's humming vitality. As one of line+ studio's most prominent construction projects, the Hangzhou Qiantang River Museum project took fifteen months of repeated discussions and design modifications before construction commenced. Construction officially started on December 18, 2019, and the civil engineering portion was completed around the end of 2021.

Qiantang River Museum is located at the geographic intersection of Hangzhou's most important rivers—the Beijing-Hangzhou Grand Canal and Qiantang River; in the distance stands the main venue of the 19th Asian Games. Its location is both geographically and historically significant, as well as sensitive. For one, the site sits at the southern part of a World Heritage site, the Beijing-Hangzhou Grand Canal, and the place where Hangzhou's two essential water systems—the Beijing-Hangzhou Grand Canal and the Qiantang River—converge. Built in sections from the Spring and Autumn period (5th century BCE) and fully unified under the Sui dynasty (605–609 CE), the Grand Canal flows through the affluent Qiantang area, bearing witness to the vicissitudes of this prosperous ancient city and the diversity among its whitewashed walls. Known as "Zhejiang" in ancient times, Qiantang River is the largest river in Zhejiang Province, as well as the source of its provincial name. One of the birthplaces of Wuyue culture, it was also a de facto governing center for the wide southeast area. As the meeting point of two water systems and their civilizations, it represents Hangzhou's "water culture."

The project is also located at the intersection of Qianjiang New Town, Phase I and Phase II; this intersection lies in Hangzhou's CBD area, which is situated close to the northern part of the project site. Across the Grand Canal is the planned River Gateway urban complex, poised to become an important urban commercial and residential landmark in central Hangzhou; the main venue of the 19th Asian Games can also be seen across the river. It is at this junction that the past, present, and future of Hangzhou converge.

Hanzhou's Qiantang riverbank

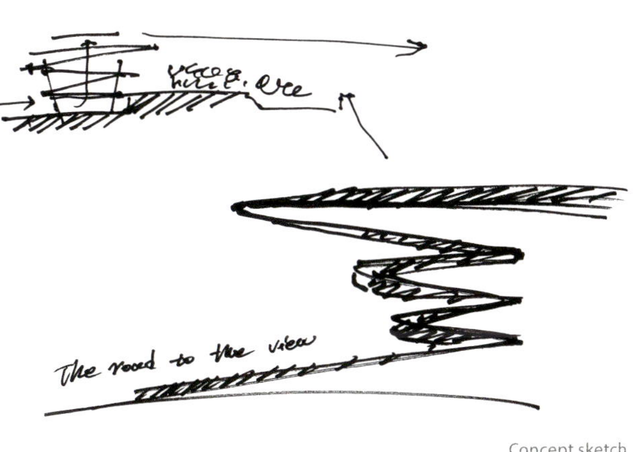

Concept sketch

Aerial view

Hangzhou Qiantang River Museum at dusk

Contemporary Seawall Construction Techniques

Unlike the direct connection between the spiraling corridor and the design concept, the formal language of the façade was inspired by the modular construction technique of the Qiantang River's seawall. With the help of contemporary digital technology, titanium-zinc curtain-wall units have been interlaced and "masoned" around the building surface such that these differently sized convex, concave, or flat titanium-zinc panels form a series of texture changes. Under different light conditions, they look like shimmering waves in a textural play that aptly embody poet Wang Anshi's notion that "waves are the water's skin."

Through an integrated design of the façade, curtain-walls, and lighting, line+ studio controls the depth of the curtain-wall units. They also subtly stagger the individual units against each other to effectively conceal the evening lighting and, ultimately, form a multilayered visual texture. The lights and shadows that dance on the walls at night cast a soft light against the grand backdrop of the riverfront. This creates the opportunity for the museum to become a new urban public landmark at the mouth of the Grand Canal along Qiantang River.

The cantilevered urban observation platform

Viewing path

Construction process

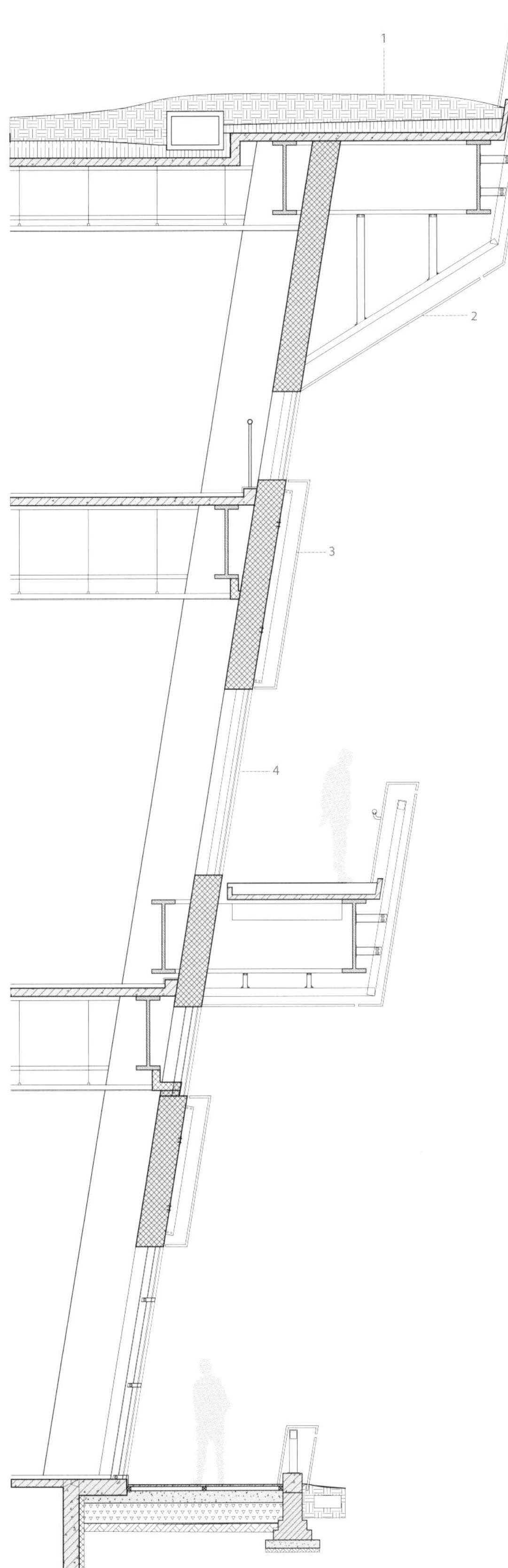

Section wall details

1. Grass-planted roofing
   300mm-thick planting soil
   Dry-laid polyester non-woven filter layer
   40mm-thick plastic drainage board
   50mm-thick C20 fine gravel concrete protective layer
   Dry-laid polyester mesh cloth, one layer
   90mm-thick extruded polystyrene insulation board with B1 combustion performance
   4mm-thick double-sided self-adhesive waterproofing membrane
   2mm-thick asphalt waterproofing coatings
   20mm-thick 1:2.5 cement leveling layer
   30mm-thick 2% slope layer
   Structural slab

2. Titanium-zinc sheet curtain-wall ceiling
   20mm-thick silver-white honeycomb titanium-zinc plate curtain-wall
   Waterproof breathable membrane
   Main and secondary curtain-wall keel

3. Titanium-zinc sheet curtain-wall façade
   20mm-thick silver-white honeycomb titanium-zinc plate curtain-wall
   Waterproof breathable membrane
   Main and secondary curtain-wall keel
   Cement fiber board
   Insulation rock wool board
   Beige interior decoration board

4. Glass curtain-wall
   High-transmittance low-e curtain-wall
   Heat-insulating aluminum bar, main and secondary curtain-wall keel

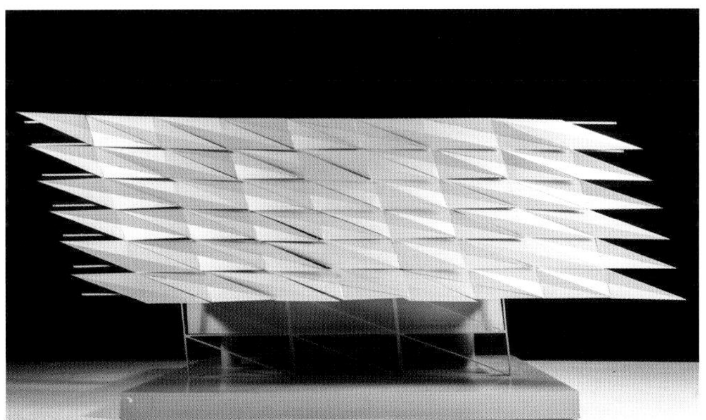

Façade model

Cantilevered urban observation platform

View toward the river from the outdoor terrace

Viewing platform

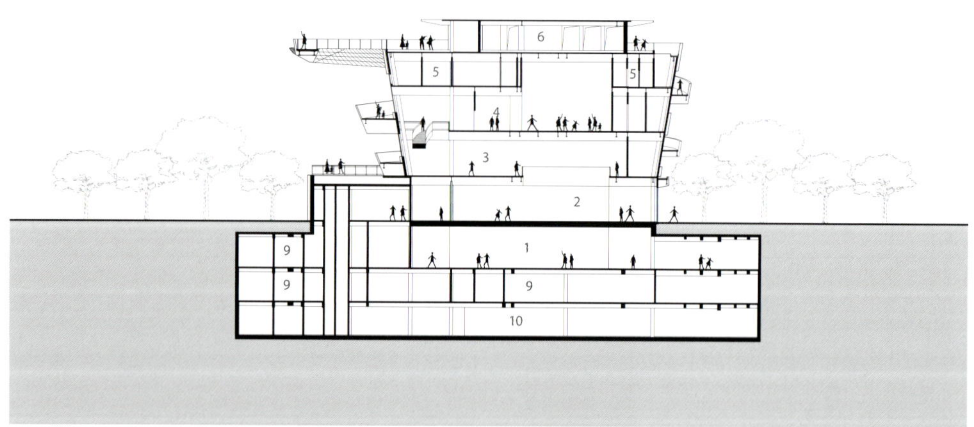

Section

1. Temporary exhibition room
2. Introduction room
3. Exhibition room 1
4. Exhibition room 2
5. Office
6. Roof garden
7. Spiral ramp
8. Mechanical room
9. Collection storage
10. Parking

Façade creating distinctive experiences at various spatial heights and dimensions

The project model and the completed building

Exhibition hall

Exhibition hall

Interior staircase

Exhibition hall

Viewing toward the urban landscape

Illuminated façade at night

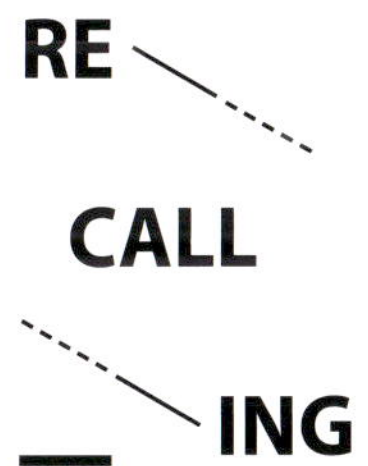

Tides of Innovation

The periodic tidal rhythms of the Qiantang River, together with its vast natural landscape, evoke a sense of the infinite cosmos, the unceasing flow of time, and the continuity of life. The Qiantang River Museum responds to these elements through architectural language that reinterprets the region's cultural essence. By integrating modern design elements, the building aligns with the spirit of innovation in Qianjiang New City, while also drawing on the river's natural rhythms and the area's historical significance. The museum, therefore, creates a seamless connection between past, present, and future, enriching the experience of both the space and its surrounding context.

Mansion on Lotus Mountain

A Leaf is Buddha

Although the private Mansion on Lotus Mountain is not representative of the culture of a region or the soul of an era, the residents' memories, daily behaviors, lifestyles, and spiritual beliefs embodied within it required line+ studio to pursue a design that is a tapestry of individual experiences and specific collective memories.

Location: Northeast China
Design firm: line+ studio
Principal architect: Meng Fanhao
Architecture design team: Zhu Min, Wang Yubin, Xu Hao, Wan Yuncheng
Interior design team: Jin Xin, Zhang Ning, Wang Lijie, Zhao Jiaqi, Lu Yue, Hu Jinwei, Zhang Ding, Li Chonghao, Zhou Lujie, Chen Yaqi, Li Chunyang, Shi Jie, Zhao Tiantian
Landscape design team: Li Shangyang, Jin Jianbo, Chen Xiaorong, Chi Xiaomei
Area: 41,010 square feet (3,810 square meters)
Design period: March 2018–June 2020
Construction period: June 2020–2023
Photography: line+ studio
Model photography: Chen Xi Studio, Sun Lei

Site context

A Family Mansion

In a valley in the northeast of China, line+ studio was commissioned to design a private mansion on a site surrounded by a tranquil environment of hills with dense vegetation and water. The project was to satisfy multiple functional requirements: both spiritual life—for Buddhist worship, meditation, and contemplation—and to function as the family's residence. The site is located in the transition zone from the Songliao Plain to the Changbai Mountains, surrounded by mountains and a serene scenery. In recent years, there have been many private residential complexes and guesthouses constructed on the outskirts of cities by urban elites returning to live in the countryside, but who still wish to be close to the city. In this private mansion project, it was imperative for line+studio to understand the inward orientation of the family, as that was what would define the privacy and spirituality of the building.

The design follows the mountain terrain, with three groups of geometric volumes scattered throughout a valley which is high in the north and low in the south, and steep in the west and flat in the east. The first set of buildings serves as living spaces enclosed by four artificial "boulders," conveying the cultural accumulation and eternal heritage of "family" through the strong anchoring force of "stone." The most important spiritual space, as part of the ancestral lineage concept, is located in a more secluded part of the valley, up a mountain path, and includes the Buddha Hall and the leaf-shaped Ancestral Hall.

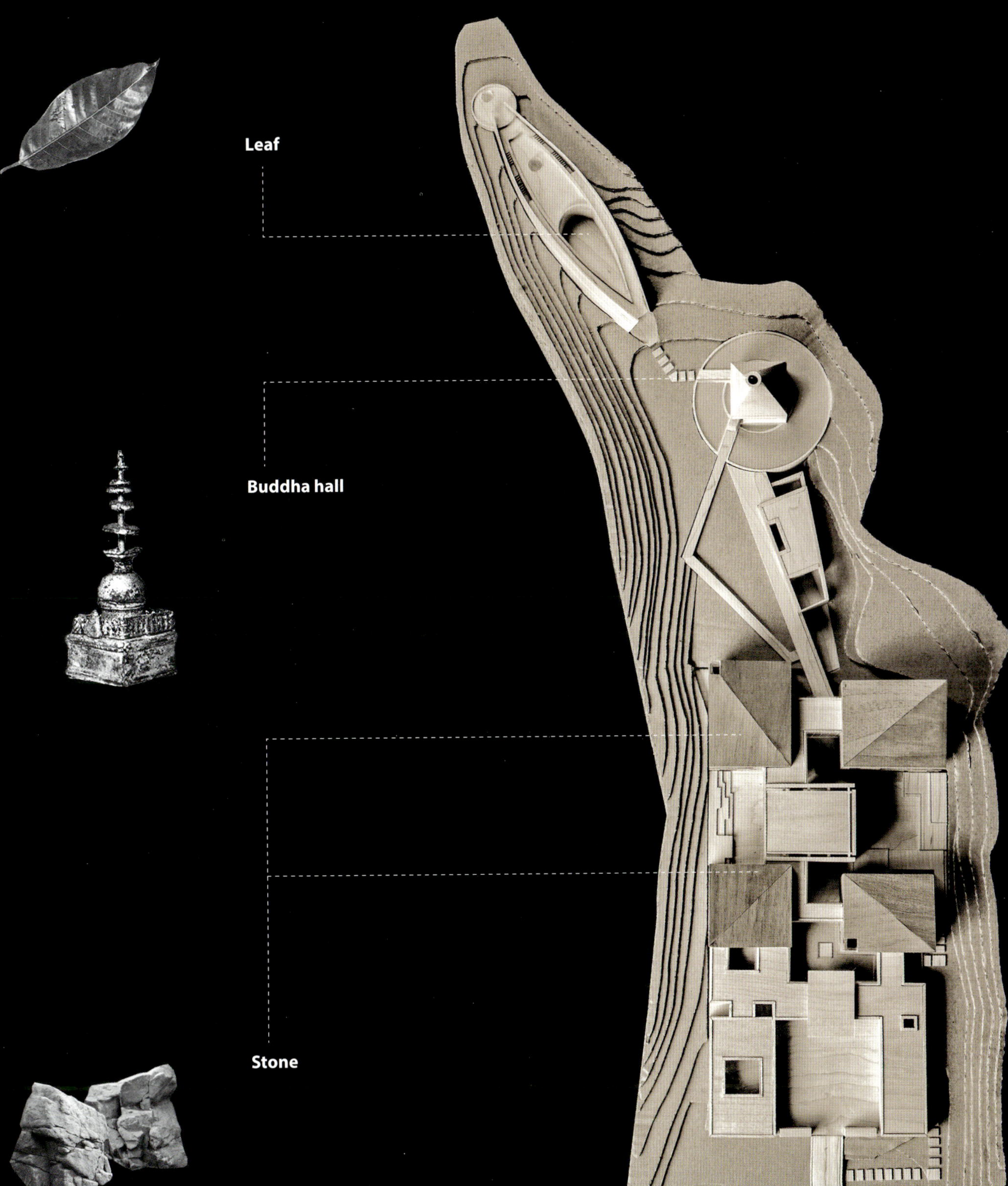

Concept and model

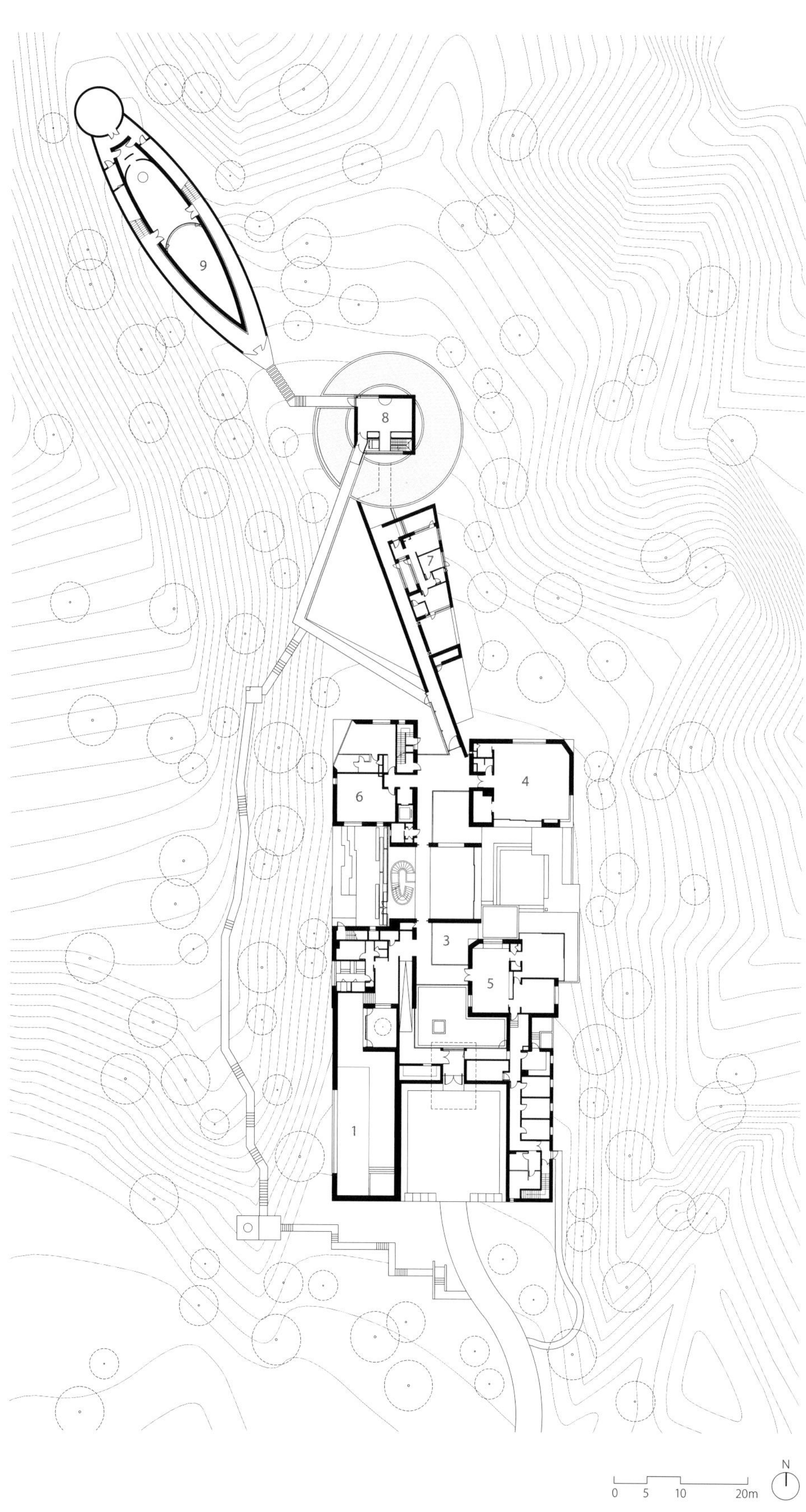

Ground-floor plan

1. Swimming pool
2. Maid's room
3. Living room
4. Lounge
5. Chinese and Western kitchen
6. Master bedroom
7. Dharma Master bedroom
8. Buddha Hall
9. Ancestral Hall

Model

Construction site

Buddha Hall, Ancestral Hall, and Dharma Master's residence

A Shelter for the Spirit

As a shelter for human beings, architecture can not only accommodate physical bodies, but also connect us back to spirituality. The family members of the project owner are devout Buddhists and requested that the Buddha Hall be made the spiritual core of the private mansion. By interpreting and reorganizing Buddhist and ancestral elements, line+ studio designed three functions that incorporate family memories and religious spirit: the Buddha Hall, the Ancestral Hall, and the Dharma Master's personal residence.

Unlike the usual earth-sheltered or semi-subterranean design strategies used for religious properties, the Buddha Hall at the center of the building sequence is the combination of a towering conical volume modeled after a pagoda, that sits atop a volume with a square base, in whole replicating the form of a stupa.

A stupa is usually a hemispherical monument that symbolizes the burial mound of Buddha, in which the relics of Buddha are contained. Often, stupas also contain the relics of monks, nuns, and revered Buddhist teachers, and commemorate the teachings of Buddha; many devout Buddhists faithfully visit stupas to meditate, venerate the relics within, or to circumambulate the stupas and chant (keeping count of chants with prayer beads), and spin prayer wheels to make merit. Following the introduction of Buddhism into China during the Han dynasty, "heaven," which was originally believed to be located on the ground, was raised to the sky and supported by a square-shaped flat pavilion below, thus creating the traditional Chinese belief that "heaven is round and earth is square."

Ancestral Hall construction details

Ancestral Hall construction details

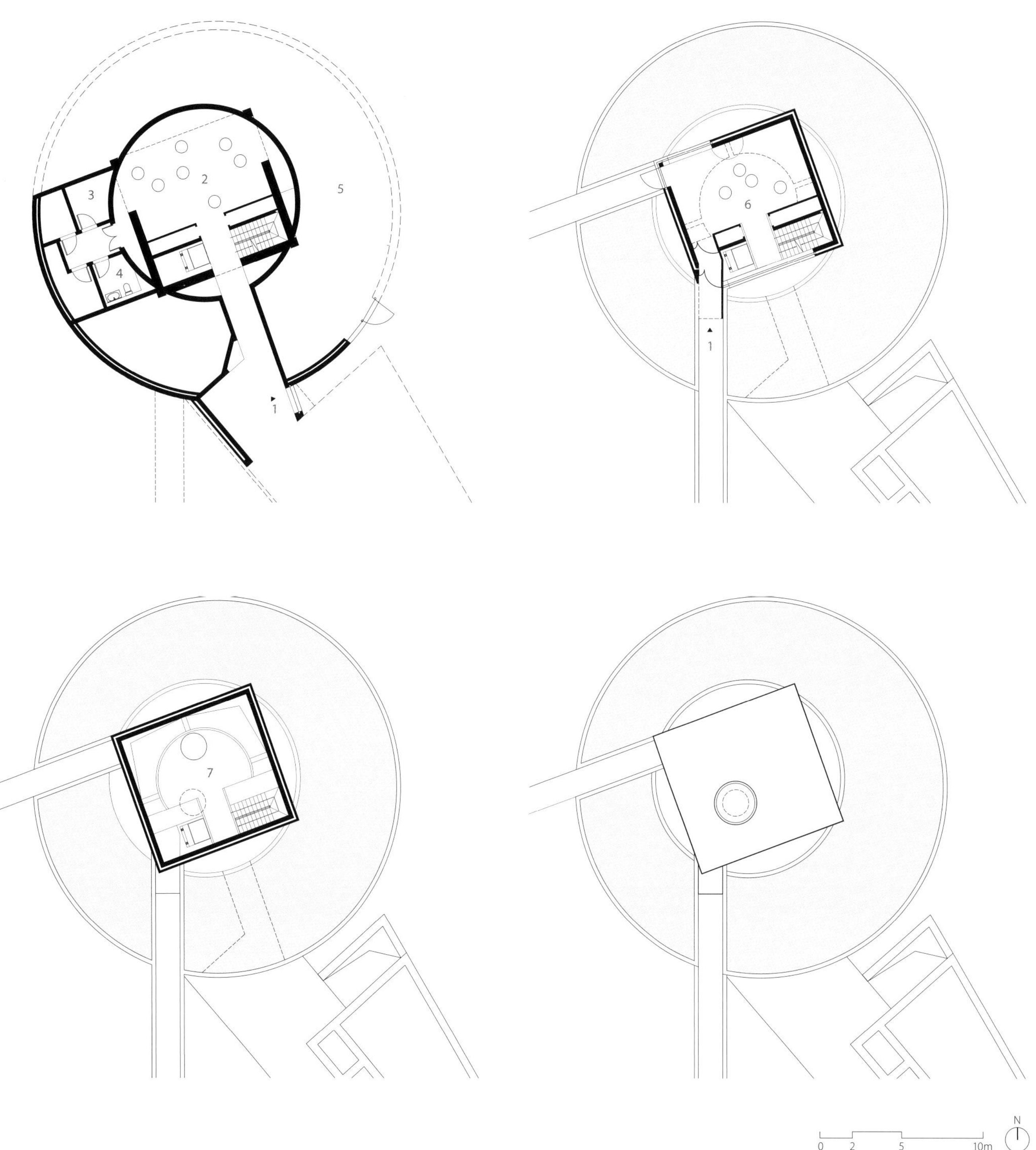

A	B
C	D

A. Basement-floor plan
B. First-floor plan
C. Second-floor plan
D. Roof plan

1. Entrance
2. Meditation room
3. Mechanical room
4. Restroom
5. Open area
6. Rest area
7. Meditation room

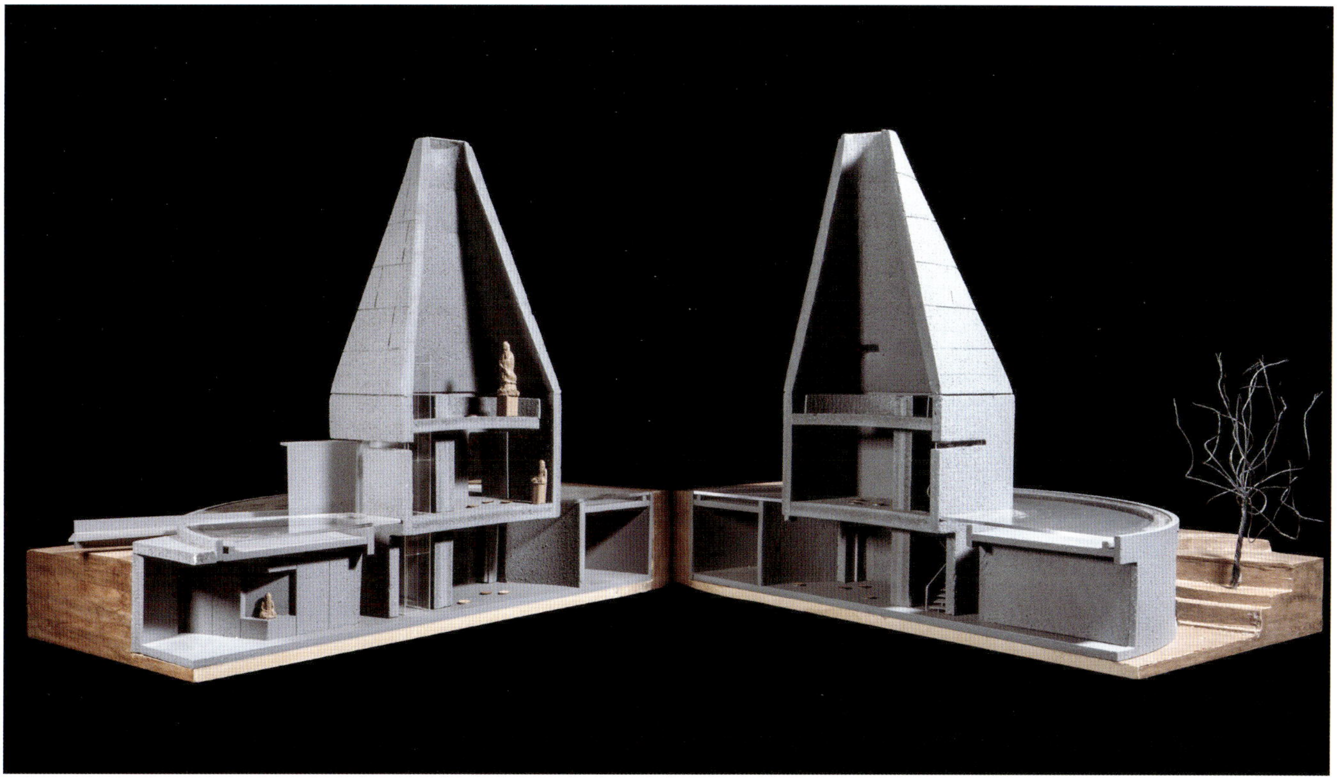

Model of Buddha Hall

The Buddha Hall comprises three floors: the basement connects to the living area, from which the owner can take the elevator directly to the private meditation area on the second floor. The first floor is an open, public meditation area for priests and visiting meditators to use and live in. This circulation route facilitates the movement of users' movement while ensuring privacy. Soft light flows in from above the Buddha Hall, creating a sacred spatial atmosphere that lulls visitors into a calm, spiritual state.

Buddha Hall

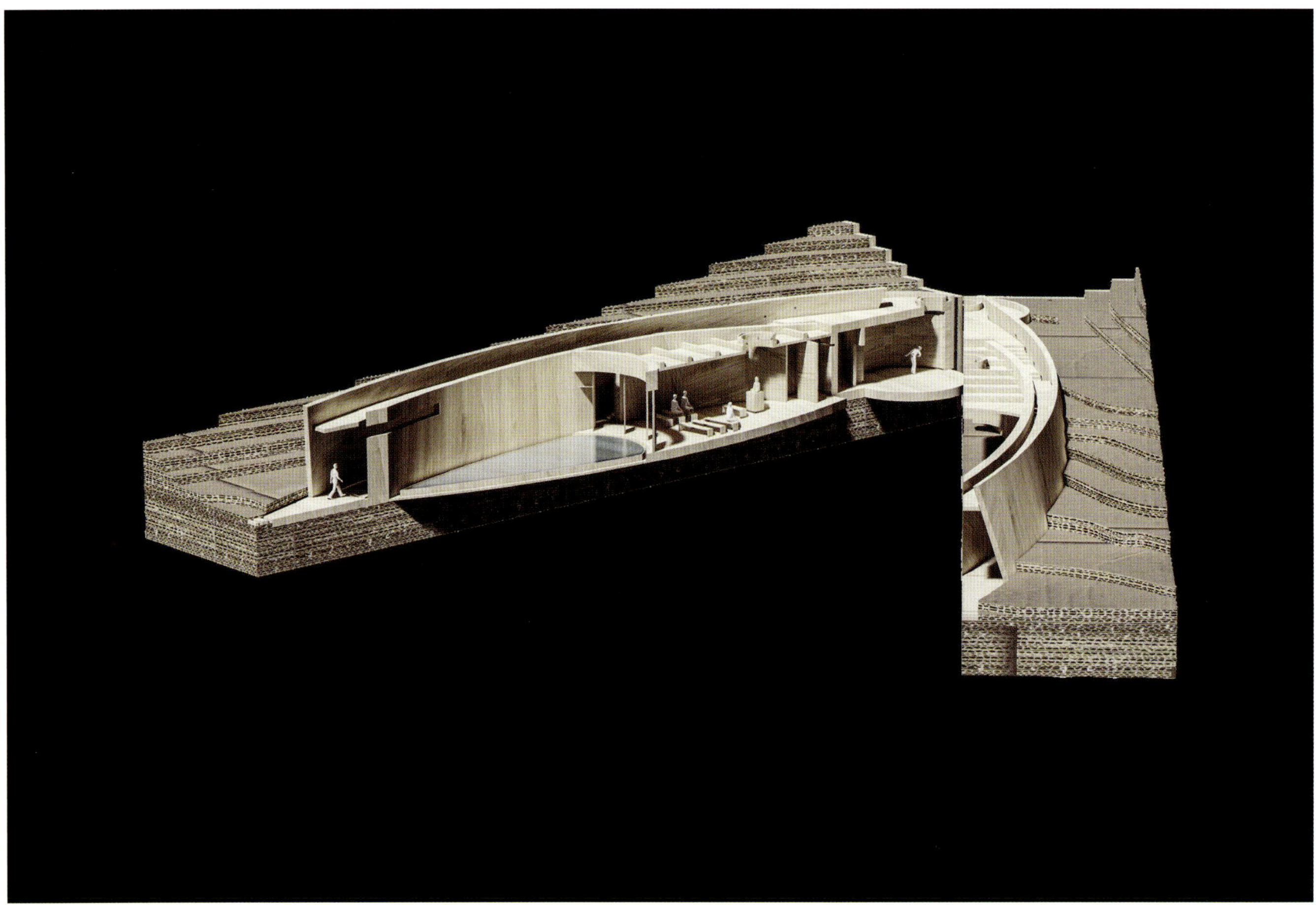

Model of the Ancestral Hall

The Ancestral Hall marks the end point of the whole building sequence. The concept of an elongated "fallen leaf returning to its roots" is used to pay tribute to departed family members who have passed on and entered another life—symbolizing completing the cycle of rebirth and rooting down memories. The design uses positive and negative shapes to organize the space. "Positive spaces" with physical functions and "negative spaces" that are left empty give the building a sense of balance, allowing the space to shift between inside and outside, and between imaginary and real, making it more expressive and experiential. The building is "cut open," and the cavity where people and light pass through simultaneously forms a simple figure-ground relationship, which enhances the spirituality and sublimity of the place.

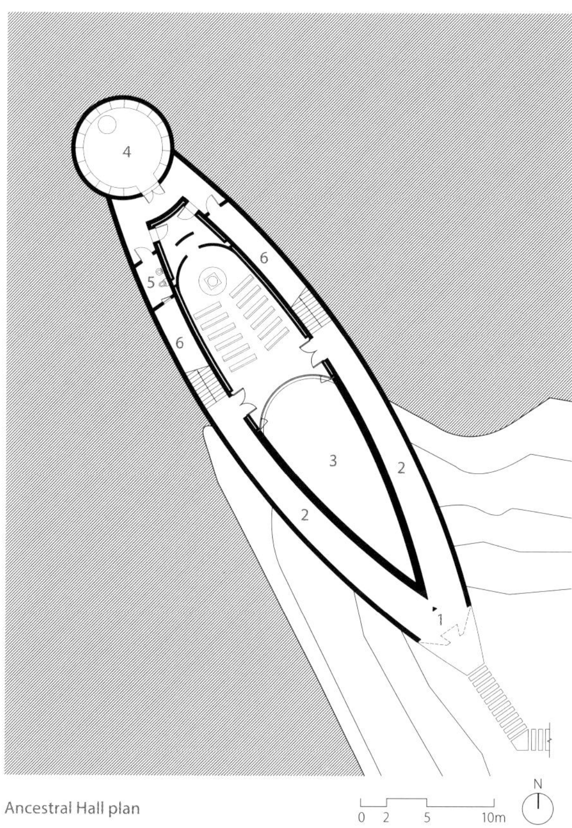

Ancestral Hall plan

1. Entrance
2. Corridor
3. Ritual space
4. Underground palace
5. Restroom
6. Mechanical space

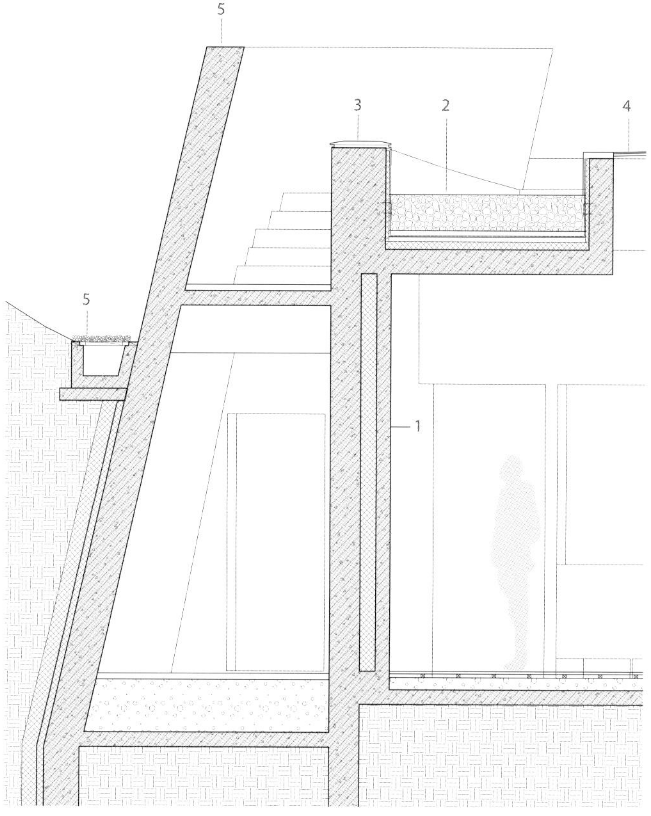

Wall detail

1. Bare concrete with insulation sandwich
2. Crushed volcanic stone roofing
3. Metal compressed roof
4. Glass skylight
5. Bare concrete wall
6. Landscape guttering

Ancestral Hall

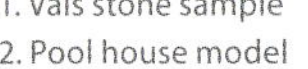

1. Vals stone sample
2. Pool house model

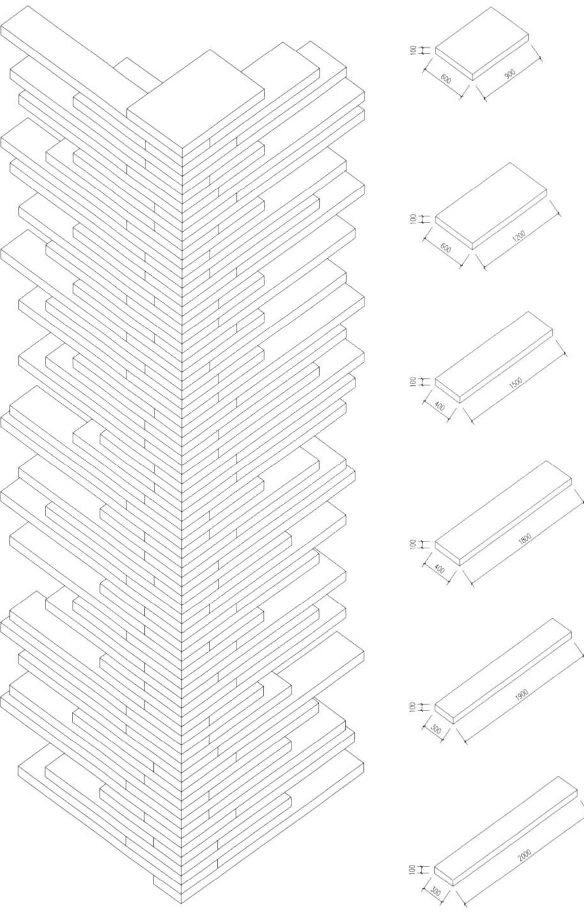

Stones splicing

Six stones module units

Two façade materials: concrete (left) and stone (right)

Residential area

The materials selected for the project correspond to the natural properties of the site, which highlight rustic timelessness. Plain fair-faced concrete and black stone constitute the two main façade materials, each distinctive in its own right yet echoing the other, forming an orderly hierarchy. Here, the plastic quality of fair-faced concrete aids to restore the inherent character of the space, avoiding superfluity, so that the spatial quality of the space can be fully experienced. The public area at the center of the residence is also made of fair-faced concrete, forming a vast cavity that envelops the family's numerous and varied activities. The façade of the monolithic "boulder" is made of black stone; the joints between the façade stones are key to producing a coherent stone texture. By using a modular approach with six standardized stone units—starting with the corner alternations, and then forming the plane with staggered joints—the desired effect on the building's body is achieved.

Living area

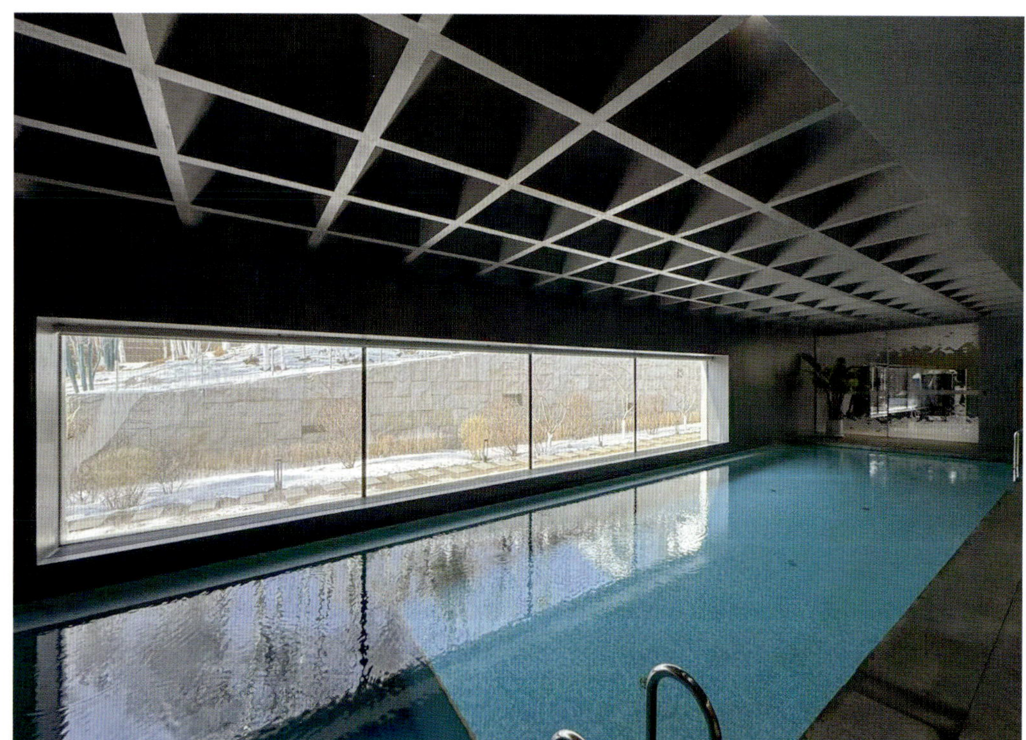
Pool house interior

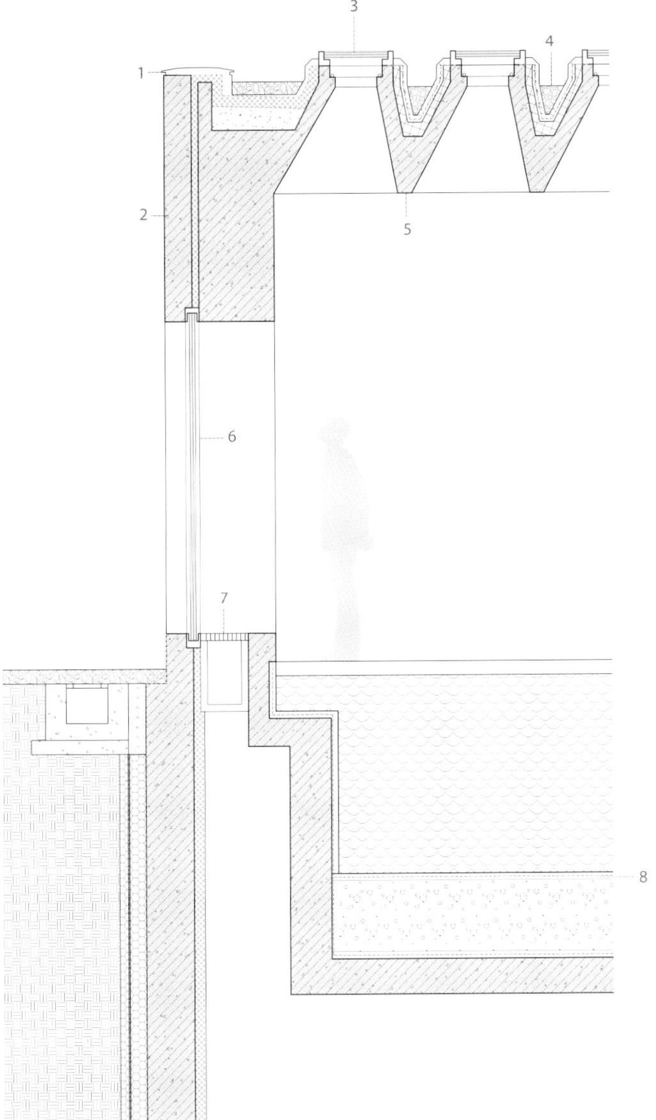

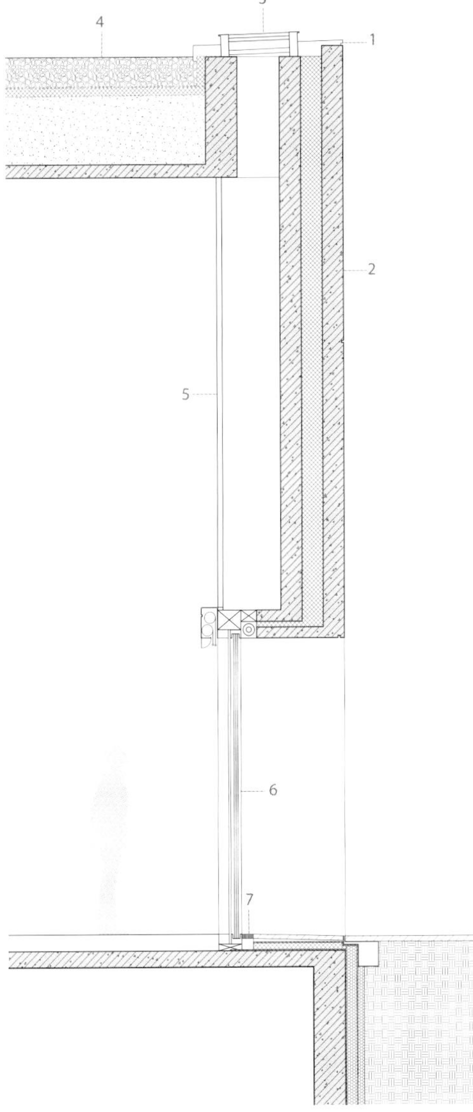

Pool house wall detail

1. Dark-gray compressed metal roof
2. Steel-molded bare concrete with double-layered insulation sandwich
3. Hollow ultra-white glass skylight
4. Crushed volcanic stone
5. Steel-molded bare concrete lightwell
6. Triple-layered hollow low-e glass
7. Anti-fog air-conditioning inlet
8. Pool surface layer

Residential area wall detail

1. Dark-gray compressed metal roof
2. Steel-molded bare concrete with double-layered insulation sandwich
3. Hollow ultra-white glass skylight
4. Crushed volcanic stone
5. Wood fence
6. Triple-layered hollow low-e glass sliding door
7. Linear metal guttering

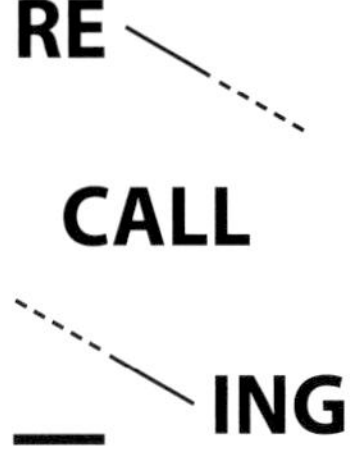

Recovering Memories

Memories are the most intimate and personal of possessions of every human being. They can be hidden deep down, or they can be passed on to become the next piece of history. In his book, *On Collective Memory*, French sociologist Maurice Halbwachs states that memories require constant nourishment from a collective source, and are sustained by social and moral pillars. Just as God needs us, memories also need other people, which means that memories can't be preserved in a context separate from the collective; their retention requires specific circumstances. Although the private Mansion on Lotus Mountain is not representative of any culture in the region or is a stamp of any era, the memories, daily behaviors, lifestyles, and spiritual beliefs of the resident family required that line+ studio present a design that includes individual experiences and specific collective memories.

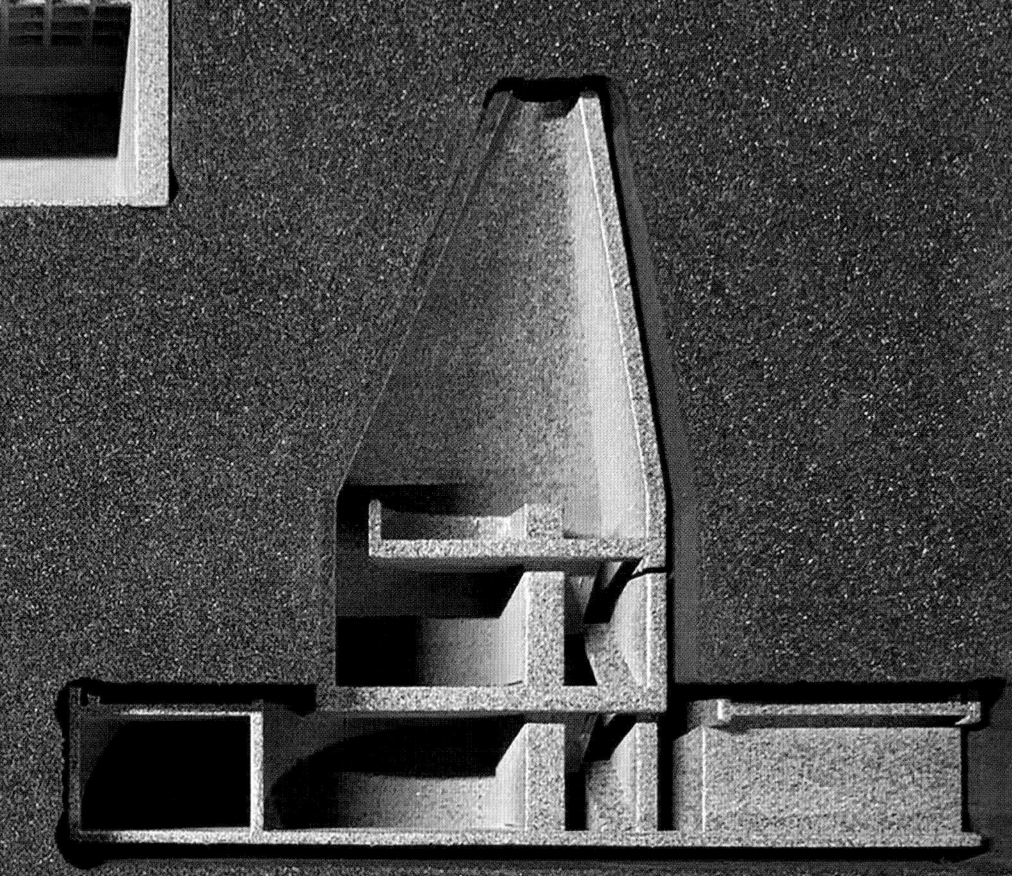

BUDDHA TEMPLE

ANCESTRAL TEMPLE SECTION

Hangzhou Lingyin Temple Extension (design competition project)

In Search of Lost Spirit

In today's modern era that has been taken over by sometimes detached contemporaneity, the design of Lingyin Temple Extension seeks to rediscover a religious space that is both spiritually powerful and open, through the shaping of space, the selection of materials, and the use of light.

Location: Hangzhou, Zhejiang Province, China
Design firm: line+ studio
Principal architect: Meng Fanhao
Architecture design team: He Yaliang, Xu Hao, Tao Tao, Li Renjie, Liu Chao, Zhu Xiaojing, Xing Shu, Hao Jun, Yuan Dong, Chen Zexin, Fan Zhen
Interior design team: Zhu Jun, Deng Hao, Fan Xiaoxiao, Yang Li, Ge Zhenliang, Zhang Sisi, Chen Wen
Landscape design team: Li Shangyang, Li Jun
Area: 217,431 square feet (20,200 square meters)
Design time: 2020
Client: Hangzhou Buddhist Association
Model photography: Chen Xi Studio

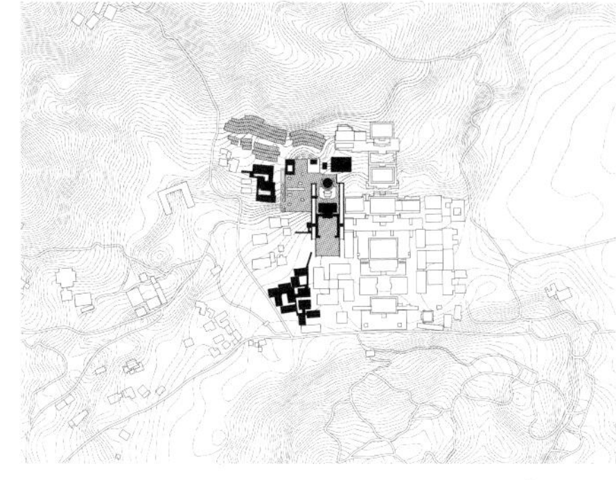

Site plan

Renewal of a Thousand-Year-Old Temple

Located in eastern China, about 124 miles (200 kilometers) from Shanghai, Hangzhou is a city famous for its local culture and over 2,000 years of history. It is known as a "Paradise on Earth" for its magnificent West Lake and the mountains surrounding it. Built in the first year of the reign of Emperor Xianhe of the Eastern Jin dynasty (326 CE), Lingyin Temple, also called Temple of the Soul's Retreat, is located to the west of West Lake, between two mountain peaks—the Beigao Peak at its back and the Feilai Peak to its front. Though the temple has undergone several major renovations, its essence remains strong, embodying a rich history of more than 1,700 years, which intertwines with the lingering scent of incense, which burns to this day. The historical city of Hangzhou has developed over time to become a major hub for the internet economy. Now the city's ancient Buddhist culture and related spaces, too, face new functional challenges. For example, the demand for large-scale Buddhist events such as Buddhist conferences and communal meals has challenged the decentralized layout of traditional temples.

In 2020, line+ studio was invited to participate in an international design competition for the extension of Lingyin Temple's western side. The project site is located on a narrow strip of land, running north to south between the original main building complex of Lingyin Temple to the west, and Zhu's Mansion and the buildings of the Buddhist Association to the east. It consists of two plots: the eastern plot (plot 3)—with a land area of about 35 mu (247,570 square feet [23,000 square meters])—is intended for religious use; the western plot (plot 2)—with a land area of about 11 mu (75,347 square feet [7,000 square meters])—is intended for recreational and cultural use. On the eastern side, the project site borders the main temple area of Lingyin Temple, which is dominated by traditional Chinese temple architecture. The project lot itself is covered with ancient trees, making it secluded and scenic. The scenery is completed with rockery and landscaped paths that offer a precious resting place for monks and visitors. According to the competition's requirements, the new expansion would need to include areas of around 67,813 square feet (6,300 square meters) above ground and 129,167 square feet (12,000 square meters) below ground; a construction area of approximately 79,050 square feet (7,344 square meters) was available for the expansion.

This created several challenges on how to meet the temple's new spatial demands while echoing the spatial order of Lingyin Temple within the limited plot. How could the team symbiotically integrate the traditional temple architecture of yellow walls, black tiles, and wooden doors and windows using contemporary design and construction methods? How would they take into account the surrounding nature, so as to reduce excavation, while maintaining and restoring the original ecology as much as possible? While these questions were created by the external constraints of the site, the most important question arose from the space itself: how could the site be used as a vector to evoke an ancient spiritual source in an era of such rapid change?

Master plan—aerial view

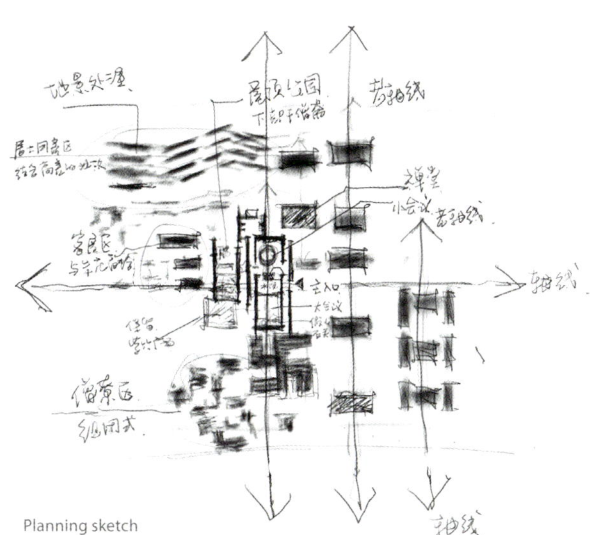

Planning sketch

Section model

An Implicit Order

Like many ancient Chinese places of worship, Lingyin Temple has a strong axial layout and sense of order. The main axis is dominated by Daxiongbao Hall, while a side axis to the east features the Abbot's Hall. In addition, a cross-axis for traffic leading from Zizhu Square to the driveway in the west was created based on modern-day needs, resulting in a distinct spatial hierarchy of "one horizontal and two vertical."

Based on this spatial layout, line+ studio proposed the following modifications in the design and layout to meet the temple's design requirements, as well as negotiate the expected design hurdles. First, a third vertical axis for Lingyin Temple was created, starting from the intersection of the project site with the horizontal east–west traffic axis. Important public spaces, such as the Counseling Center, lobby, Buddhist Culture Center, and meditation hall have been arranged along this third vertical axis. The new extension places a focus on the meditation hall, which is located to the west of Zhizhi Hall in the main cluster, where the Songtao Pavilion used to be; it echoes Lingyin Temple's main hall and its traditional shape. The third vertical axis mirrors the existing side axis of the Abbot Hall opposite the main axis of Daxiongbao Hall, to form a layout arranged in the way of a main center with support in the east and west. This design not only preserves the thousand-year-old spatial order of the temple complex, but also reinforces the original layout with a clearer hierarchical division. Private areas at the north and south ends of the project site provide resting spaces, such as monks' cells, guestrooms, staff quarters, and restrooms.

The area of the monks' cells is set at the southern end of the site, where an original building for the same purpose still remains. As the site is flat, the original layout pattern can easily be extended. The staff quarters and restrooms are located on a slope in the far north of the site, taking full advantage of the terrain to ensure good lighting and ventilation. The guestrooms are logically located to the east of Zhu's Mansion and act as a complementary resting area.

By strategically incorporating the topography of the site's vertical dimension, line+ studio consciously enhances the spatial order of the expansion area. The entire public area is intentionally lowered, while the meditation area is raised, to echo the main hall of Lingyin Temple. The guestrooms and monks' cells are enclosed in a series of courtyards, while the staff quarters and restrooms in the north align with the mountain contour and fade into the surroundings. The lowered areas have been reforested with the replanting of about 200 trees that were temporarily removed from the original site to preserve the surrounding nature during construction.

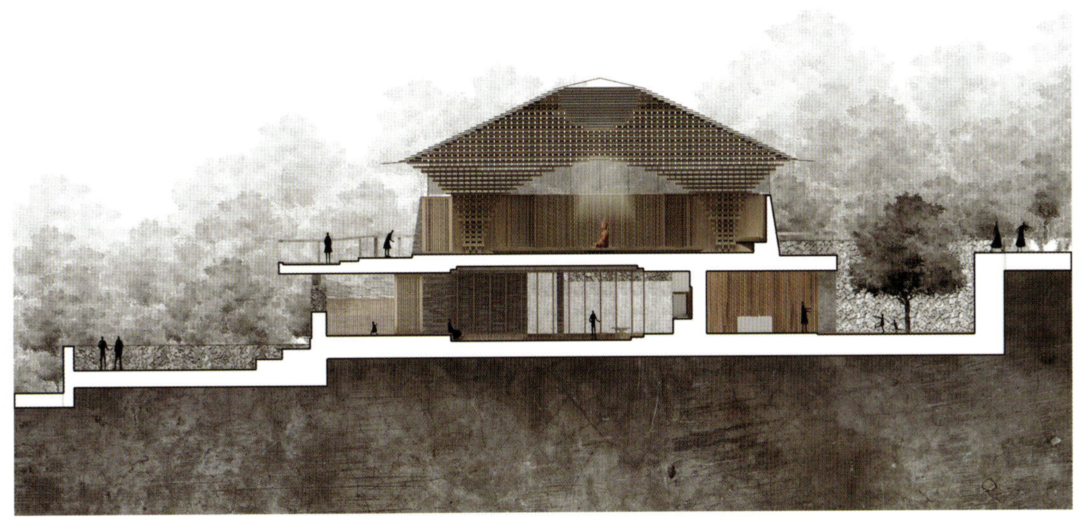

Section—meditation hall

Section—conference center

Section—corridor

Lecture hall

Conference center

A Ritualized Space

A lobby of approximately 4,844 square feet (450 square meters) connects the Exhibition Center for Intangible Cultural Heritage, the conference center, and the Buddhist Culture Center. Entering from the main cluster of Lingyin Temple or Zizhu Square on the west side, an open, water courtyard brings people to this lobby. Passing through the lobby, they reach the core area of the entire public space, the Atrium of the Great Buddha. A nearly 26-foot-tall (8-meter-tall) Buddha statue sits at the center of this circular atrium, from where vertical pathways connect the various functional areas of the public space. Thus, the Atrium of the Great Buddha becomes both the central rhythm generator of the physical space and the spiritual core of the entire expansion. The water courtyard and the atrium are also set up to immediately convey the spatial rhythm in the dim environment of the vast underground building.

The Atrium of the Great Buddha and the lecture hall, together, form the Buddhist Culture Center. The lecture hall adopts the shape of an inverted cone to reinforce the centralized character of the public area. The interior space reflects the building's actual form as the circular space gradually converges with the building's rising height, enhancing the centripetal nature of the space. The design takes advantage of the existing height difference in the terrain, creating a two-story auditorium in the lecture hall to increase its functional capacity, while limiting the construction area. The conical space opens up to the audience in the front, while the back naturally forms the background of the pulpit. Light floods in from the top, guided by simple geometric interior walls, underscoring the spirituality of this religious space.

From the Atrium of the Great Buddha, one can access the conference center on the lower level by escalator or elevator. The conference center is designed like a theater, with an official capacity of 1,000, in order to host large Buddhist conferences and cultural performances. To address the scarcity of large spaces within the site, the design makes use of modern tools, such as a hydraulic mechanism, to create a raisable seating area that allows the hall to be transformed into a large space with a flat floor, so that it can serve a variety of functions in the future.

To the west, the Atrium of the Great Buddha adjoins the Exhibition Center for Intangible Cultural Heritage. The hall has been designed to provide a ceremonial place for an annual, large-scale traditional Buddhist event known as the Feast of a Thousand Monks. The arched structure of the exhibition center follows the mountainous terrain, forming a large-span, column-free rectangular space. The arched structure rises from both sides of the central axis to form a linear opening in the center (aligned with the axis), through which daylight and views of the surrounding landscape enter. The long tables needed for the feast are arranged in rows within the large-scale rectangular space, so that the monks can enjoy their meal peacefully, in an uncomplicated manner. As natural light gently moves through the hall, accompanied by serene sceneries, the space humbly merges nature with the spirit of ritual.

1
2
3

1. Atrium of the Great Buddha
2. Entrance courtyard
3. Conference center

Meditation hall

Meditation hall:

As the core of the expansion along the new western axis, the meditation hall covers an area of approximately 10,764 square feet (1,000 square meters), divided into a formal 5,382-square-foot (500-square-meter) meditation hall with auxiliary supporting areas. In order to accommodate the main hall of Lingyin Temple, the design of the meditation hall looks to the traditional Chinese wooden arch. Incorporating the abstraction and integration of modern architectural language, it starts at the four corners and advances in layers to form a pure and smooth column-free space. A meditation space is placed on the second floor, which monks can reach directly from a trail that ascends the mountain. It is arranged according to the layout of traditional meditation halls. The central part of the building is hollow, so that the sunlight casts directly on a Buddha statue that has been placed in the hall.

Monks' cells:

The layout of the monks' cells borrows from the design of traditional Chinese courtyard architecture, breaking up the 36,059-square-foot (3,350-square-meter) building volume into eleven separate buildings composed in either two or three stories. Most of them face south, forming a small cluster, so that the monks may enjoy their own private space. The building units were inspired by typical dwellings of the region. They feature high and low pitched roofs as a starting point for the design while applying contemporary materials such as small gray tiles and combinations of stone and aluminum alloys. By combining simple overhanging eaves, a courtyard layout, contrasting exterior corridors, and water features, the monks' cells in the southern corner of Lingyin Temple are adorned with a contemporary aesthetic that displays local characteristics.

Guestrooms:

The guestrooms are located on the east side of Zhu's Mansion and are mainly used for receiving distinguished guests. The layout of the building recalls the shape of a traditional Chinese double-courtyard mansion; the first floor of the central building is open to the public. Two entrances, one in the east and the other in the west, lead to Zhu's Mansion and Lingyin Temple respectively. Compared with the scale of the monks' cells, the guestrooms and courtyard spaces are larger.

Staff quarters and restrooms:

The staff quarters and restrooms are located on the hillside. Through the integration of the difference in elevation, three distinct zones have been created: fully lit bedrooms, a central walkway that allows daylight to enter, and an underground bathroom. By staggering the upper and lower levels, the building volume—of about 43,056 square feet (4,000 square meters)—blends with the mountain and dissolves into them.

Exhibition Center for Intangible Cultural Heritage

Courtyard in monks' cells

Monks' cells

Restored Nature

Confronted with the natural landscape on the site, the expansion adopts an approach of light intervention, aiming to preserve the sustainable vegetation of the site after the expansion is completed, as well as maintaining the temple's green and lush ecological mountain scenery.

The entire expansion area, from south to north, and from bottom to top, combines different programs to form a pattern of interconnected secularized gardens, grand spiritual spaces, and secluded meditation halls. Between the buildings, shaded paths wind up the hill and past murmuring mountain streams, resembling traditional Chinese landscape paintings.

Considering the excavation and construction process, the design sorts out the existing trees on the site along a workable plan for local transplantation, keeping the original trees in the public spaces while transplanting trees that conflict with the construction scope. Ultimately, 200 trees will continue to grow on the site in harmony with the new buildings; additionally, nine scenic spots will be set up in the expansion area to merge the religious context with the site's landscape.

Front façade of the Buddha Hall

Future Lingyin Temple as a traditional Chinese long scroll painting

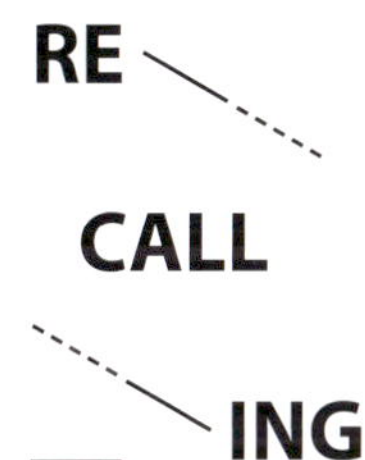

Rediscovering a Spiritual Space

Faced with the vicissitudes of history and time, the design sets off by responding to nature, in an effort to address the contemporary demands of a Buddhist space within the constraints of site and function. In today's fast-changing contemporary times, the design seeks to rediscover a religious space that is both spiritually powerful and open, through the shaping of space, the selection of materials, and the use of light.

The architecture, borne in response to these times, will, together with Lingyin Temple, usher in a new millennium of the temple's legacy.

RE — CON — NECT — ING

Sharing Through Space

In the post-*danwei* era, the growing disintegration of the intermediate group in the social connection mechanism led to the phenomenon of social atomization. While atomization has, to a certain extent, enabled individuals to express themselves more freely and pluralistically, it has also led to a gradual weakening of interpersonal ties and an increasing alienation between individuals and the public sphere.

As people commune, *danwei* buildings of the past have encouraged a collective life through spatial organization, but there still exists the question of how space today can create new bonds among individuals through the act of sharing. Since ancient times, architecture has had a capacity for inclusion. By opening itself to different social groups and users, it fosters a sense of community among them. As such, line+ studio believes that a shared communal space that is open to all is crucial in all building types.

The projects listed in this chapter include a wide range of building types, such as infrastructure, factory, school, creative park, and even a corporate headquarters. Although their uses incorporate people of different ages, occupations, and personalities, in each of these projects, line+ studio attempts to shape a stronger bond between them through a shared communal space. From service stations providing for the public to an industrial park regenerated from former industrial relics; from a landscaped courtyard inspired by classical Chinese *shanshui* paintings to an educational hub that encourages children to explore freely, these projects focus on the openness and accommodating character of architecture as a spatial container. Through sharing, they aim to *re-connect* individuals in today's contemporary society.

03

Re-connecting

Education Hub,
Hangzhou International School

Shaping Education

The Education Hub at Hangzhou International School reorganizes and redefines the entire campus space. In doing so, it encourages a more exploratory, spontaneous, and unstructured learning model that extends beyond the classroom, and creates a more dynamic campus environment through reimagining the educational space.

Location: Binjiang District, Hangzhou, Zhejiang Province, China
Design firm: line+ studio
Principal architect: Zhu Peidong
Architecture design team: Sun Xiaoyu, Wu Haiwen, Huang Yunting, Du Mengying, Yang Xiaoyu
Area: 528,108 square feet (49,080 square meters)
Design period: June 2018–August 2019
Construction period: August 2019–August 2022
Client: Hangzhou International School
Photography: schranimage, line+ studio, Chen Xi Studio

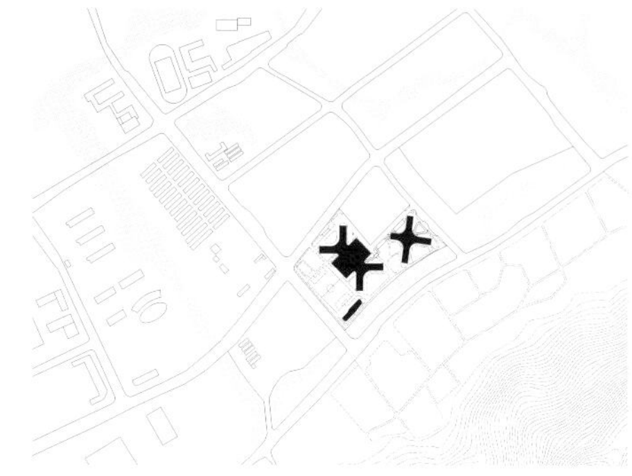

Site plan

A New Educational Space

The rapid development of Chinese society and cities in China have given rise to a new type of educational institution: international schools. These schools were set up after China's reform era to see to the education needs of expatriates and residents from then Hong Kong, Macau, and Taiwan. As time went on Chinese parents became increasingly accepting of the open interaction espoused in the education philosophy of international schools and took to enrolling their children in them.

Hangzhou International School (HIS) was the first school in Zhejiang Province to admit expatriate students, as well as students from Hong Kong, Macau, and Taiwan. Organized and managed by the International Schools Foundation (ISF), the school adopts a K-12 system in line with international standards. Its first campus was situated on the banks of the Qiantang River in Hangzhou's Binjiang District, across the river from Liuhe Pagoda. The new campus designed by line+ studio is built along Baima Lake—a move meant to meet the ever-expanding needs of the school. Of all the ISF schools worldwide, HIS is the only school designed by local designers.

The project site sits on the shores of Baima Lake in Binjiang District, across the river from the main part of Hangzhou. Although Binjiang District is well known as the home of many tech companies' headquarters and industrial parks, Baima Lake remains untouched by urbanization, still retaining many of its attractive natural features. Within the context of a nascent urban culture, the design considerations for HIS stemmed mostly from general reflections on the internal organization of schools as a building type.

The starting point for the studio's concept sprang from HIS' educational philosophy, which focuses more on emotional experiences and open interaction, in contrast to rigidly structured classroom-focused learning models. Compared to ordinary school buildings, K-12 schools are often part of a long phase in their students' educational upbringing, which provides room to elevate the role of architecture and space in their growing-up years.

Old campus

Aerial view

Site condition

Playground with the main building in the background

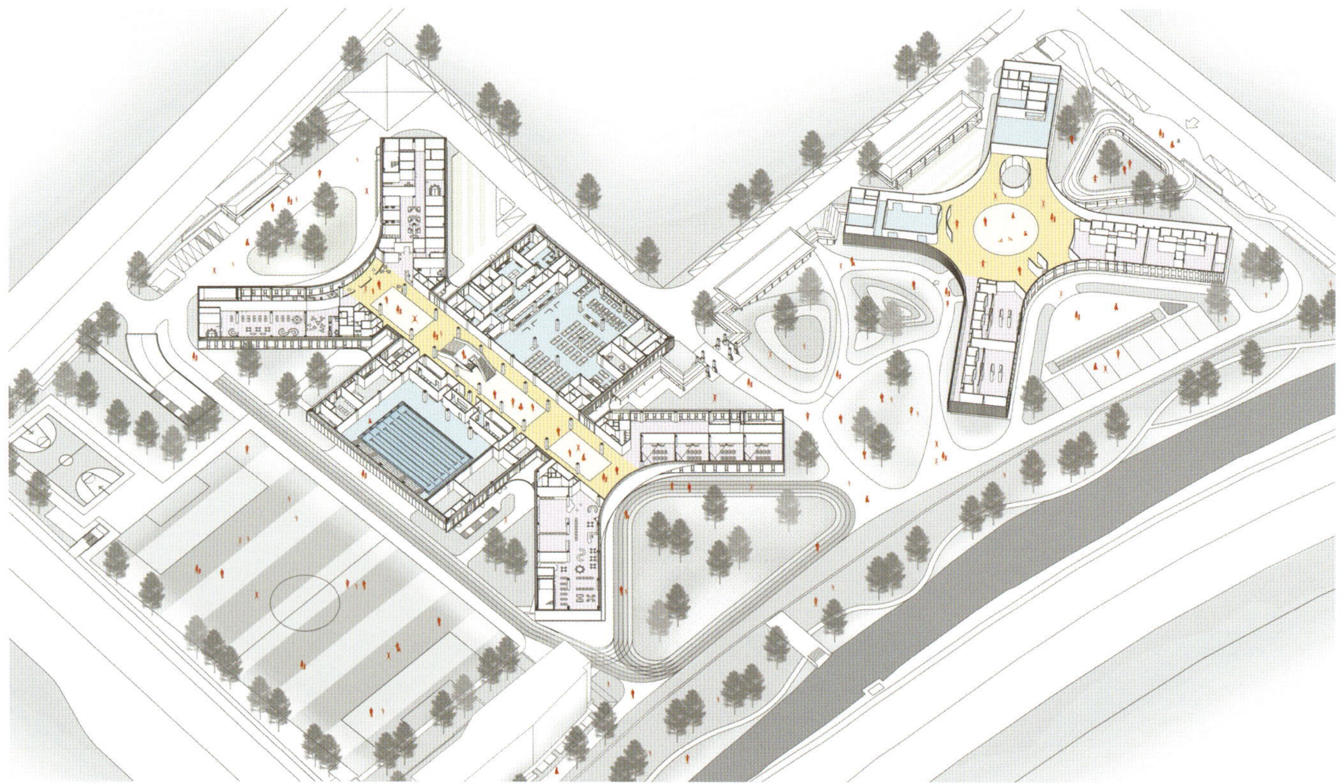

Ground floor—axonometric view

Single-unit Detached

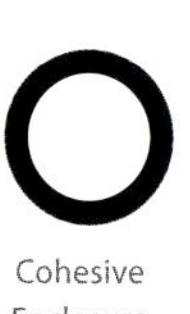

Cohesive Enclosure

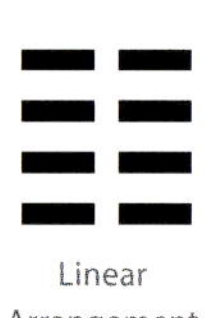

Linear Arrangement

Courtyard Style

Fishbone Layout

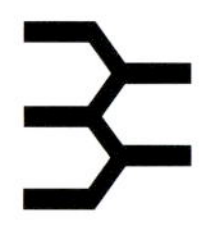

Branching Layout

Evenly Distributed

Dispersed Settlement

Typical school layouts

Traditional school layouts often adopt a "hallway-to-classroom" layout, where long, one-directional hallways connecting to different classrooms create an orderly spatial organization. The philosopher Michel Foucault once pointed out that schools' hierarchical layouts are the source of the disciplinary effect they have on students. Cultural anthropologist Edward Hall has also argued that space is a "hidden dimension" that can transmit information as language does, thus influencing people's lives and behaviors. Given that, can adapting a new model for the school space provide a diverse environment in which children of all ages can foster respectful interactions and be nurtured to possess behavioral traits that are carried into their adult lives?

Aerial view

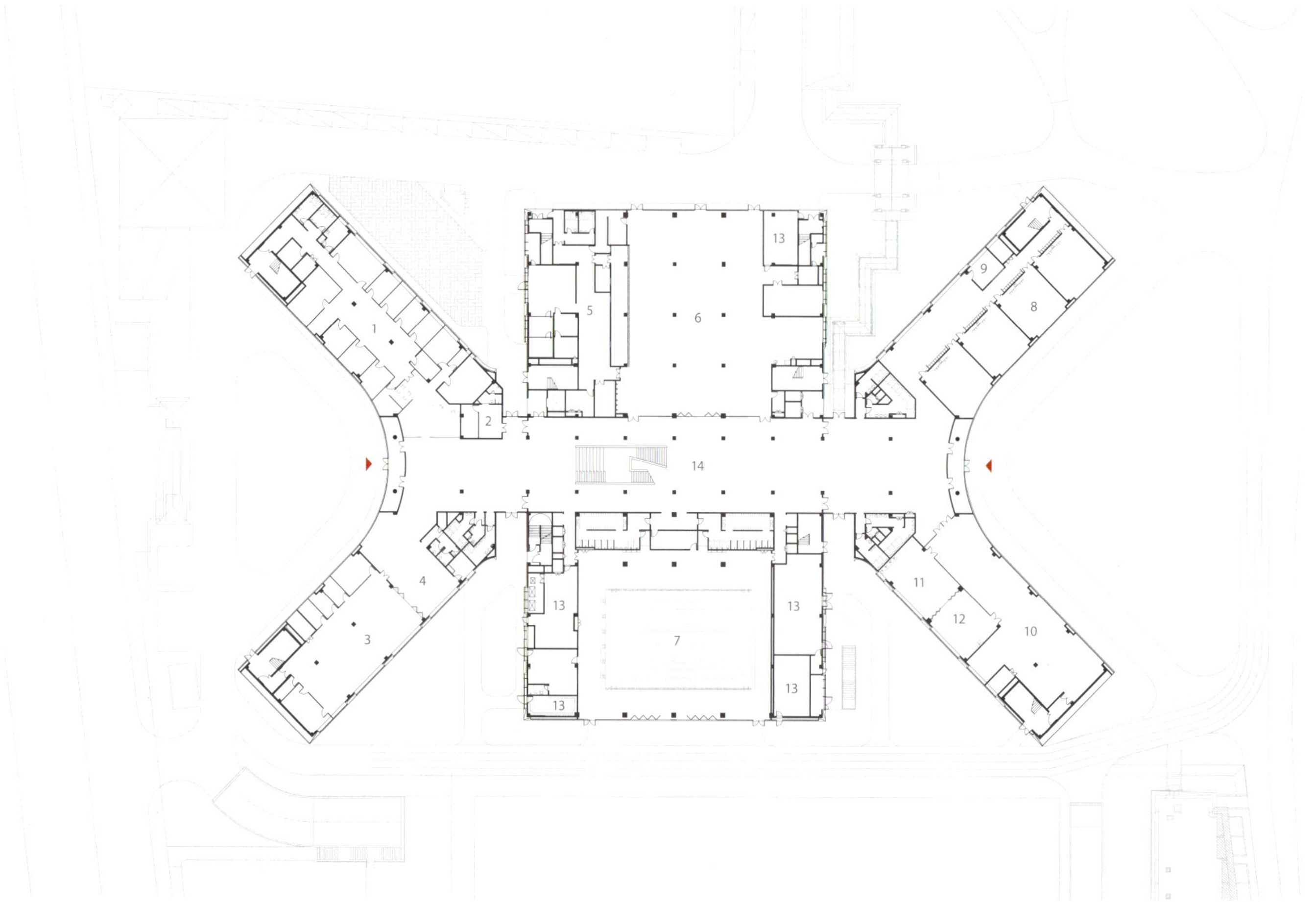

Main building—ground-floor plan

0 5 10 20m

1. Administration office
2. Medical room
3. Library for middle-school students
4. Café
5. Kitchen
6. Canteen
7. Swimming center
8. Classroom
9. Multiuse room
10. Library for primary students
11. Art center
12. STEM center
13. Mechanical room
14. Atrium

Football field with the main building in the distance

View of the Education Hub space (main building)—from the ground floor

View of the Education Hub space (main building)—from the ground floor

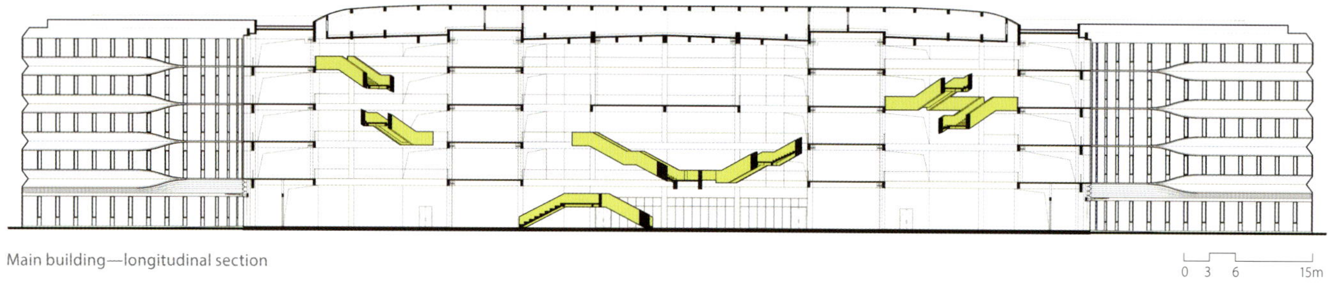

Main building—longitudinal section

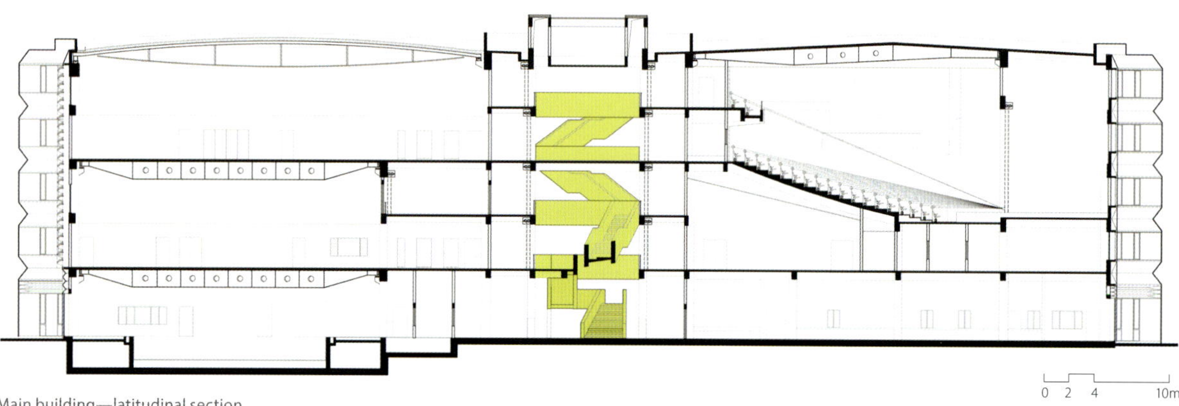

Main building—latitudinal section

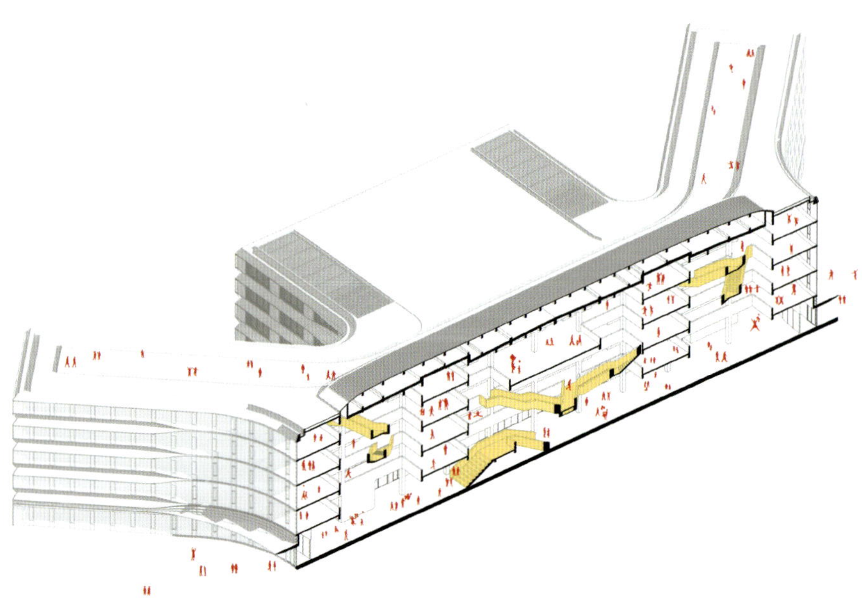

Axonometric view of the Education Hub space (main building)

Education Hub interior (main building)

Education Hub–West
1. Secondary gymnasium
2. Primary gymnasium
3. Swimming pool

Primary gymnasium

Secondary gymnasium

Swimming pool

Black Box Theater

Canteen

Grand Theater

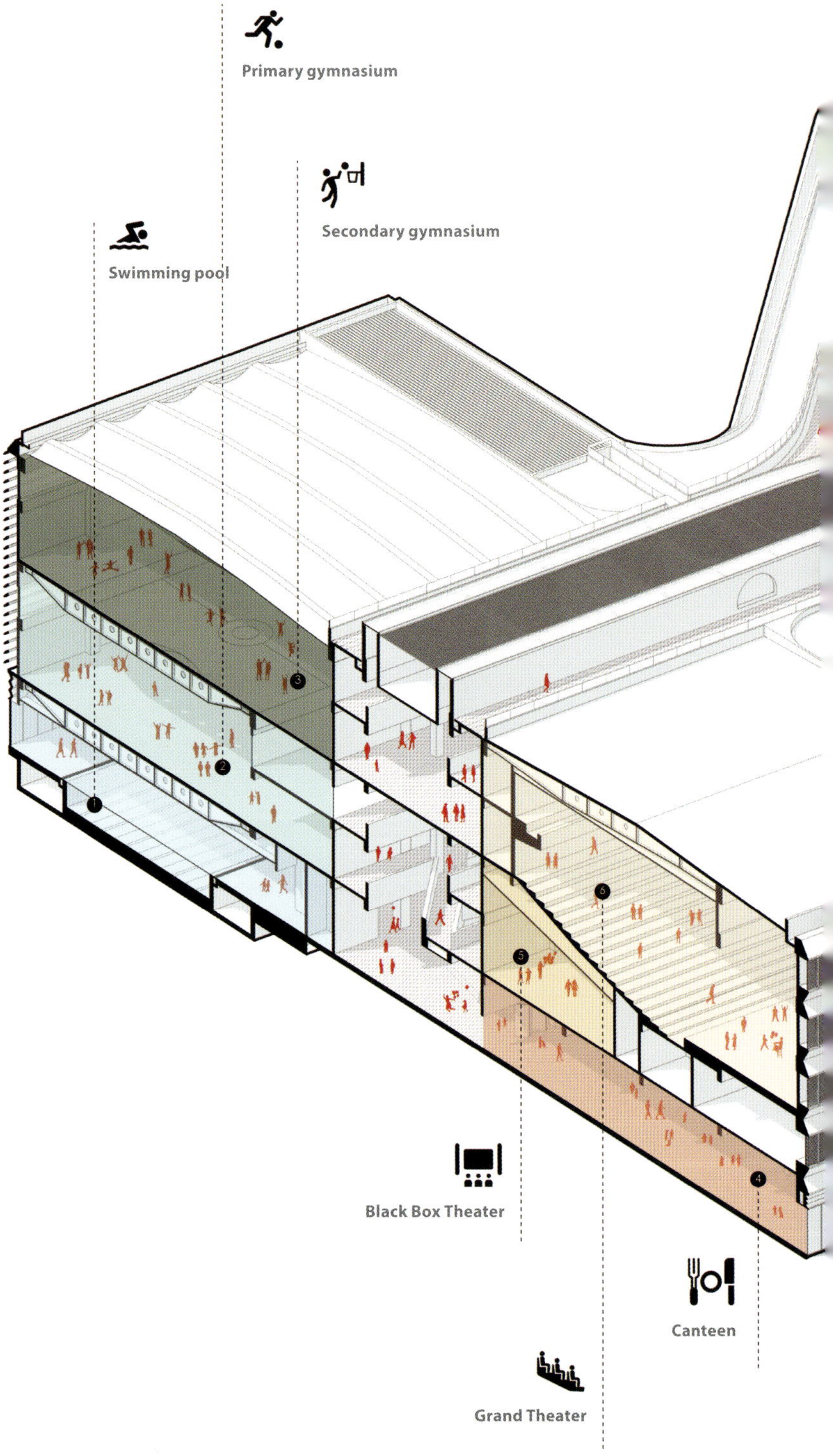

Education Hub–East

4 4. Grand Theater

5 5. Black Box Theater

6 6. Canteen

Education Hub–West

Education Hub–East

Kindergarten

Education Hub

Hangzhou International School's design departs from the typical, rigidly structured, classroom-focused learning model, underscoring line+ studio's commitment to breaking down the classroom-driven spatial model at the school. To that end, the studio uses a central, compact Education Hub to reorganize and redefine the campus space to focus on sharing and interaction. This approach also carves out lots of outdoor space for the children to explore. Spatially, the Education Hub is an open space that flows up and down, welcoming children of all ages to explore the grounds freely. Functionally, it is complex; it encourages diversity, and the simultaneous use of its many spaces, and acts as the hub of the entire campus.

The project site takes an irregular L-shape. To achieve an intensive and compact layout, the design began by determining the location of the running track and grass field, which helped to free up as much open space as possible, and plan reasonable pathways. While traditional schools are laid out in rows, both the main building and the kindergarten at HIS diverge from that form through extensions that radiate from each of their Education Hubs. Inside the kindergarten's Education Hub, the library, pool, cafeteria, multipurpose classrooms, art center, and STEM center are arranged around a five-story atrium hall. In addition to ensuring that each school department can access the multipurpose activity spaces, the hub's design also increases potential encounters and interactions between students and teachers. As a complement, the system of social spaces formed by the connected large steps, stairs, and hallways also frees stairs in the interior from their traditional enclosed design and transforms them into a varied, intriguing spatial landscape.

Similarly, the floor plan of the kindergarten is centered on the atrium, while the outdoor area is shaped into activity spaces with four different interfaces. Inside, the stairs resemble slides and connect to the circular hallway, creating a multidimensional, interactive space. Organizing the space around the behavioral patterns of younger children inspires them to explore and be enthusiastic about exploring the space. The building façade of both the main campus and kindergarten are highlighted by horizontal lines to create a pure architectural image. Constructed from anodized aluminum panels, the façade of the main teaching building features futuristic concave horizontal lines running along the surface, while the façade of the kindergarten is made of large floor-to-ceiling windows and perforated metal panels to guarantee the uniformity and softness of the indoor lighting. The overlay of louvers and metal façades produces a visual effect on the building façade, as if it extends infinitely into the horizon.

Kindergarten's Education Hub space

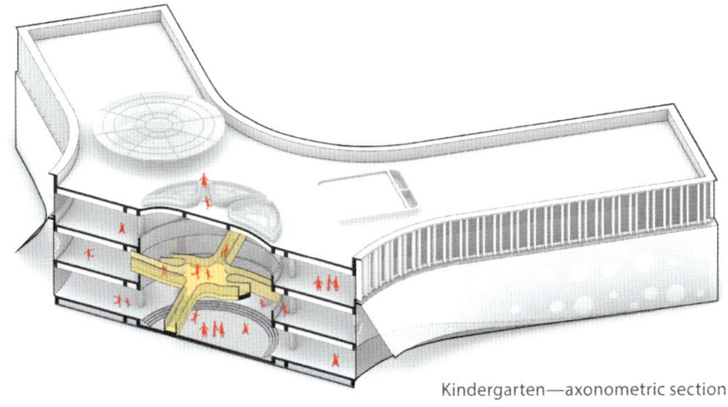

Kindergarten—axonometric section

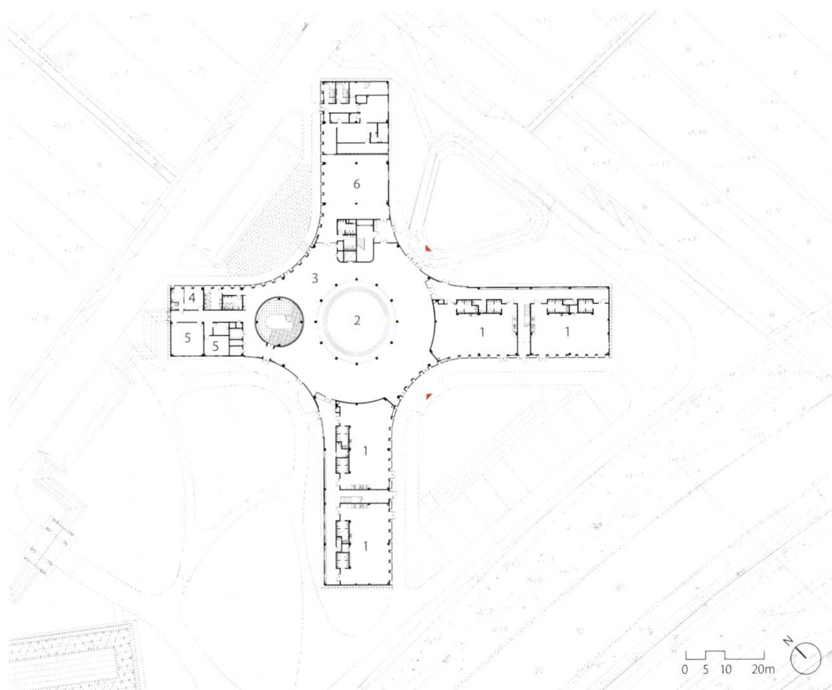

Kindergarten—ground-floor plan

1. Activity room
2. Atrium
3. Morning-inspection room
4. Medical room
5. Office
6. Cafeteria

Main building façade

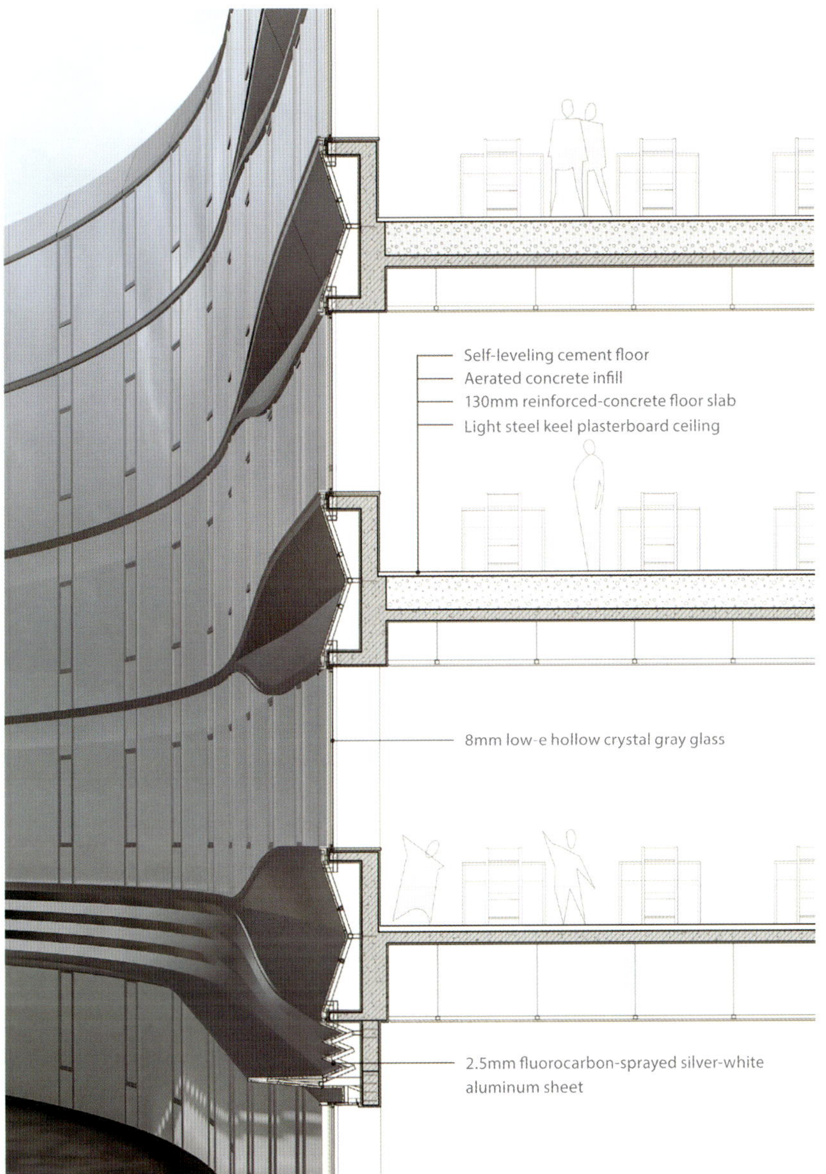

Construction detail

Main building façade

Campus in daily use

Basketball playground

RE ⟍ CON
⟋
NECT
⟍
— ING

Environment as Education

Track with the main building in the background

The central, compact Education Hub reorganizes and redefines the entire campus space. In doing so, it encourages a more exploratory, spontaneous, and unstructured learning model that extends beyond the classroom, creating a more dynamic campus environment that restructures the idea of an educational space. This spatial environment that accompanies the children's development will become an important memory of their childhood. Inspired by Thomas Pritchard's concept of "environmental education," line+ studio hopes to foster interactions and sharing in every facet of the students' academic lifestyle through the comprehensive role of a dedicated spatial organization.

Zhejiang Perfect Production Factory Integrated Renovation

Shaping Industry–Shan Shui Factory

Industrial parks are no longer a storage space for unfeeling machines. Rather, they have become compound clusters of spaces with highly efficient production capabilities, comfortable work environments, and human-centered shared work and living experiences.

Location: Haining, Zhejiang Province, China
Design firm: line+ studio
Principal architect: Zhu Peidong
Architecture design team: Sun Xiaoyu
Interior design team: Jin Yuting, Liu Jia, Cai Xiaoyu, Shi Jianguo, Liu Moran, Chen Weilong, Gu Chuanjie
Landscape design team: Li Shangyang, Jin Jianbo, Su Chenjuan, Tang Ruixian
Area: 279,862 square feet (26,000 square meters)
Design period: February 2019–April 2019
Construction period: May 2019–October 2019
Client: Zhejiang Perfect Automobile Technology Co. Ltd
Photography: Arch-Exist Photography, Wen Studio, Jianzhi-Arch Photography

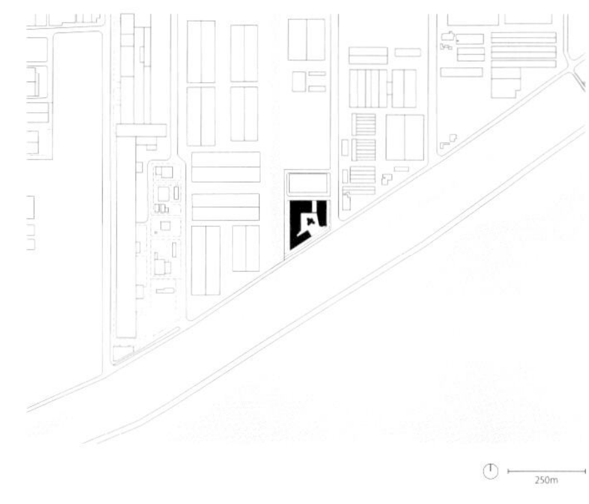

Site plan

Tradition and Modernity in Industrial Parks

From the time of the Industrial Revolution, factories in the West have usually taken the form of long-span, open spaces, but that is not the case in this particular project. Through the containment of the functional space and an undulating interior circulation route, line+ studio endeavored to transform the shape of the entire industrial park into a traditional settlement with a local narrative context. With the natural landscape as the core, encircled by an inward, quasi-enclosed space, this settlement creates a sense of security, shelter, and identity.

Borrowing from the traditional Chinese paintings in the *Manual of the Mustard Seed Garden*, line+ studio twines through the project a design logic that uses a "typological" perspective to deconstruct the elements of traditional landscape paintings—like mountains, stone, buildings, water, hedges, terraces, accessways, and so on—and contrast them with a contemporary architectural vocabulary.

Mountains (*shan*):
Through the connection of their volumes and roofs, the four building clusters fit on the periphery of the site, forming the fundamental topography of a mountain; they open up to the southeast corner, shaping an enclosed, yet misaligned pocket space.

Stones:
Prefabricated concrete blocks are stacked to reconstruct the idea of rockery.

Water (*shui*):
A shallow pond sits at the center of the site facing the open space. The water feature brings with it a sense of spirituality and tranquility.

Buildings:
To avoid the pressure of the canteen and the service center on the small, mountainous courtyard, the building shapes are broken up and transformed into three interconnected clusters of small, mountain-esque structures by the water.

Hedges:
The linear sequence of modular, white gradient colored glass defines the boundaries of the site, while maintaining an openness to the visuals and resources of the surrounding environment.

Terraces:
An observation platform is constructed in the southwest corner, on the top floor of the main research and development (R&D) office, so that people can lean against the railings and gaze out at the river that fills up when the tide rolls in.

Walkways:
Red walkways are used as the core element. The bright hues of the twisting bridges and walkways are central to the visual presentation of the architecture, just like how similar constructions are to the spatial language of a landscape painting. This main thread connects all the "images" previously mentioned.

Courtyard

On the outside of these volumes formed by a traditional narrative are white corrugated steel panels. These panels cover the outer walls, as vertical windows, a corrugated texture, and ridged roofs mimic the texture of the mountains. On the inside, connected U-shaped glass lends the structure a semi-transparent look that also diffuses the internal scenery, such that daily activities within the building are visible yet indistinct in this factory perched by the water.

Aerial view of factory

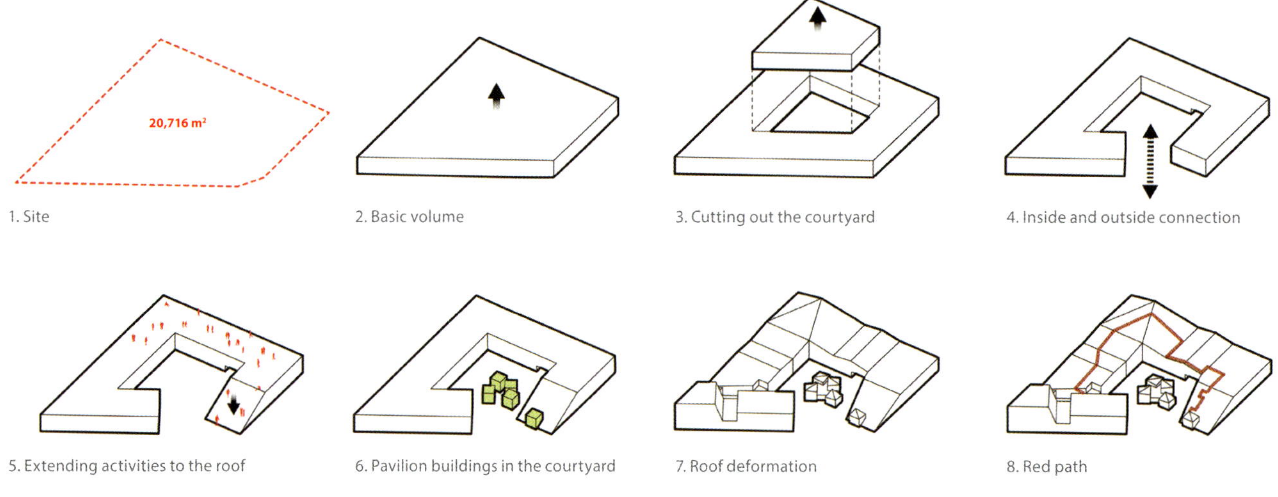

Generation process

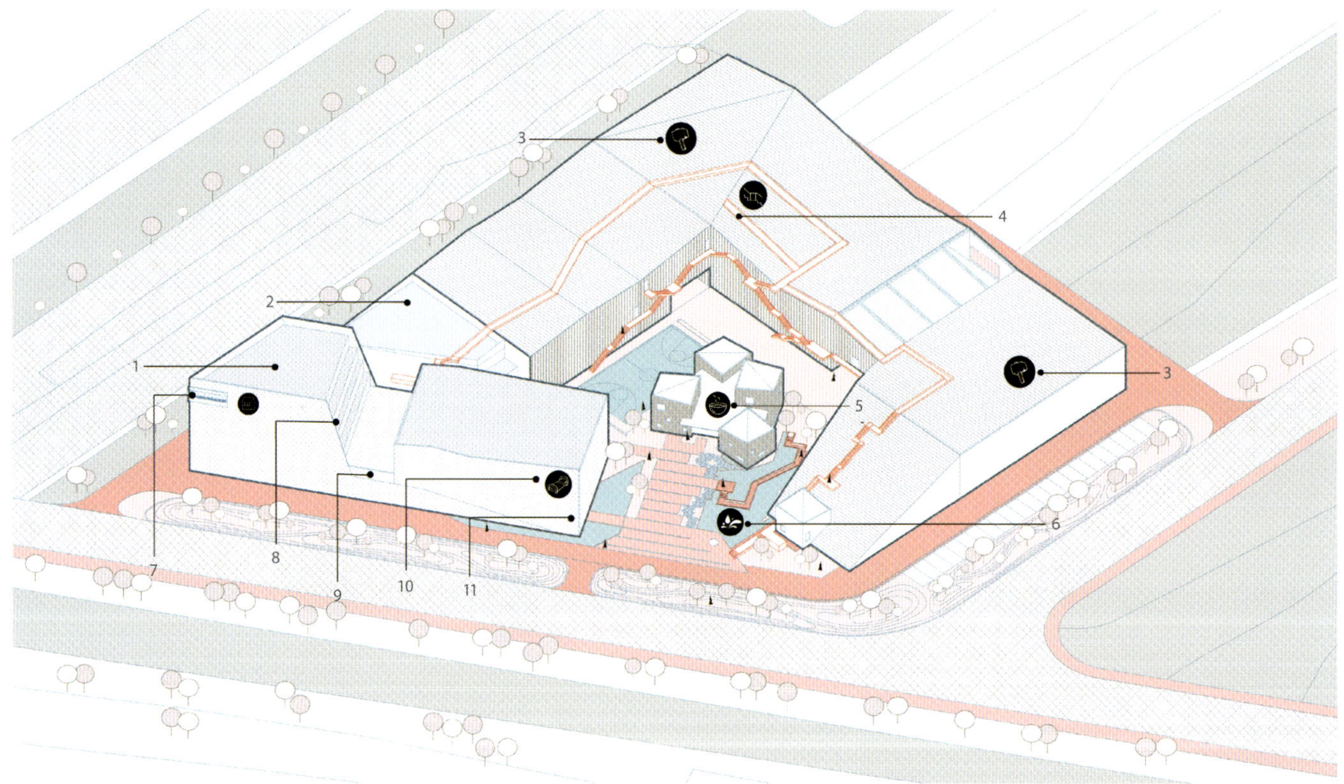

Axonometric diagram

1. Multifunction building
2. Research institute
3. Factories
4. Red path
5. Cafeteria
6. Pool area
7. Viewing space
8. Clubhouse
9. Public area
10. Dormitory
11. Foyer

Mountain-like building volumes

U-glass façade at nightfall

Factory building and the water courtyard

Reconstructing Circulation

The automobile production plant that Detroit (United States) architect Albert Kahn designed in the 1910s—with spacious interiors framed by long-span steel trusses and wide windows that brought in natural light and ventilation—came to define the "daylight factory," which became a model for industrial architecture constructed under Ford-style production circumstances. However, modern industrial production in China and around the world has gradually changed from an extensive, concentrated work mode to a refined, smart, and human-centered one. Given that, the large-scale continuous operation, work allocation, and labor management that once prevailed, as well as the barracks-inspired layouts or matchbox-style rooms centered entirely on the need for production efficiency, have been in urgent need of modification. Influenced by post-Ford production methods, companies like Google and Facebook have adopted more creative communal office spaces in an effort to improve their employees' work environment and spatial experience. It is against this backdrop that line+ studio strives toward a different possibility: industrial parks as production buildings.

The site sits along the river in Jianshan New District, Zhejiang Province. The image of the rushing waters at the mouth of the vast Qiantang River stands in stark contrast to the still waters of the floodway to the west. Its environmental features lend themselves to an inward, balanced layout, which links the atmosphere of the surrounding industrial area with the swift development of the innovative industry, all while striking a distinction from traditional industrial parks with their closed management style.

The most fundamental elements behind the logical functioning of this production base are the processes required for industrial production, the freight circulation routes, and circulation routes carved by the workers' and managers' work lifestyles. These three aspects also give shape to the building's architectural form. Considering the production logistics, line+ studio divides the volume into five building blocks. They expand four of the buildings along the edge of the site and connect them to the surrounding streets to streamline logistics: the customer-service workshop is located to the east; the basic production area to the north; the cleanroom and laboratory along the floodway to the west; and the R&D offices and living complexes to the south, facing the scenery of the Qiantang River. Finally, the fifth building block, which is the canteen and service center, is placed in the center, serving as the spot where lifestyles converge, forming an inner courtyard that belongs to the people.

Wall detail

1. Flashing
2. 0.8mm-thick 65/430 aluminum and titanium vertical seaming roof panel
   0.49mm waterproof ventilation membrane
   100mm insulation layer
   1mm leveling steel plate
   0.6mm HV-900 profiled galvanized steel plate
3. 50×50mm galvanized square steel
4. Main steel structure
5. 0.6mm galvanized steel inner liner
6. 50×50mm square steel
7. U-shaped tempered glass
8. Steel stair
9. 40×25mm corner steel
10. 0.6mm galvanized steel inner liner
11. Steel column
12. PVC cushion
13. Aluminum clamping piece

Made of weathering steel, the fire escapes of the workshops, the access road to the solar panels on the roof, the path across the pond, and the indoor stairways of the office building are presented in an unified red color lending cohesiveness to the design; some are made visible while some are concealed, and others are interwoven through the buildings, reminiscent of mountain paths in traditional Chinese landscape paintings, with their faintly discernible and ostensibly fragmented and winding appearance. A series of walkways also loops through the different functional areas.

Symbiotic with that are a range of motional experiences: "watching the shores," "climbing mountains," "walking along a cliff," "crossing bridges," and "swimming." Seeing each other's reflection in the water is like watching the shores; making your way upward is like climbing mountains; the building façade resembles walking along a cliff. The connecting pathways lay out bridges to cross, while the twisting and turning walkway on the water is a symbolic representation of swimming.

Traditional Chinese painting

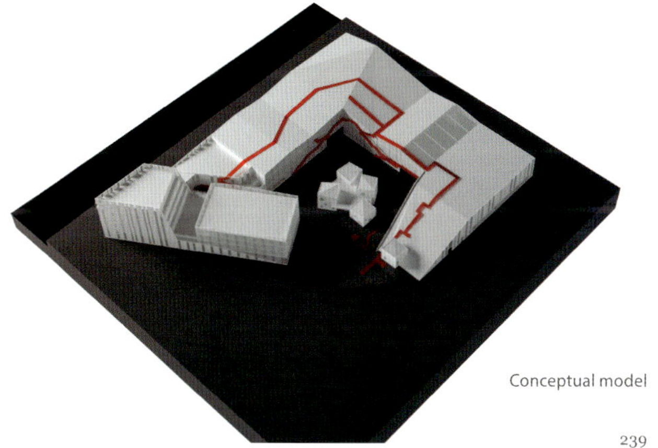

Conceptual model

Courtyard inside the factory campus

Overhead floor of R&D center

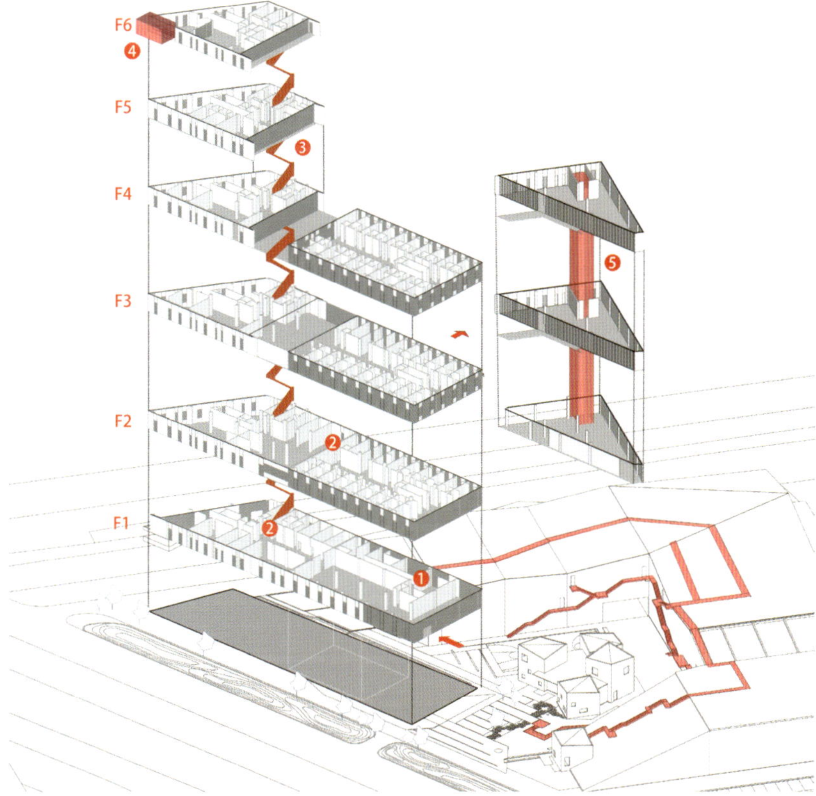

Exploded axonometric diagram

1. Mountain-like ceiling
2. Public area
3. Red path
4. Viewing space
5. Vertical stair

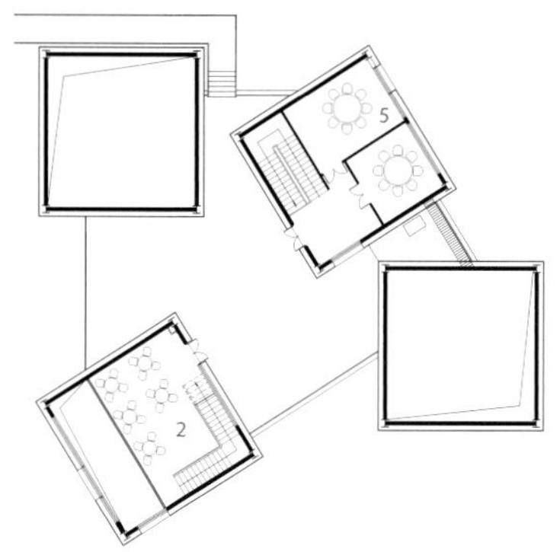

Ground-floor plan of the cafeteria

Second-floor plan of the cafeteria

1. Foyer
2. Cafeteria dining area
3. Kitchen
4. Disinfection room
5. Boxes

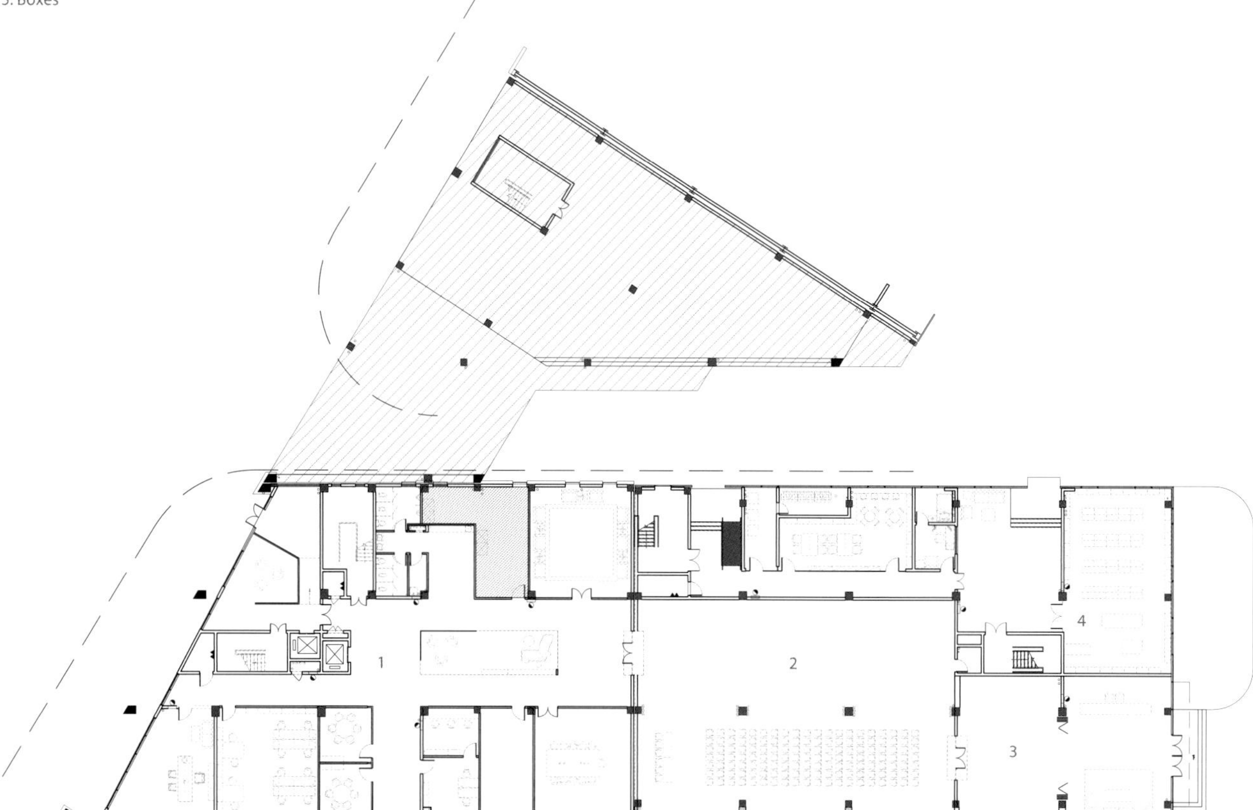

Ground-floor plan of the multifunction building

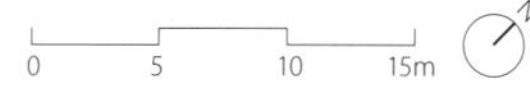

1. Office
2. Multifunction hall
3. VIP reception
4. Meeting room

1. Entrance to office
2. Multifunction room
3. Staff dormitory
4. Meeting room

Black box office

Staff entrance behind the cafeteria

Experiencing *Shan* and *Shui*

The philosophy of line+ studio has always revolved around the integrated design of architecture, landscape, and interior, and this project represents a continuation of that idea. The interior of the office building carries the tone of traditional culture, while on the exterior, integrated iterations of elements in traditional landscape paintings create an all-new modern office experience. This "experience" is composed in four parts: "Encounters," "Early Explorations," "Ascent," and "Gazing Afar."

"Encounters" begins in the foyer, where bent weathered steel conveys a sense of ritual while buffering the transition between the interior and exterior space. The ceiling introduces semi-transparent extended metal grids as the primary element, combining T8 bulbs and linear light strips with the exposed original building structure.

"Early Explorations" starts with a space in the center of the office area that is semi-enclosed by a light metal mesh, and awash in warm hues. It serves as both a communal workspace and an interior "courtyard" for relaxing.

"Ascent" offers a continuation of the red walkways that thread through the entire structure. Connected at all levels, the steel staircase inside the building spirals upward, echoing the walkways outside.

"Gazing Afar" occurs in the owner's private reception and office space on the top floor. The suspended ceiling and the walls in its entrance area are constructed from wood to resemble water ripples, echoing the waves of Qiantang River in the distance, as if one is gazing into the distant waters, letting thoughts drift on.

Outdoor staircase as part of red path

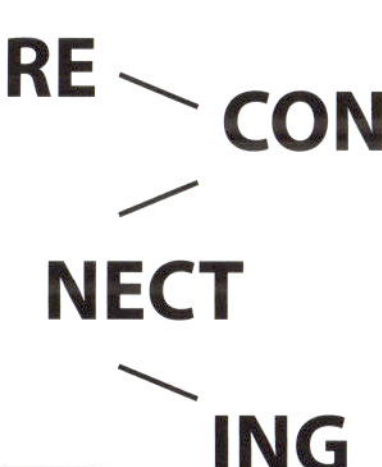

Rethinking Industrial Architecture

How can we provide a space for urban manufacturing and enable it to encourage production to take root and thrive in cities? What is the factory of the future from the perspective of economics, architecture, and urbanism? At a time when manufacturing is constantly evolving and reforming, what form should industrial architecture adopt in response, and to what extent will this affect cities? These questions were not merely considerations for line+ studio in this project, but also represent foreseeable challenges that will confront the construction of urban industrial parks in the future.

New building types at one time, sites engaged in manufacturing, assembly, and production in those days provided a new, independent model for urban development, but the political and economic environment of today, as well as modern industrial production methods, have placed higher demands on industrial buildings. Such industrial parks are no longer a storage space for unfeeling machines. Rather, they are compound clusters of spaces with highly efficient production capabilities, comfortable work environments, and human-centered, shared work and living experiences.

Hangzhou LOFT49 Regeneration

Urban Jinshan, Vitality Block

"The renovation of industrial relics is not only a tribute to history but also a service to the present and a vision for the future. By adopting the Jinshan approach, we aim to infuse urban center with a unique vitality that merges historical memory with contemporary spirit."

—Zhu Peidong

LOFT 49

Entrance to LOFT49

Regenerated building 10 façade

Transforming an Enclave into a Vibrant Hub

In late 2018, LOFT49 initiated a regeneration project focused on preserving industrial heritage. Buildings 6 and 10, notable for their industrial-era character, were fully preserved, while less significant structures were demolished to make way for future development. The project not only retains key heritage buildings but also introduces nearly 969,960 square feet (90,000 square meters) of new space.

The design focuses on preserving the factory's layout, centering around the heritage buildings and placing new structures along the periphery. This approach creates a welcoming urban interface by opening boundaries and controlling the scale of new additions.

The regeneration transforms the factory into an open public platform, blending offices, leisure, ecology, and cultural activities. Two high-rise buildings complement the existing office structure, while multistory buildings are strategically placed along the boundaries, ensuring a balanced urban scale.

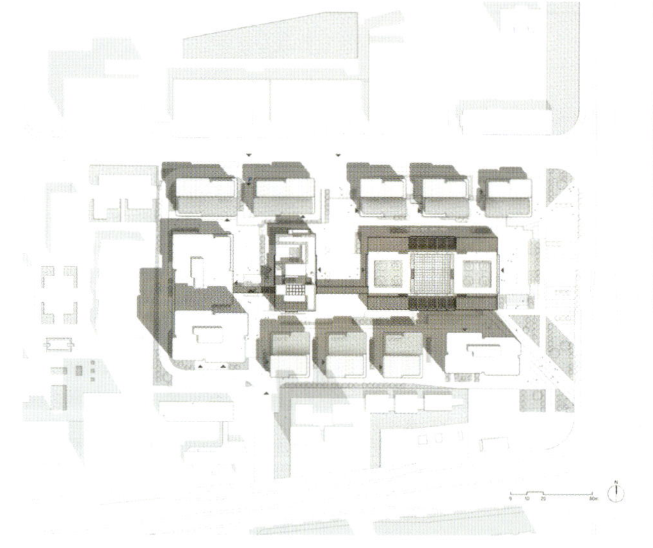
Site plan

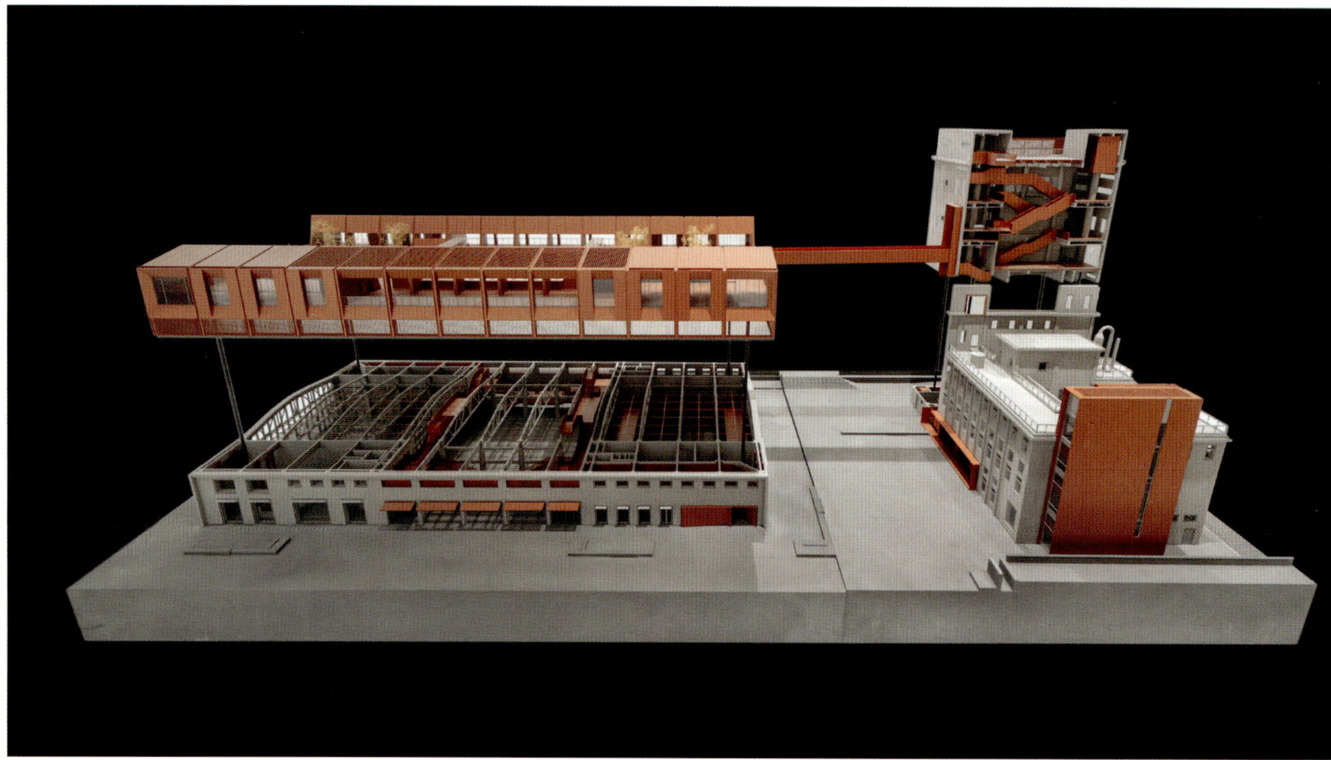

Model

Relics Regeneration: From Static Space to Dynamic Platform

Building 10, the primary production facility of the original factory built in 1987, is a large-span steel-framed structure that still houses pioneering industrial equipment. Building 6, constructed in 1990 as the acrylic sock workshop, also retains several key production features. During the cultural transformation phase, artists modified both buildings—mainly by repainting walls and altering window openings. In the current renovation, the primary goal is to preserve authenticity while enhancing performance and functionality with minimal intervention.

line+ studio employed a threefold strategy from the Jinshan concept: integration, intervention, and connection, to create a unified narrative in form, function, and experience. By reinterpreting the overlapping relics and original production elements, they transformed industrial flow into a fluid spatial circulation that forms the foundation of an industrial narrative.

Both buildings now feature an actively open ground floor that integrates seamlessly with the surrounding park, making the previously confined space more accessible. Elevated walkways connect the upper levels (at 39 feet [12 meters]) to form a cohesive exhibition of industrial heritage. Interior functions have been reallocated based on the original layout, blending historic and new uses, while refreshed external façades establish clear connections between the buildings and the park.

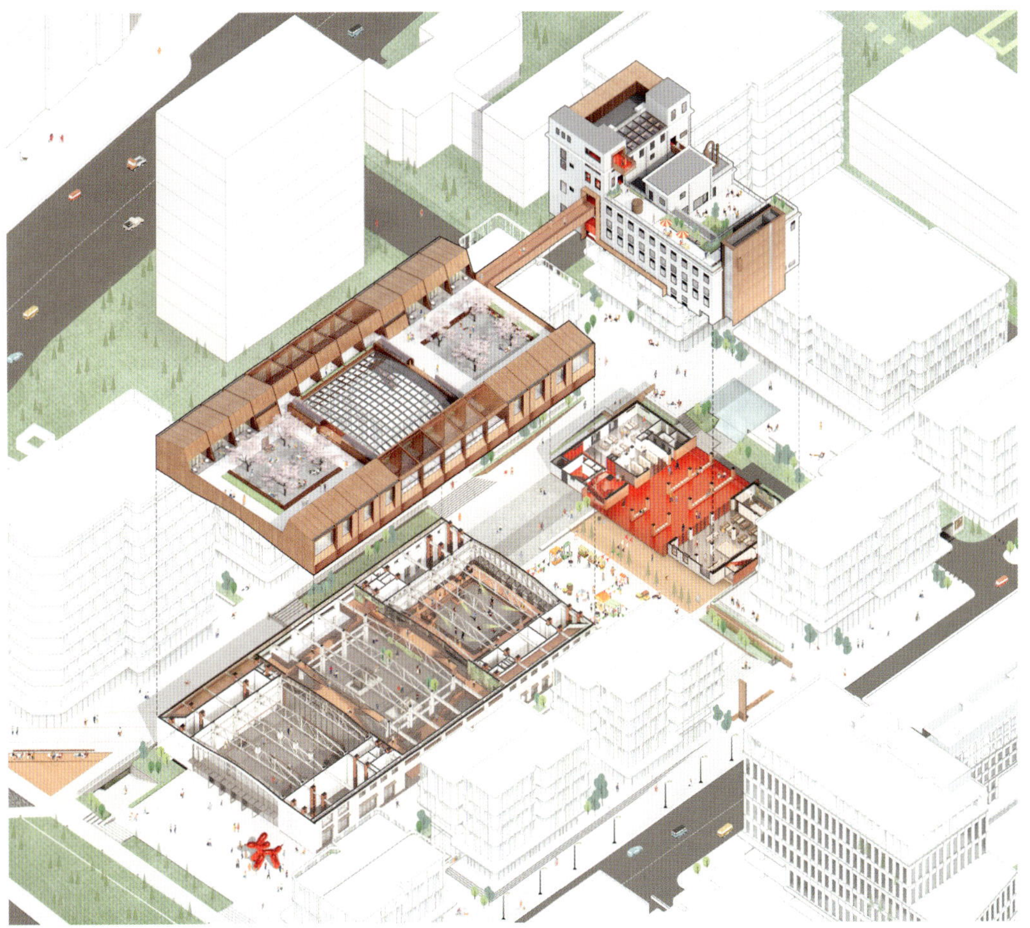

Exploded structural diagram

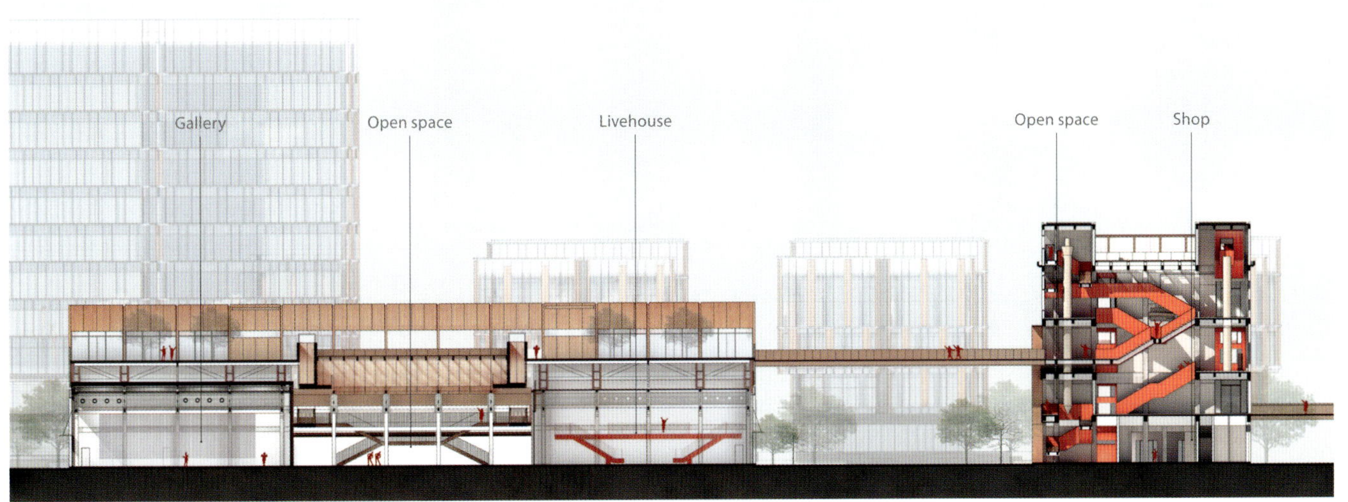

Section diagram

Building 10 entrance

Building 10 :

In Building 10, the north and south façades maintain a classic industrial character—preserving window proportions, wall materials, and select alterations from the creative park era. The central entrance is expanded into a public atrium, while openings in the east and west reveal internal truss systems and equipment, reinforced through grouting and structural improvements.

To address the deteriorated roof condition of the original structure, a new weather-resistant roofing system was installed, detached from the original framework and supported by sixteen lattice columns. This vertical extension creates an elevated platform that now serves as a rare urban rooftop garden and public space.

Building 10's interior retains its central large-span area and peripheral smaller units, divided horizontally into three zones suitable for exhibitions and performances—enhanced by folding doors that offer flexible space configurations. A central courtyard connects the north and south areas, linked by a multilevel circulation core.

Before and after comparison of Building 10

Building 10 interior after renovation

1. Renovated staircase of Building 6
2. Renovated elevator hall of Building 6
3. Renovated façade of Building 6

Building 6:

Building 6 preserves its unique form with varying spans and retains original features such as window placements and industrial pipes. Its layered roof creates dynamic activity platforms, while modern detailing—such as updated window frames—introduces new visual experiences.

The interior, organized around the remnants of production equipment, features opened walls with weather-resistant steel panels and micro-cement finishes, fostering a dialogue between old and new and creating a continuously accessible, contemporary industrial museum experience.

Building 6 façade after renovation

Before and after comparison of Building 6

Exhibition hall after renovation

Section wall details

1. Aluminum composite panel eaves
2. Aluminum alloy profile lines
3. Green roof
4. Aluminum composite panel backing
5. 6 low-e + 12a + 6 high-reflective tempered glass
6. Glazed ceramic rods, glazed ceramic panels
7. Aluminum alloy concealed frame horizontal bar
8. Aluminum composite panel backing
9. Honeycomb aluminum panel
10. 6 low-e + 12a + 6 high-reflective tempered glass
11. Aluminum canopy
12. Aluminum alloy grille
13. 12 low-e + 12a + 12 ultra-clear tempered glass
14. Weathering steel plate
15. Stainless-steel sink
16. 6 low-e + 12a + 6 ultra-clear tempered insulating glass
17. Weathering steel grille
18. Metal light trough
19. Dark gray steel window frame
20. Existing exterior wall, reinforcement treatment
21. New lining wall, lightweight block wall
22. Weathering steel plate edge bead

Business Evolution: From Singular to Diverse

As businesses grow and lifestyles change, spatial flexibility, adaptability, and accessibility have become key considerations. The traditional creative park model no longer fits LOFT49's evolving needs. Combining industrial legacy with cultural inventiveness, LOFT49 drives sustainable industrial site restoration, shifting from "manufacturing" to "creation."

The design prioritizes spatial flexibility to support diverse business models. Beyond offices, LOFT49 incorporates live-music venues, art galleries, and entertainment, fostering a "Live-Work-Play" (L-W-P) environment. This strategy revitalizes surrounding commercial and residential areas, breathing new life into the urban fabric.

In the future, LOFT49 will not only be an all-day industrial museum but also a hub for exhibitions, performances, fashion shows, markets, and various urban events. These functions will coexist, creating a vibrant space for diverse cultural activities. Meanwhile, LOFT49's open and welcoming environment will act as a creative incubator for artists, encouraging spontaneous cross-industry partnerships and building a vibrant new mixed-use zone. This merger of sectors will rebrand LOFT49 as a symbol of synergy and usher in a new era of "co-creation."

Public leisure space

Exhibition hall

Construction process

LOFT49 regeneration

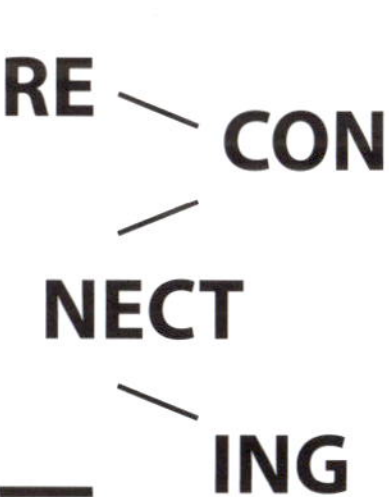

Reviving Industrial Heritage

Does industrial heritage today serve merely as a relic or a landscape? In the case of the regenerated LOFT49, the prominent architectural structures and industrial equipment cannot be overlooked. They embody the unique identity of this place and the necessity of preserving its history. By creating open public spaces that encourage gatherings, the project doesn't just preserve the past; it actively continues the narrative of that history. In this way, the building becomes a catalyst for reconnecting people with the historical and social fabric of the place, inviting new interactions while honoring the old.

iFLYTEK AI Headquarters Campus (Phase 1)

Future Echoes

"Artificial intelligence is a broad interdisciplinary and frontier science. As a Chinese AI company with global influence, iFLYTEK Global Headquarters not only represents an image of the company, but also showcases the Eastern wisdom and humanism in its technological architectural language. We have tried to create a hyperlinked, strongly conducted, and growable system, and an open and shared urban park through a 'super cell body,' so that work, life, and natural scenes can be interwoven to create a spiritual home full of creativity and vitality for iFLYTEK staff."

—Meng Fanhao

Location: Hefei, Anhui Province, China
Design firm: line+ studio
Principal architect: Meng Fanhao
Design team (competition): Zhu Min, He Yaliang, Chen Guanxing, Xing Shu, Huang Ye, Li Jing, Wang Yubin, Xu Hao, Huang Jiaofeng, Zhang Erjia, Li Renjie, Liu Chao, Pan Yiming, Shi Yuhang, Chen Bin, Shen Rui, Xu Yifan, Ji Xin, Ye Huazhou, Ge Jiaqi (Architecture); Zhu Jun, Zhang Sisi, Yang Li, Ge Zhenliang, Deng Hao, He Yukuan, Fan Xiaoxiao, He Zhiyi, Lu Siqi (Interior); Li Shangyang, Lu Yuping, Chi Xiaomei, Li Jun (Landscape)
Design team (SD to DD phase): Zhu Min, Li Xinguang, He Yaliang, Chen Guanxing, Hao Jun, Liu Chao, Li Hang, Li Jing, Huang Yukun, Huang Ye, Shi Yuhang, Xu Yifan, Xu Hao, Xing Shu, Li Renjie, Lin Yu, Zhang Wenxuan, Hong Yang (Architecture); Su Kelun, Zhang Sisi, Deng Hao, Ge Zhenliang, He Yukuan, Yang Li, Fan Xiaoxiao, He Zhiyi, Wang Ziyi (Interior); Li Shangyang, Lu Yuping, Jin Jianbo, Zhang Wenjie, Rao Feier, Chi Xiaomei, Li Jun (Landscape)
Architecture construction drawing: Shanghai Shuishi Architectural Planning & Design Co. Ltd, Qingdao Beiyang Architectural Design Co. Ltd
Landscape constructing drawing: Zhejiang Lansong Landscape Design Group Co. Ltd
Interior cooperative: Suzhou Gold Mantis Architectural Decoration Co. Ltd, Cheng Chung Design (HK)
Lighting consultant: Architectural Lighting Institute of Tongji Architectural Design (Group) Co. Ltd
Transport consultant: Shenzhen Urban Transport Planning Center Co. Ltd
Curtain-wall consultant: Hangzhou Zhongchuang United Construction Technology Co. Ltd
Contractor: Greentown Management
Area: aboveground—2,616,700 square feet (243,100 square meters) underground—1,700,700 square feet (158,000 square meters)
Design period: November 2021–November 2022
Construction period: Under construction
Client: iFLYTEK Co. Ltd
Photography: Arch-Exist Photography, AOGVISION, line+ studio
Model photography: line+ studio

Site plan

Headquarters in the Park

The project is located in Hefei High-tech Zone, Hefei, Anhui Province, with a total planned land area of 33 acres and a construction area of about 4,305,600 square feet (400,000 square meters). As iFLYTEK's corporate headquarters, it includes a national-level open research platform for artificial intelligence, as well as other such research units, such as a key laboratory for cognitive intelligence. It can host 15,000 industrial and R&D employees.

As a pioneer in the intelligent voice and artificial intelligence industry in the Asia-Pacific region since its establishment in 1999, iFLYTEK has been committed to building a better world with artificial intelligence through innovation and perseverance. And for its new headquarters in Hefei High-tech Zone, it sets high expectations and goals: to be the highest level of corporate headquarters in the global intelligent voice and artificial intelligence industry; the most desired industry-city integration base for young technological and entrepreneurial talents; and the benchmark of such intelligent parks, to lead the era of artificial intelligence. iFLYTEK Global Headquarters is also expected to embody the company's wisdom and imagination of Eastern philosophy: sunshine and nature; kindness and harmony; simplicity and permeability; and creativity and inspiration.

Following iFLYTEK's vision for the future, line+ studio proposed Park X as a planning concept and Campus X as spatial type to create an urban park that is both a functionally efficient and accessible campus, and also one that is based on human scale. The concept of "headquarters in a park" means that it is first a large, open park for the city and second, a headquarters that has been built in the park. From an urban perspective, the campus will grow organically as the "city lung," like an emerald embedded in the western part of Hefei. The park will mainly meet the needs of the daily leisure activities of Hefei's citizens, as well as their recreational and civic safety needs, such as cultural activities and disaster evacuation.

Aerial view of the campus

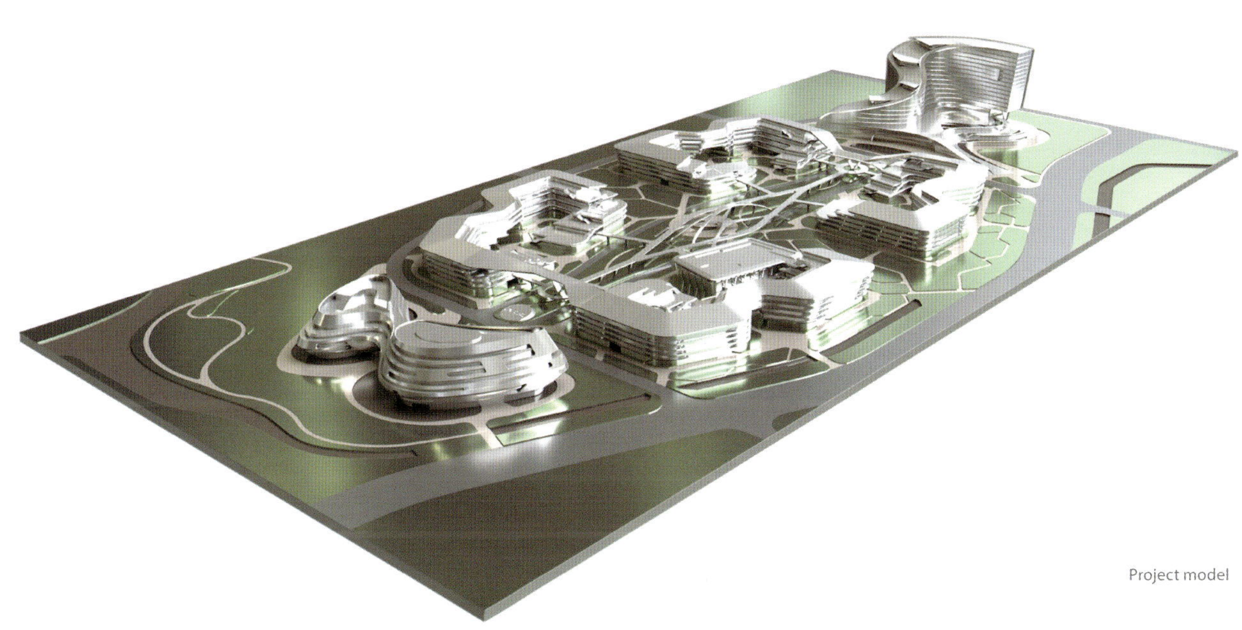

Project model

Night aerial view of the campus

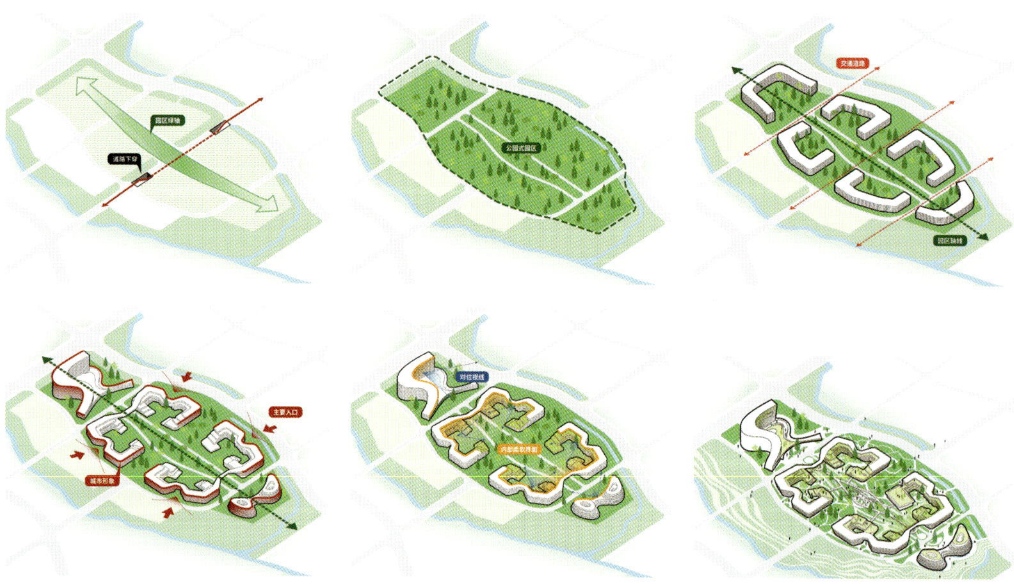

Planning generation

Night view of the campus building exterior

Aerial view of the campus buildings

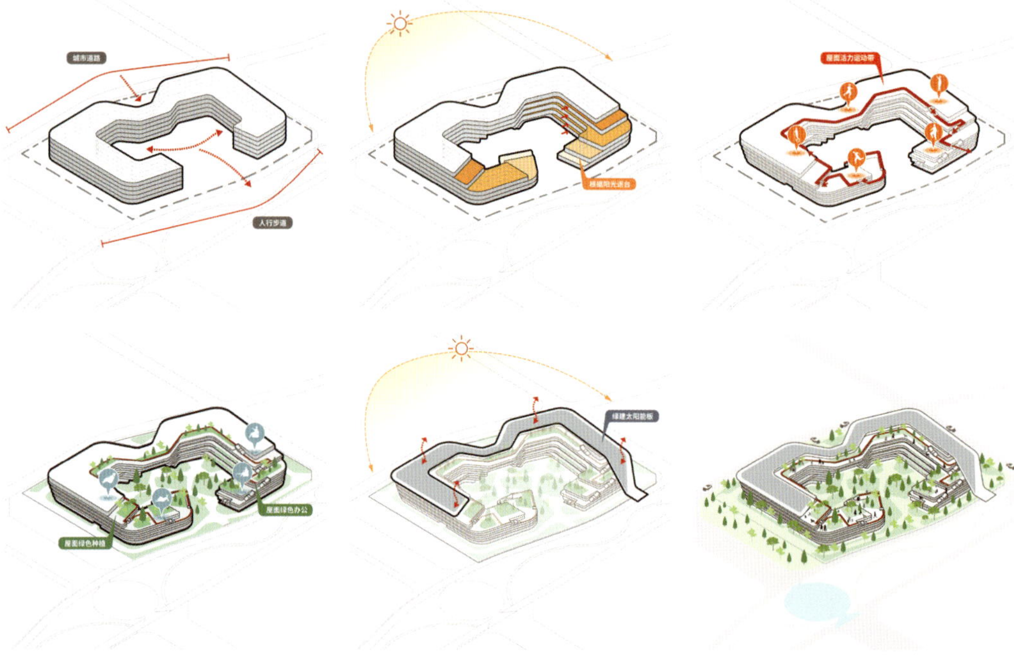

Office volume generation

Campus building and landscape

Terrace and steps

The architectural strategy of enclosing the massive volumes inward frees up a large amount of landscape space within the site. In order to better highlight the concept of "park," line+ studio designed an open and shared interface to the city, while planning a complete walking system in the park. The studio also added a continuous terrace, rooftop runway, and solar panels to maintain the ecological and enjoyable character of the building, integrating office space into a three-dimensional park. The four independent office clusters located in four lots are connected through landscape corridors, leading to a functional structure that combines clusters and public levels to meet the various needs of users.

The terrace, foyer, and rooftop runway in the office area, as well as the urban AI technology exhibition hall, the central ecological corridor, and several dotted AI interactive landscape installations, together with the waterfront garden and waterfront walkway outside the park, form a comprehensive urban park, fostering a new experience that combines nature, culture, and technology.

Terrace and steps

The campus as an urban park

Campus entrance

Future-oriented Campus

Drawing on the innovative spirit of contemporary universities, the concept of Campus X emphasizes openness and urbanity, so as to create a campus-style headquarters that looks toward the future.

The integration of the human scale and place-experience into the super-scale architecture creates a young, energetic, and inspiring atmosphere. By emphasizing sunlight and nature in interior spaces, line+ studio believes that the office space, in the future, will be ecologically sustainable, intelligent, rich in experiences, and full of social activities. A flexible and borderless shared space can stimulate creativity and enable efficient collaborations.

Within the flexible modular system for office space, programs are divided into four modules: office, meeting, energization, and communication. Using a combination of modular space layout and furniture design to create interior aesthetics enables flexibility in the interior look as these elements can be updated and replaced if needed, even after they have been installed. This ensures a high customization benefit, as well as cost optimization within iFLYTEK's headquarters.

North atrium

1	3
2	

1. Shared space
2. Office space
3. South atrium

Model

Exterior of the campus buildings

A New Image for iFLYTEK

iFLYTEK, as one of the leading Chinese AI companies, has a growing global influence. The design process of iFLYTEK Global Headquarters also led line+ studio to build a new image for the cutting-edge high-tech enterprise, so as to tailor a cohesive representation of the organization across all aspects of its presence.

The organization's technological and futuristic business interface strongly presents it as a technological enterprise, but it is the construction of a physical place that truly gives a profound meaning to it. The construction of iFLYTEK Global Headquarters also ties in well with iFLYTEK's grand vision of "Building a Better World with Artificial Intelligence." In the Eastern context, "a better world" implies harmony between human beings, between human beings and places, and between buildings and places. Within the context of the project, it is also the relationship between the high-tech surface and the humanistic spatial experience that interpenetrates each of these characteristics.

Office building cluster

The strategy of the architectural interface was executed along a simple approach. The design uses low-e super-white glass, colored glazed glass, and silver-gray aluminum panels as the main materials to form the curtain-wall system. The colored glazed glass glazing points have been generated by AI, thereby enriching the interface details. The intervention of transparency makes the relationship between inside and outside more natural, and closer.

1. Campus entrance
2. Office building
3. Office building lobby entrance

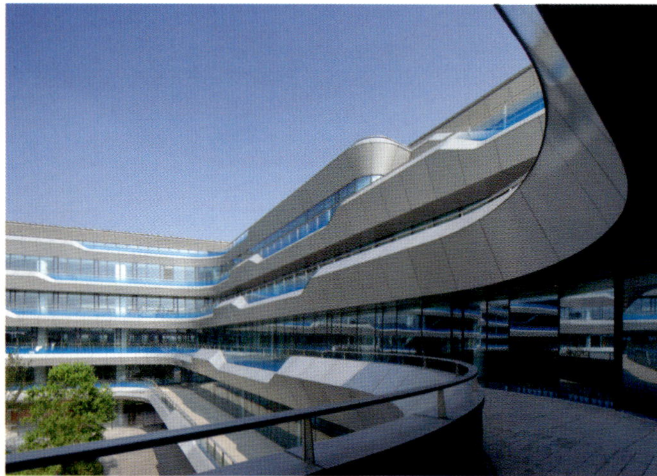

1. Terrace
2. Aluminum panel
3. Façade details

Refined Implementation Control

To address the complexity of the irregular curved surfaces, line+ studio utilized Revit's parametric families for efficient modeling. The team optimized the curtain-wall's division through algorithms and conducted multiple 1:1 mock-ups on-site to select materials and analyze construction nodes, ensuring precise control over the structural and façade outcomes.

Steel structure:

The main office structure of the building utilizes a combination of steel and concrete frame construction. A steel truss system is employed at the main entrance's large span to emphasize openness, while the remaining areas utilize a concrete frame structure. Expansion joints are placed between the two structural forms.

Curtain-wall system:

The curtain-wall's interlayer façade primarily features silver-gray aluminum panels, characterized by sharp angles and continuous metallic lines, creating the overall façade expression of the campus.

During the design development phase, line+ studio meticulously considered post-processing costs and on-site construction feasibility, categorizing the interlayer aluminum panels based on position, size,

Details

1. Aluminum alloy beam
2. Linear light slot with glass cover, 5% drainage slope
3. Linear floodlight
4. 50x50x4mm hot-dip galvanized square steel pipe
5. Fireproof rock wool
6. Fireproof sealant sealing
7. 3mm aluminum angle code
8. 3mm single-layer aluminum panel
9. Aluminum panel joint drip groove
10. 1.5mm hot-dip galvanized steel plate
11. 40mm rock wool insulation board
12. Hot-dip galvanized embedded parts
13. Cast-in-place reinforced concrete
14. Drainage hole
15. 6mm low-e + 12a + 6mm tempered insulated glass

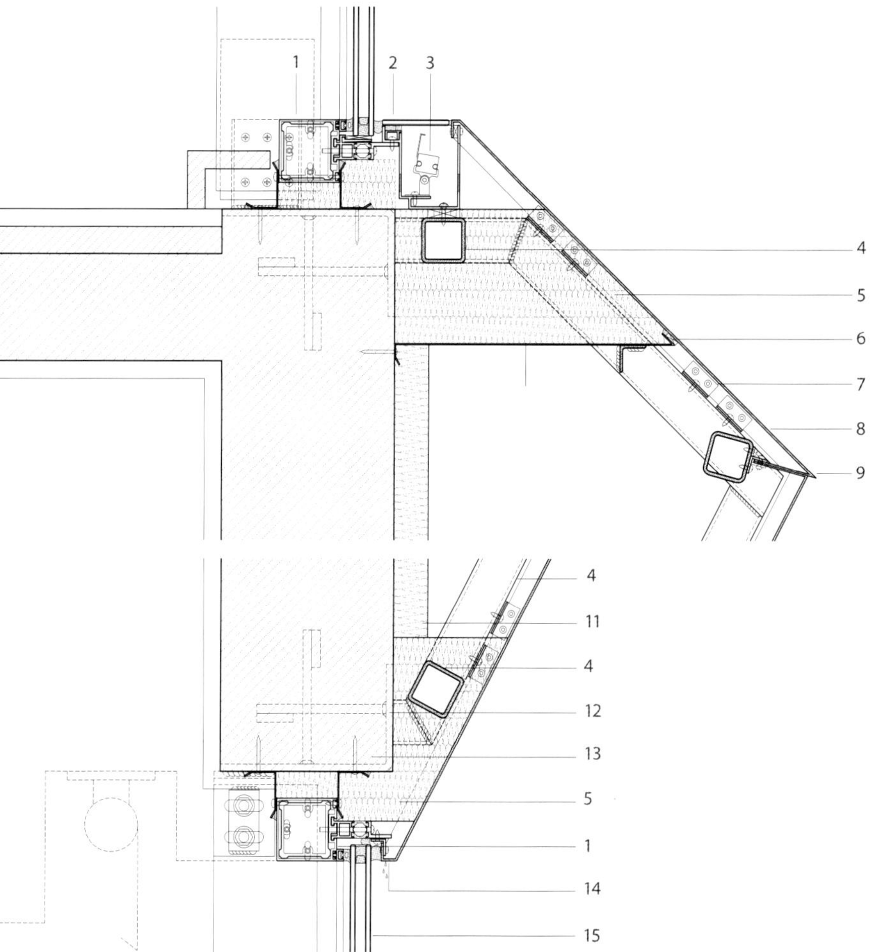

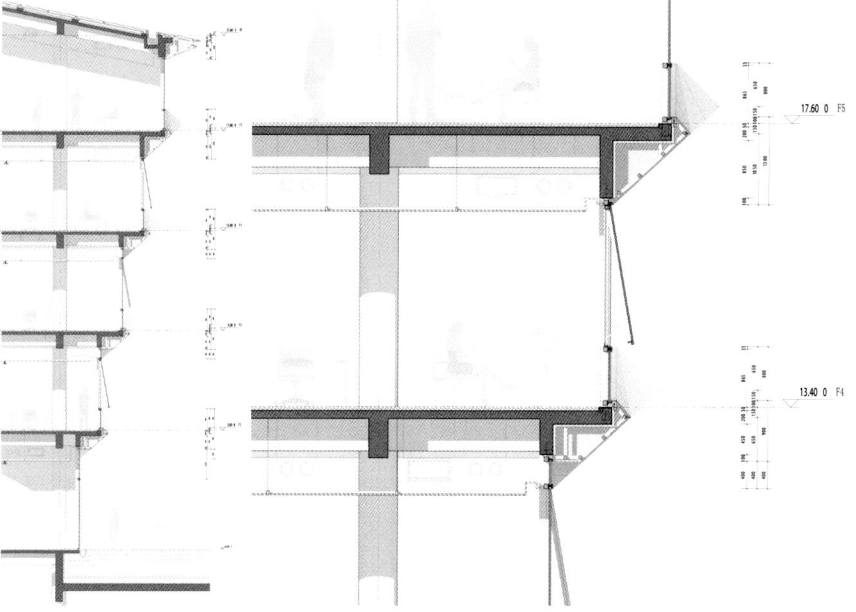

and function—such as protruding sections, terrace areas, and steel structure zones. The panels were classified into 13 categories with detailed annotations. Early in the construction phase, line+ studio conducted on-site mock-ups to test and validate the drainage methods for linear aluminum panels, hyperbolic aluminum panels, and the pointed ends of the panels before proceeding to production and installation.

Colored glazing glass

A1

A3

Type of colored glazing glass

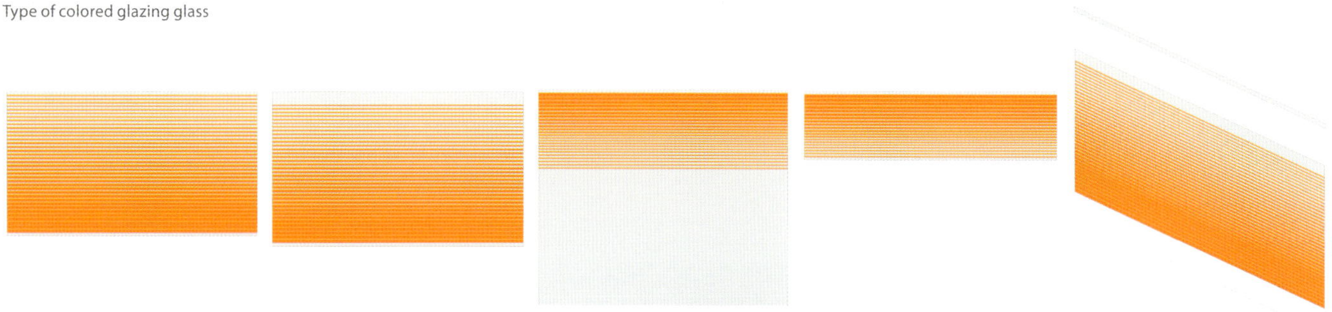

Lower section of inter-floor glass curtain-wall

Terrace glass balustrade

Upper section of inter-floor glass curtain-wall (first floor)

Upper section of inter-floor glass curtain-wall

Outdoor staircase glass balustrade

Façade details

Façade details

Façade details

Blue glazed glass

Orange glazed glass

Colored glazed glass:

To enhance the identity of each building while maintaining a cohesive overall appearance, line+ studio incorporated various colors of glazed glass alongside silver-white aluminum panels and low-e glass. Each building features a unique theme color, reflecting the young and vibrant corporate culture of the technology company. After multiple rounds of deliberation on the overall unity of the campus and the color vibrancy of the glazed glass, line+ studio ultimately selected a gradient horizontal stripe pattern.

Roof-mounted photovoltaics:

The solar panels utilize a BIPV (building-integrated photovoltaics) design, combining silver aluminum, cadmium telluride thin-film modules, and gray back-glazed glass. This integration creates a seamless roof while showcasing iFLYTEK's logo and AI representation. Parametric design tools standardized roof sections to minimize non-standard panels, controlling construction complexity and costs. The layout optimizes about 4,000 square meters of panels for efficiency, with unsuitable areas replaced by matching glass for consistency.

Overall aerial view of the campus

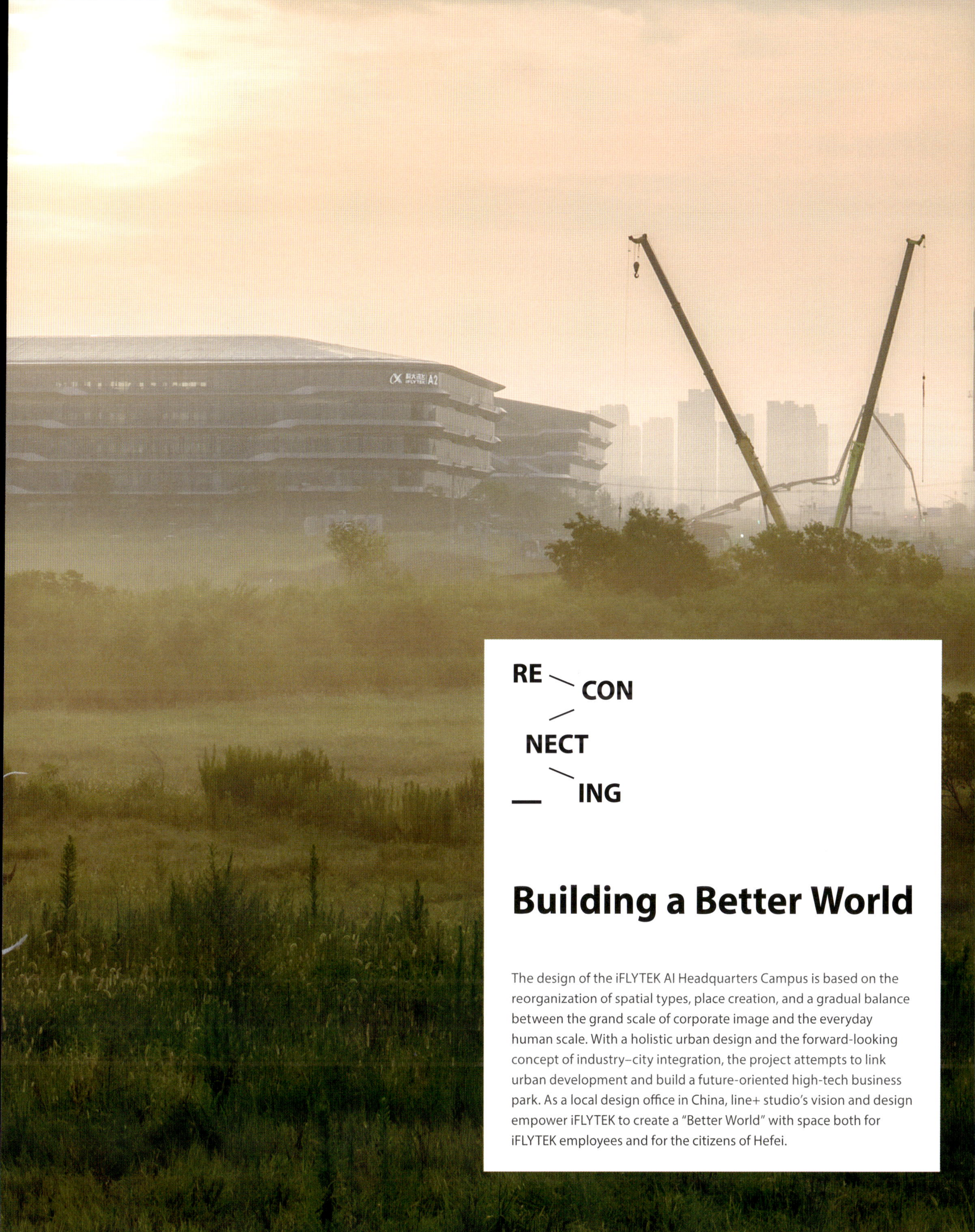

RE — CON — NECT — ING

Building a Better World

The design of the iFLYTEK AI Headquarters Campus is based on the reorganization of spatial types, place creation, and a gradual balance between the grand scale of corporate image and the everyday human scale. With a holistic urban design and the forward-looking concept of industry–city integration, the project attempts to link urban development and build a future-oriented high-tech business park. As a local design office in China, line+ studio's vision and design empower iFLYTEK to create a "Better World" with space both for iFLYTEK employees and for the citizens of Hefei.

Shenzhen Yunhai Forest Service Station

Amidst Mountains and Seas

"The outdoors has become the new destination for modern tourism, offering an unparalleled environmental experience. The allure of nature is magnified by the mountain and sea setting of the Yunhai Forest Service Station. Our goal was to amplify this dream through architecture, transforming it into a sensory experience and a visceral journey."

—Meng Fanhao

Location: Shenzhen, Guangdong Province, China
Design firm: line+ studio
Principal architect: Meng Fanhao
Project architect: He Yaliang
Architecture design team: Xing Shu, Liu Chao, Xu Hao, Xu Yifan, Zhu Xiaojing, Li Changhao, Jin Lingbing (Intern), Wei Xuzhen (Intern), Shen Han (Intern), Yu Qizheng (Intern)
Interior design team: Zhu Jun, Jin Yuting, Yang Li, Zhang Sisi, Lv Siqi
Landscape design team: Li Shangyang, Jin Jianbo, Rao Feier, Wang Xinyu
On-site architect: Xing Shu
Area: 14,962 square feet (1,390 square meters)
Design period: August 2021–March 2022
Construction period: July 2022–January 2023
Client: Yantian District People's Government of Shenzhen
Photography: Arch-Exist Photography, line+ studio
Model photography: line+ studio

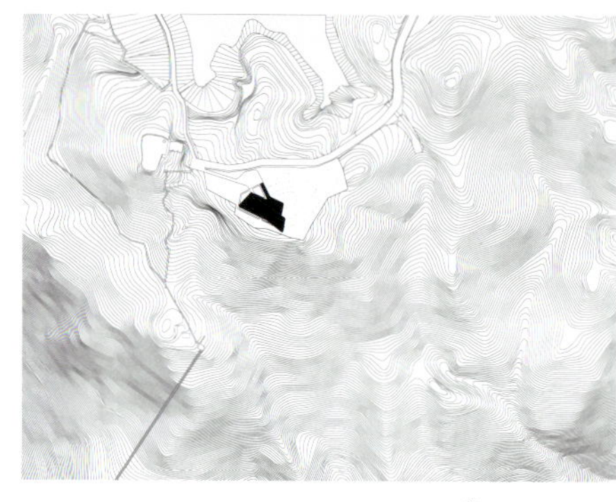

Site plan

Shenzhen, a city that blends rapid urban growth with a respect for nature, stands at the forefront of China's transformation. As the city advances, it continues to integrate green spaces, like the Yunhai Forest Service Station, which serves as both an environmental restoration project and a popular outdoor destination.

In line with the ecological construction goal of "Mountain-Sea Connected City, Beautiful Green Shenzhen," the local government has initiated several projects aimed at environmental restoration while catering to the growing outdoor activity community. The Yunhai Forest Service Station is one such initiative.

Nestled at an altitude of 380 meters on Maluan Mountain, with sweeping views of both the bustling port and the pristine forest, Yunhai Forest Service Station occupies a unique site. Inspired by the tension between nature and the urban landscape, line+ studio transformed the architectural space into an experiential journey, blurring the lines between infrastructure and outdoor landscape while encouraging public engagement.

Existing site

New building

Aerial view

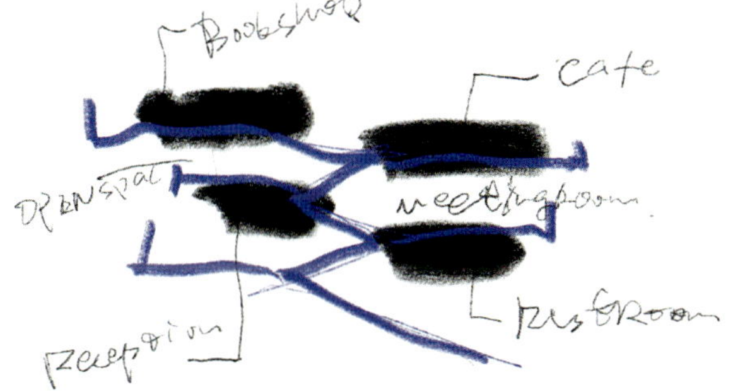

Concept sketch

Aerial view

360-degree Panoramic Folding Platform

The station's design maximizes its compact footprint, offering sweeping 360-degree views of Dapeng Bay, Sanzhoutang Reservoir, and surrounding mountains. line+ studio focused on maximizing viewpoints within the station's compact footprint.

After a hazardous three-story building collapsed, the site was left with a foundation pit. The restrooms were strategically placed here for accessibility, connected by a dedicated pathway. Above, reception rooms, meeting areas, open spaces, a café, and a bookstore are arranged in half-level increments, creating a Z-shaped, multilevel path that winds through the building. This design links the visitors' movement with the surrounding environment, providing observation platforms and expansive, open gray spaces.

The circulation pathways also function as outdoor platforms and flexible spaces. Wide, gently sloping paths, glass terraces, and large steps offer places for pausing and contemplation, enriching the sensory experience.

As the design took shape, the concept of iconicity emerged. The challenge was to transform infrastructure from a supporting function into a destination in itself. The Yunhai Forest Service Station is not just a scenic structure; it draws attention from varying heights and perspectives, becoming an integral part of the landscape. Transparent, lightweight materials and a streamlined form enhance the station's visual presence within its mountain–sea setting.

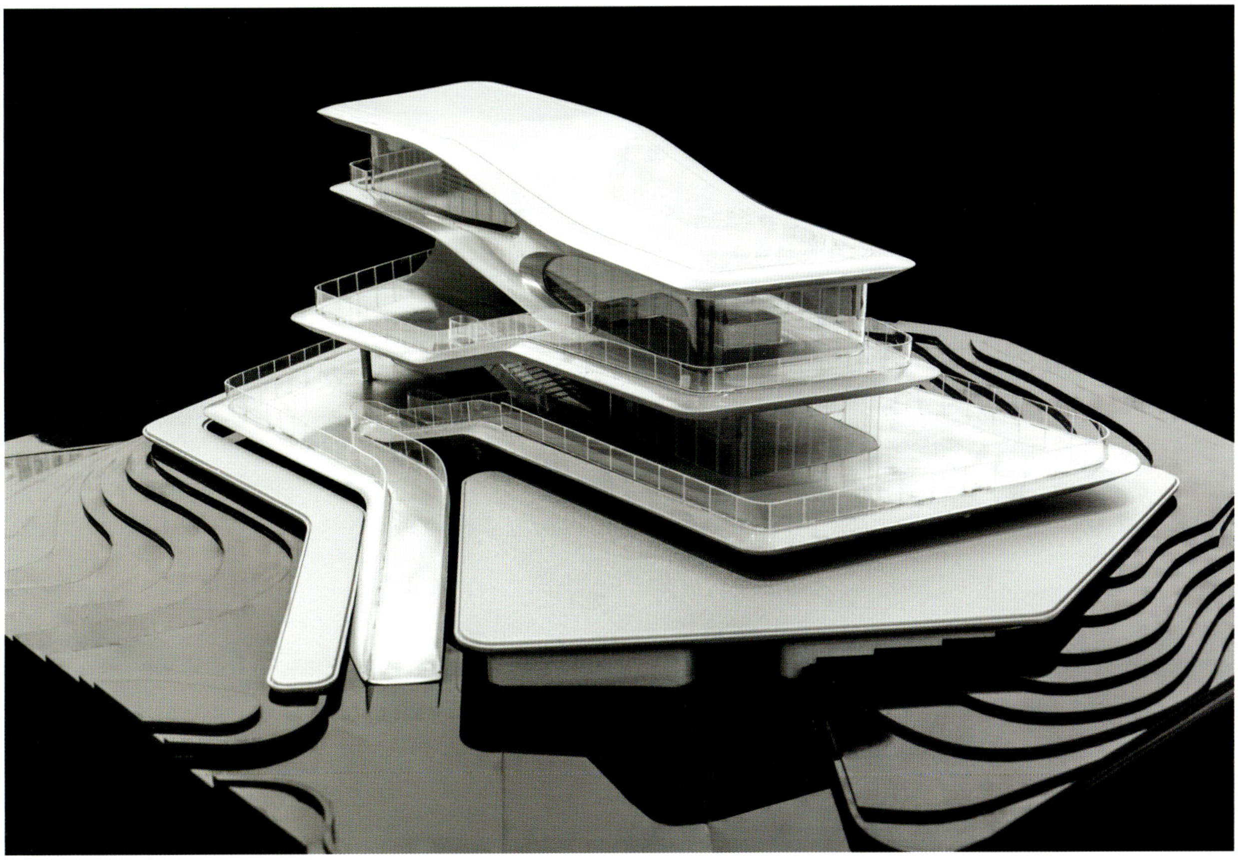

Model

1	2
3	4
5	6

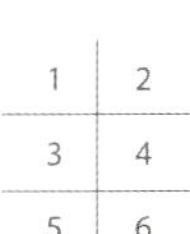

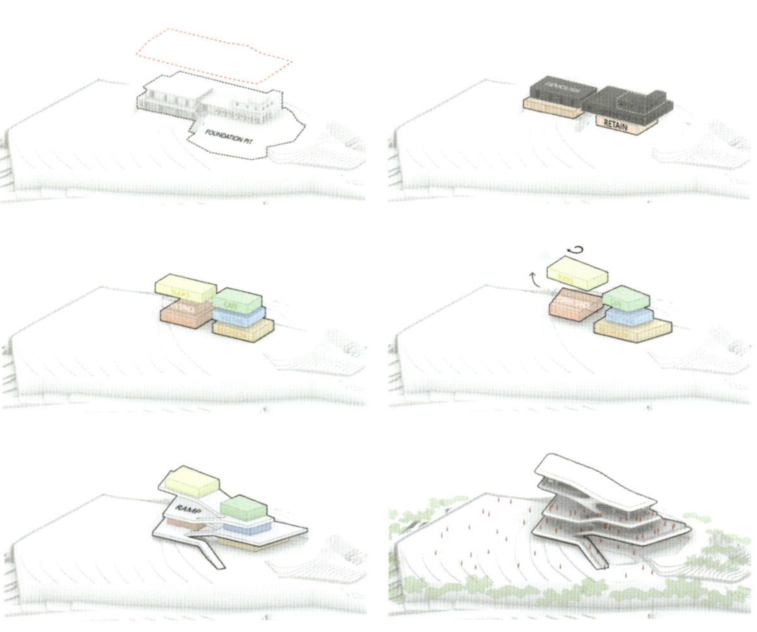

Generation process

1. Site
2. Renovation
3. Program
4. Sightline Analysis
5. Connecting
6. Morphing

Night view at distance

An Otherworldly Experience

The interior design creates an otherworldly atmosphere, with curved walls and flowing forms enhancing the sensory experience.

The floor plan is in harmony with the architectural flow, punctuated by art installations that capture attention at key moments. Notably, a metal installation between the three-story café and reading area serves both functional and artistic roles, integrating book displays with the coffee preparation area. The contrast between the irregular stainless-steel surfaces and the white terrazzo floors evokes a cyberpunk aesthetic, set against the expansive mountain and sea views.

The restroom on the first floor adds another layer of surrealism to the design. A full-height, irregular metal installation at the entrance and a translucent curved acrylic wall mark the beginning of this otherworldly journey. Inside, the space is organized around a central circular installation, with metal plates accentuating the flow of space while maintaining privacy.

Streamlined exterior form

Integrated interior installation design

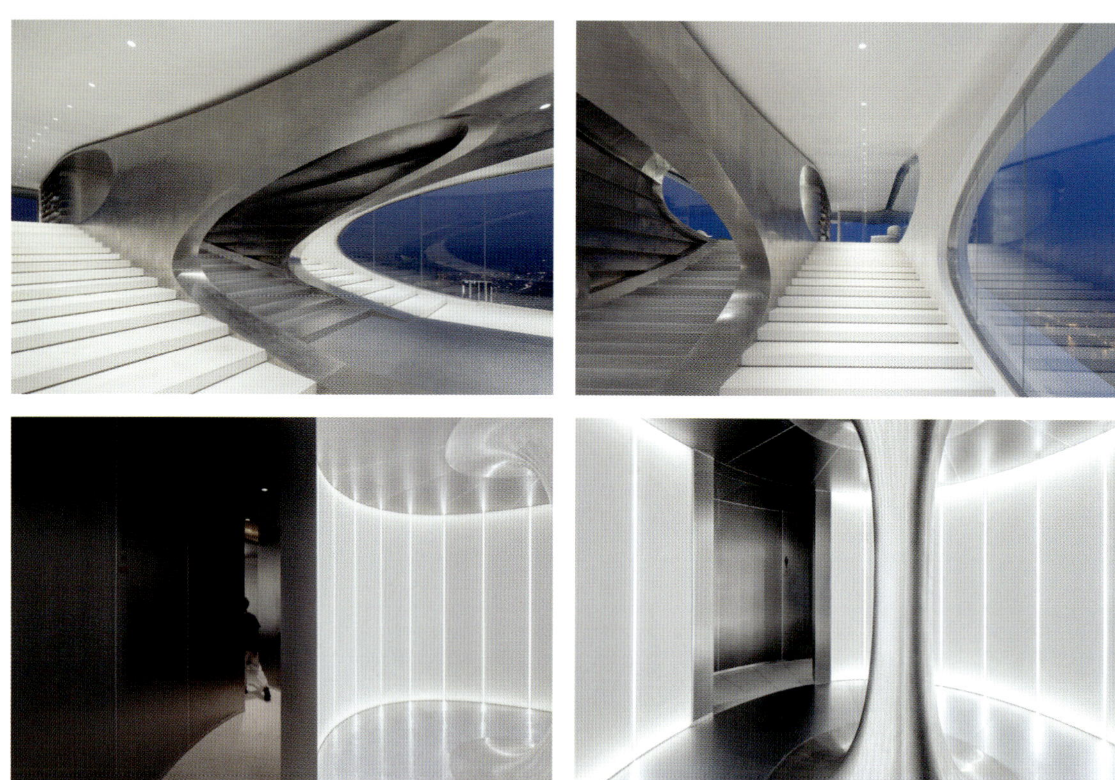

Futuristic interior design

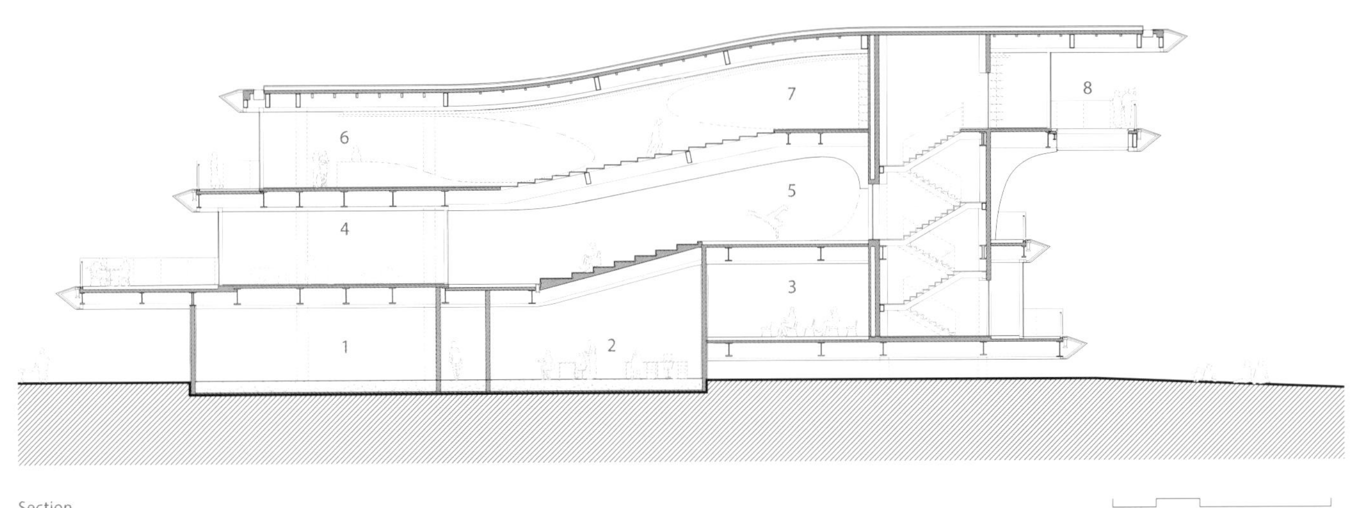

Section

1. Toilet
2. Office
3. Reception hall
4. Lounge
5. Viewing terrace
6. Coffee bar
7. Reading lounge
8. Glass terrace

Model

Façade

Material and Structure

Material and structural choices were driven by considerations of construction feasibility, environmental resilience, and the desire for large-span, column-free spaces. The steel framework and curtain-wall system of the building were prefabricated off-site for rapid installation.

Steel structure:
The eccentrically arranged core tube and the frame structure at the rear collectively achieve the large-span and multidirectional cantilever of the viewing platform. Through a structural feasibility analysis, it simulates the response to the wind pressure and load conditions at the mountain top.

Building skin:
The exterior walls use UHPC panels for their durability, impermeability, and ability to form complex curves. Panels were divided into smaller sections (3 feet [1 meter] by 6.5 feet [2 meters]) for easy transport and installation. After installation, seams were sealed, surfaces polished, and protective coating applied, with drainage grooves along the edges.

The outdoor ceiling features tightly installed fluorocarbon-coated aluminum panels, with hidden drainage pipes. The core tube is wrapped in seamless, curved stainless-steel panels coated in white paint. The terrace is covered with prefabricated terrazzo slabs. The curved glass curtain-walls are framed by a steel subframe, with laminated glass and curved corner panels.

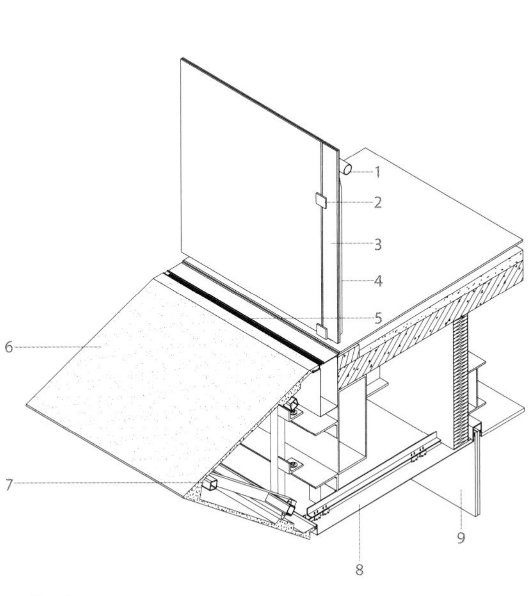

Details

1. 50mm stainless-steel round tube handrail
2. 304 stainless-steel spider fitting
3. 8+21.5PVB+8 laminated tempered glass
4. 80×16mm stainless-steel flat bar
5. Stainless-steel slotted drainage cover
6. 20mm UHPC panel
7. 50×50×5mm hot-dip galvanized steel
8. 3mm fluorocarbon-coated white aluminum panel
9. 15+2.3SGP+15 laminated tempered glass

Façade details

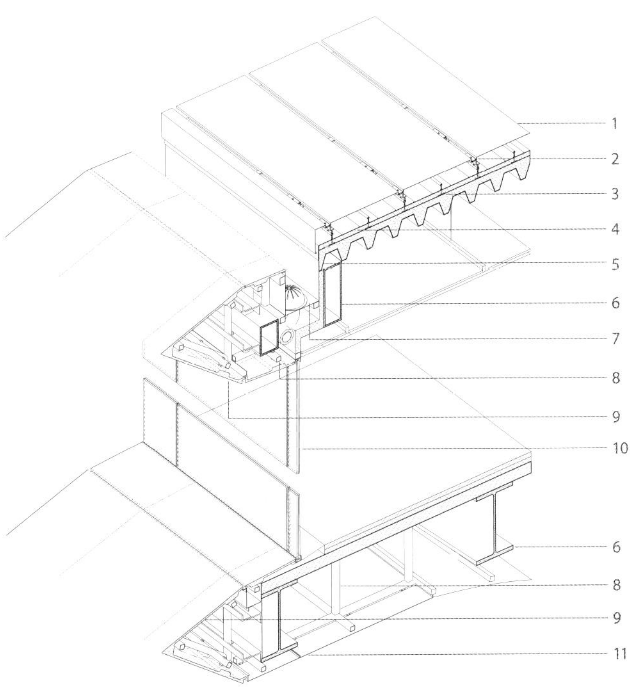

Details

1. 3mm aluminum panel
2. L50×4mm hot-dip galvanized angle steel
3. Aluminum alloy fixing components
4. Glass fiber insulation wool
5. 1.5mm high-rib steel deck, filled with sound-absorbing cotton
6. Steel structure frame
7. 304 plate
8. 20mm UHPC panel
9. 50×50×5mm hot-dip galvanized steel
10. 15+2.3SGP+15 laminated tempered glass
11. 3mm fluorocarbon-coated white aluminum panel

Curved shaped glass curtain-wall

Glass terraces:
The glass terraces, using oversized triple-laminated panels (up to 8.9 feet [2.7 meters] by 13.5 feet [4.1 meters]), maximize transparency and provide unobstructed views of the surrounding landscape.

Interior design:
The interior maintains the same color and texture as the exterior, with white stainless-steel dominating the walls and ceilings. Equipment is discreetly concealed, with air vents hidden between metal forms and water pipes integrated into side walls.

Glass terrace

Semi-outdoor terrace and platform

Curved shaped glass curtain-wall

Layered activity platforms

Space for event activities

The Yunhai Forest Service Station quickly captured the attention of Shenzhen residents, becoming a popular outdoor destination and one of the city's most iconic new landmarks.

Surpassing architectural expectations, the station has inspired visitors to use the space in ways not originally anticipated, such as enjoying coffee in the clouds or hosting wedding ceremonies. On social media, it has earned the nickname "Sky Cruise Ship at the Peak of Mountains and Seas," further highlighting Shenzhen's distinctive landscape.

Beyond serving as a public attraction, the Yunhai Forest Service Station has evolved into a platform for spontaneous creativity, with images and videos circulating widely online. Recently, it has also hosted events for high-end brands like Ferrari, Porsche, Avita, and Roewe, solidifying its role as a key cultural and commercial hub that promotes social interaction and exchange.

RE — CON

NECT

— ING

A Social Landmark

Streamlined exterior form

In the media age, the role of public buildings has evolved beyond mere landmarks or subjects for dissemination. They now serve as physical platforms that bring together people, ideas, and communities. The Yunhei Forest Service Station, with its capacity to inspire and engage, fosters social interaction and becomes a space where diverse imaginations converge, enhancing the societal relevance of architecture.

Veranda in the Zhejiang Conservatory of Music

Floating Cornice on the Brook

"Where nature completes the images of time, where nature lingers and time slips by."

—Friedrich Hölderlin, *The View*

Location: Hangzhou, Zhejiang Province, China
Design firm: line+ studio
Principal architect: Zhu Peidong
Principal landscape designer: Li Shangyang
Architecture design team: Sun Xiaoyu, Zhou Yang
Landscape design team: Jin Jianbo, Zhang Wenjie, Chi Xiaomei
Structure design team: Li Baozhong, Gao Yi
Area: 4,413 square feet (410 square meters)
Design period: July 2020–September 2020
Construction period: April 2021–September 2021
Client: Zhejiang Conservatory of Music
Photography: Zhu Runzi, line+ studio, Yao Li

Site plan

The Zhejiang Conservatory of Music—where the Floating Cornice on the Brook is located—is the tenth independently established professional music education institution in China. Ten years ago, in a design competition for the Zhejiang Conservatory of Music, Zhu Peidong (then one of the project principals at gad) was prompted to reflect on the enclosed layout of colleges and universities in China while considering concepts, which led him to adopt the approach of an "open music and art park," breaking away from the traditional scale and interface of typical Chinese university campuses. By borrowing the formal language of landscaping and settlements, he manifested a new model of campus architecture that allowed for more freedom and openness.

During the period from 2015 to 2020, after the conservatory's inauguration, the management team became keen to declare the campus a "4A cultural and tourist attraction"—a ranking that grades tourist attractions in China according to their importance. This provided line+ studio with the opportunity to expand the identity of the campus from a conceptual "open campus" to a social-ecological "public landscape" through on-site micro-renewals, transforming the campus into an urban public park connecting students, faculty, and residents from the neighborhood.

Bird's-eye view of the campus

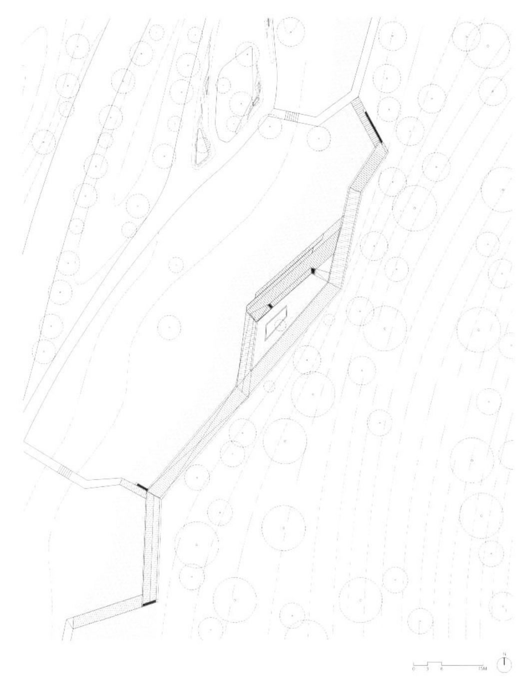

Plan

A Connecting Linear Structure

Influenced by the local terrain, Zhejiang Conservatory of Music's campus layout is divided into two major building clusters at the north and south of a small mountain. The north side presents a landscape architecture embedded into the mountains, while the south side features a ceremonial space with clear artificial boundaries. Located in the middle of the two main areas, Floating Cornice on the Brook preserves the original landscape of the site, connecting the north and south clusters with a flowing, bending walkway, winding with a brook on the site to follow the mountains and the natural landscape. In order to secure the conservatory's "4A cultural and tourist attraction" ranking, reinforcing the public character of the campus's middle section became the main design intention in a micro-renewal project.

Based on the campus design concept, the new demands of the campus, and the surrounding urban development, the rain garden in the valley-like middle section of the campus was selected as the project site. The new linear pedestrian walkway, which connects the north and south building clusters, was embedded in the site with minimal disruption to the existing landscape.

The new pedestrian walkway borrows from the traditional Chinese painting technique of oblique projection and reinterprets the spatial elements of classical Chinese gardens, such as walkways, corridors, cornices, and bridges. Within the newly designed winding space, multiple focal points, spatial forms, and behavioral scenarios are superimposed, so that people can experience multiple spatial perspectives while walking through the corridor and observing the surroundings. This provides students, faculty members, and the public with a new walking environment as they journey between the north and south of the campus.

Veranda against the site context

Veranda against the site context

A Dialogue Between Two Corridors

The new Floating Cornice on the Brook runs parallel to the existing Cloud Corridor in the Valley of Music, which has been in use for many years, and which blends in with the natural mountain scenery at the center of the campus. Designed a decade ago, Cloud Corridor in the Valley of Music exhibits a wave-like structure that echoes the flowing landscape of the campus. Its solid, fair-faced concrete, with a subtle texture of the wood-grain formwork, provided the starting point for the structural and material design of the new Floating Cornice on the Brook. line+ studio aimed to establish a dialogue between the new and existing corridors through the contrast between light and heavy, void and solid, and zigzagging and meandering, creating a transition space between the Zhejiang Conservatory of Music and the natural, gently sloping mountain landscape at the center of the campus. Cloud Corridor in the Valley of Music forms a semi-open, fair-faced concrete corridor that also acts as a sound barrier against the noise from a nearby expressway. In contrast, the Floating Cornice on the Brook forms a permeable steel and wood corridor that elegantly connects people with nature.

Floating Cornice on the Brook is located along the foot of Wangjiang Mountain, zigzagging across an existing brook. Based on the archetypical elements of classical Chinese gardens—such as walkways, corridors, cornices, and bridges—Floating Cornice on the Brook creates a rich spatial experience by adopting spatial themes such as "embracing the mountains," "trickling water," "facing the brook," and "a twisting path."

Undulating roof

Space beneath the roof

Echoing the water features

Folding roof gently touching the ground

Entrance

Walkways

In order to avoid affecting the local environment, the walkway is elevated above the stream—as close to the water as possible—and evades existing trees at every bend of the corridor, while conforming to the slope of the mountain.

Corridors

Columns along the walkway hold up the cornice and bend in harmony with the mountains. In just a few steps, people passing through can reach the river, where they can sit comfortably by the side of the stream, allowing the structure to combine behavioral functions like sitting, standing, observing, and strolling in one entity.

Cornices

The ridge and eaves of traditional Chinese sloping roofs were simplified into a lightweight and retreating shape. Adding to that, the cornice has also been contorted to form a seating bench, as well as buttresses that define the ends of the corridor.

Bridge

The brook forms a small pond in front of the campus cafeteria, over which a slightly sloping steel "bridge" has been erected, cantilevered on one side and gently passing through the creek's slope to the main walkway on the other.

Hidden in nature

Folding forms

A Light Structure

The roof structure of Floating Cornice on the Brook is made of a central box girder with cantilevered I-beams on each side. This creates an abstract shape with double-pitched and polygonal tented roof sections. Underneath the roof, the ceiling forms inverted pyramids, with apexes that extend into slender steel columns. Expanding across 371 feet (113 meters) from north to south, the roof is supported in the ground by only five columns. Seen from a distance, these columns resemble tree trunks that blend with the forest behind the corridor. Thus, the undulating roof seems to float above the stream, and becomes a part of the surrounding landscape.

In terms of materials, Cloud Corridor in the Valley of Music has a strong morphological expression through the use of fair-faced concrete. In contrast, the new Floating Cornice on the Brook accentuates its human-centered scale and its relationship with the surrounding mountains through the use of wood. The top of the roof and the sitting area are made of dark-gray burnt fir boards treated with charcoal, in order to effectively counteract the effects of weathering; the ceiling and the corridor buttresses are made of red cedar boards to provide a natural color and warm texture.

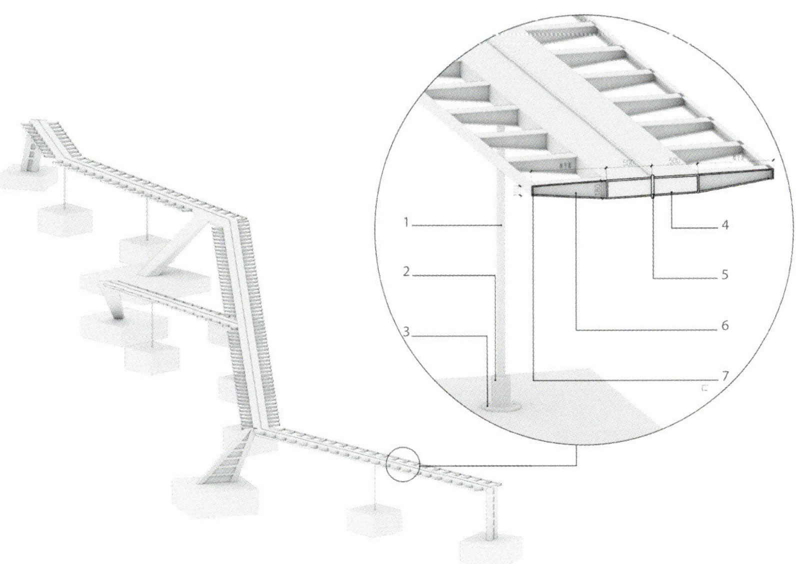

Material Comparison: Concrete (from Cloud Corridor, left) and Wood Panels (from Floating Cornice, right)

Structure detail

1. Seamless round steel pipe columns
2. Concrete ring
3. Welding mat
4. Box-type steel beams
5. Stiffening ribs
6. Overhanging I-beam
7. Hot-rolled V-shaped steel bar

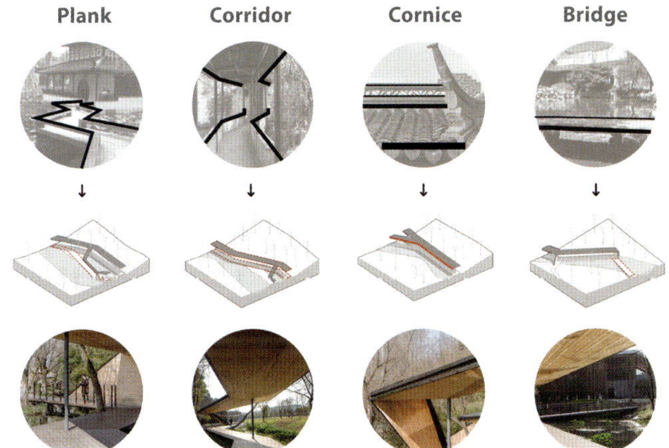

Veranda detail

Detail section

1. 2mm-thick gray metal covering plate
2. 15×80×1,200mm gray Shou Sugi Ban
3. 30×30mm hanging strip
4. LED lighting strip
5. 2mm-thick gray aluminum bar
6. 30×30mm counter batten
7. Stainless-steel plate waterproof layer
8. Slope-finding purlin
9. Square steel beam
10. I-shape steel beam
11. Ceiling wooden keel
12. Red cedar board

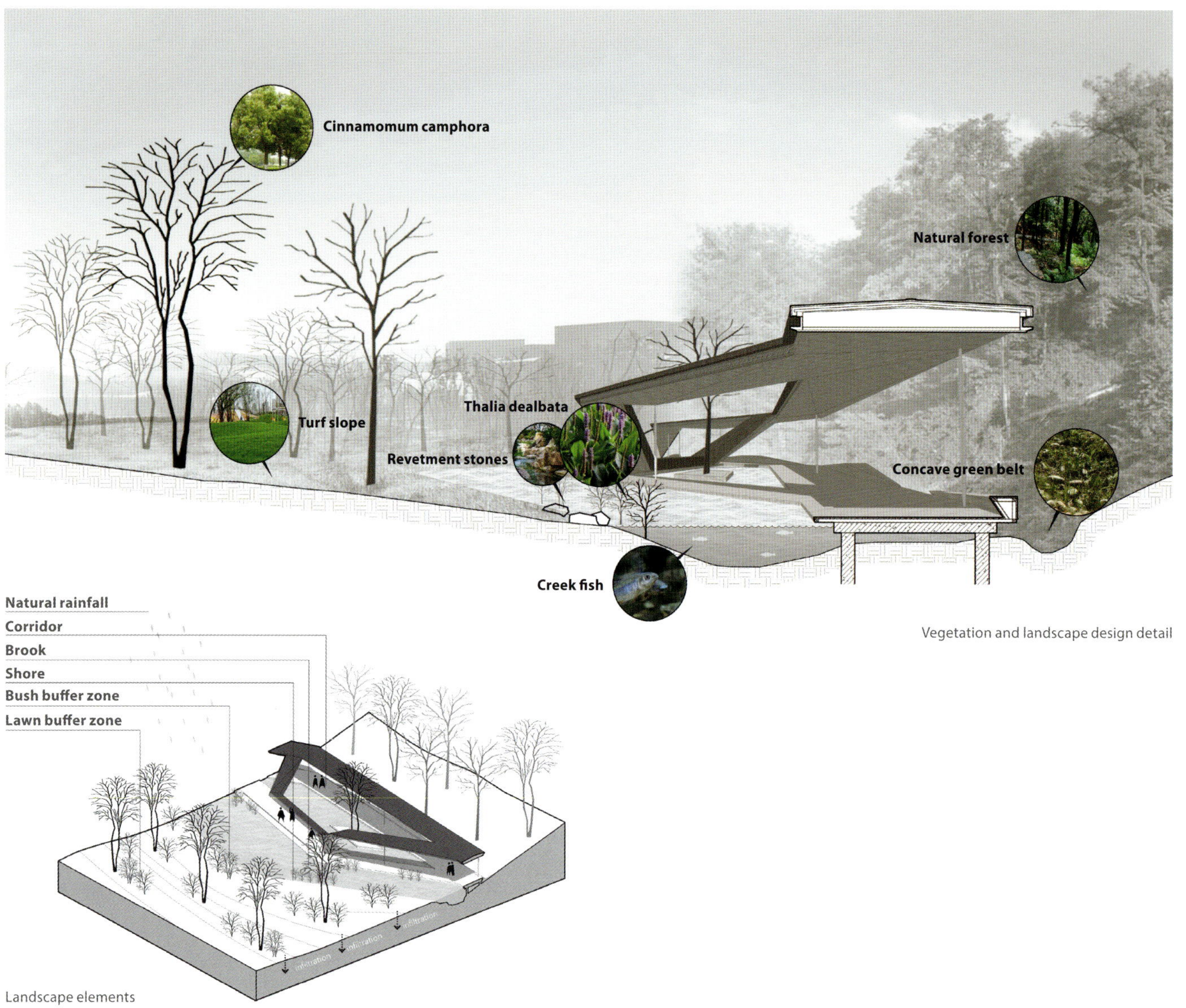

Vegetation and landscape design detail

Landscape elements

Eco-friendly Sponge Landscape

Based on the concept of the "rain garden" and the principle of minimal intervention, the local campus water system, mountains, trees, and meadows were preserved and integrated into the spatial design, creating, an eco-friendly sponge landscape that combines ecological sustainability with landscape art and participatory behaviors. Through a buffer zone of lawns, bushes, and the brook's landscape belt, a natural transition exists between the parallel brook area, the vehicular and pedestrian paths, and the Cloud Corridor in the Valley of Music at the center of the campus. The covered bridge is elevated above the water, and on both sides of the winding corridor, gentle slopes enter the water that is filled with aquatic plants. Through the combined purification by the plants and the sand surrounding the brook, rainwater filters into the soil, nourishing the groundwater and replenishing the waterscape.

Veranda in a natural setting

RE — CON

NECT

— ING

Open to All

In the years since its opening, the Zhejiang Conservatory of Music has hosted a number of music and art events for the public. In this music park, the Floating Cornice on the Brook connects the northern and southern building clusters on campus by creating a corridor in sync with nature. It forms a public art and cultural space that is open and accessible to the city, as it is permeated with nature.

With regard to the campus overall, Floating Cornice on the Brook improves the campus infrastructure, as well as the artificial ecological environment, while providing benefits to various public groups. Yet, on a microscopic, local, ecological scale, it is a unique resting place founded on biodiversity.

Los Angeles Hilton Hotel Expansion in Universal Studios

Dynamic Grids

"Respond to environment, create experience, and create memory"—it is hoped that the experience accumulated from our previous cultural tourism projects in natural landscapes can inject new experience and vitality into Hollywood's Universal Studios, a world-famous cultural tourism landmark.

—Zhu Peidong

Located on top of Hollywood Hills, between Universal Studios and Highway 101 in Los Angeles, California, United States, this project not only offers great views of the city, but is also located near other well known tourist attractions in Hollywood and Beverly Hills, and has been standing as a city landmark for the past forty years. The project is line+ studio's second overseas project following FOREST Community in San Francisco, United States. As the design architect, line+ studio led the collaborative teams working on the design stages, from conception to construction.

Valley Diamond

Night view rendering

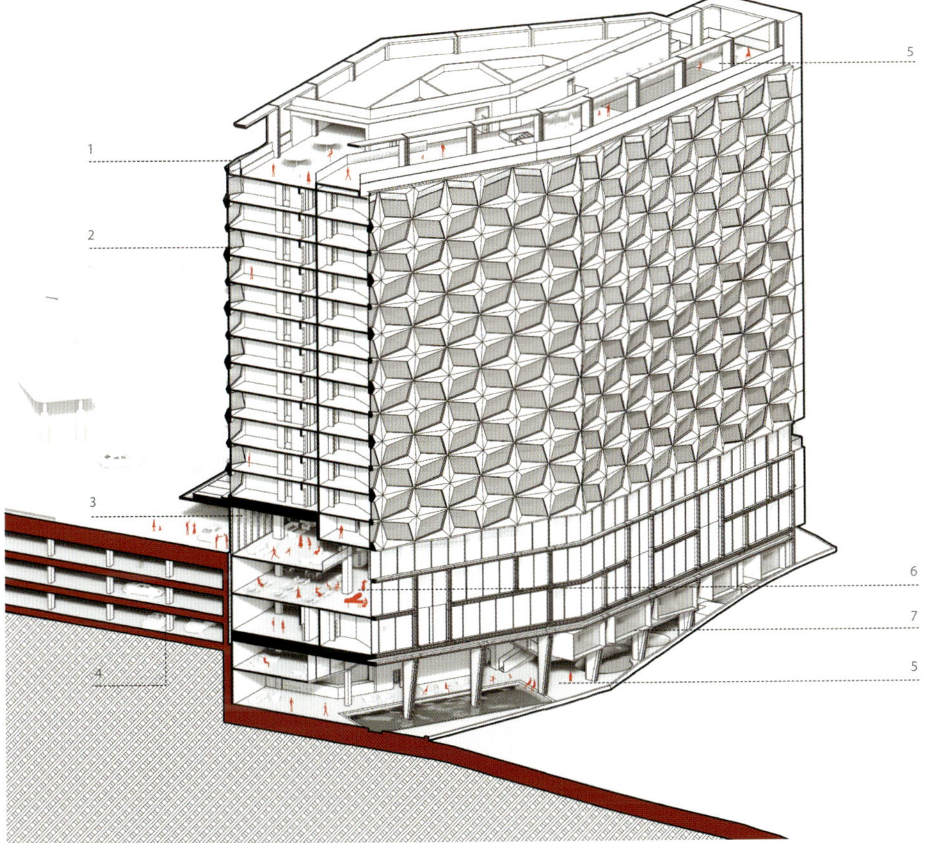

Axonometric section

1. Roof bar
2. Guestroom
3. Lobby
4. Parking
5. Swimming pool
6. Restaurant
7. Spa deck

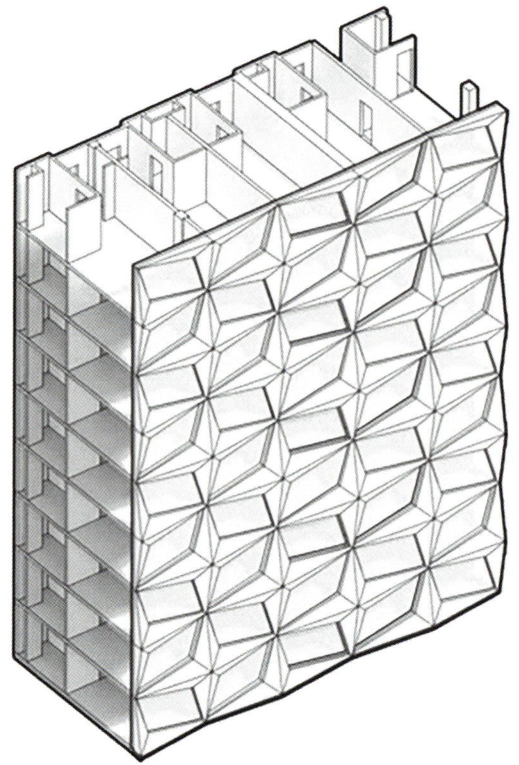

Modular façade

Façade detail

At the beginning of the design, the team adopted a modular and prefabricated overall construction strategy, which not only complies with the strict structural seismic fortification standards of Los Angeles, but also meets the owner's requirement to shorten the project period. Based on line+ studio's Rhino-Revit working platform, the design expression will connect with the technology application and produce an efficient information synchronization between the architecture of record and the contractor.

Standardized construction can make buildings with a lower carbon count and allow for higher sustainability. Observing standardization to create differentiated experiences has become an important approach in dynamic grids. Inspired by the opening (blooming) and closing dynamics of Los Angeles city's official flower, the bird of paradise (from the genus Strelitzia), the design forms a dynamic grid façade through the four-way change of a standard modular framework to respond to different weather conditions, in order to bring "surprises"–such as dynamically changing hotel outlooks and guestroom views—to hotel guests.

The star-shaped pattern, composed of silver profiled window openings, is not only an abstraction of the memory of the classic films and television of Universal Studios, but also an echo of the resplendent Hollywood city. Wrapped in the silver dynamic grid is a copper core that is composed of multiple variously sized modules—balconies, frames, and giant columns—covered by copper plates. Under the golden, robust sunshine of California, the building looks warm and passionate, vividly demonstrating the film texture and dreamy atmosphere of Hollywood and Universal Studios.

Sparkling façade

A new hotel image

Rendering of the entrance to the hotel

Partial silhouette showcases the hotel's allure

Hill–Valley Oasis

The new tower, with excellent supporting facilities, will continue to provide a luxury hotel experience for guests. line+ studio further introduces a holiday experience and space choices that are closely related to the region, so guests can experience and enjoy the interweaving of the natural scenery with the urban one.

Taking advantage of the height difference of a 56-foot (17-meter) slope, as well as the expansion of Los Angeles' abundant greenery and the optimal use of land resources, the new tower successfully arranges public areas, including the swimming-pool dining bar, outdoor spa, and gymnasium in the slope space area adjacent to the first floor. It also sets up a semi-outdoor activity space to connect the hotel's public area to urban life.

On the guestroom floor, at the middle, a diamond shape stretches out to both ends in a staggered manner. The suite at the end looks out to a 270-degree view of the landscape, forming a vertical terrace in the air against the urban background. On the top floor is a boundless swimming pool and a sunset restaurant. Guests can take the see-through elevator directly to the top floor to enjoy the inspiring urban landscape from the top, as well as the sights on the way up.

With increasing parking pressure and the impact on the landscape brought about by visitors, the design rearranges and expands the existing underground stereoscopic parking structure, incorporating a series of new parking technologies and machinery to meet Universal Studios' requirement for additional parking spaces. The roof layer of the three-dimensional parking structure will serve as the drop-off area and landscape forecastle for the old and new hotels, as well as connect with the adjacent Sheraton Hotel, to enable peak-hour parking sharing. This approach also meets the transportation needs of the surrounding workers and community residents.

1
2

1. Rendering of the hotel in the city of Los Angeles
2. Rendering of swimming pool in the evening overlooking the city

Night view

RE ＼

WOR —

／ LD

__ ING

Night view

Renewal of the Public Environment

As soon as the expansion plan of Hilton Hotel Universal Studios was proposed, it drew great concern from all involved parties, including NBCUniversal, Hilton Hotel Group, and the city council of Los Angeles city, as well as various public groups, due to the landmark attribute of the hotel. Because of the many concerns that had arisen, the expansion project had been shelved and the designer had been changed several times. line+ studio proposes to adjust the design from the "expansion" of a single hotel to the "renewal" of the public environment, with featured sustainable strategies, such as urban friendliness, an eco environment, and resource sharing, to balance the owner's requirements and the benefits of the public stakeholders. This project will provide the city of Los Angeles, the community, and the general public with a brand-new resort hotel cast in a fresh urban image, to offer a unique vacation experience backdropped by memorable vistas.

FOREST Community, San Francisco

Building for Sustainability

"The essence of living is about the restoration and settlement of both body and mind, as well as the harmony between humans and nature. While cultures and environments evolve, the architect's mission remains unchanged—to create communities where people and nature coexist in harmony, using the right technologies and methods."

—Zhu Peidong

Location: San Francisco, United States
Design firm: line+ studio
Principal architect: Zhu Peidong
Design team (competition): Hu Runzhi, Wang Zhongming, Wang Dadong, Tao Xufeng, Zhao Chensen, Zhu Jinqiu
Design team (SD to DD phase): Sun Xiaoyu, Zhou Yihan, Zhong Yifen, Huang Yinan, Chen Qi, Cao Linlin, Cai Xianghang (Architecture); Li Shangyang, Lu Yuping, Rao Feier, Li Jun (Landscape)
Architecture and AOR (LDI in the US): Ankrom Moisan Associated Architects
Area: 1,649,537 square feet (153,247 square meters)
Design period: 2021–present

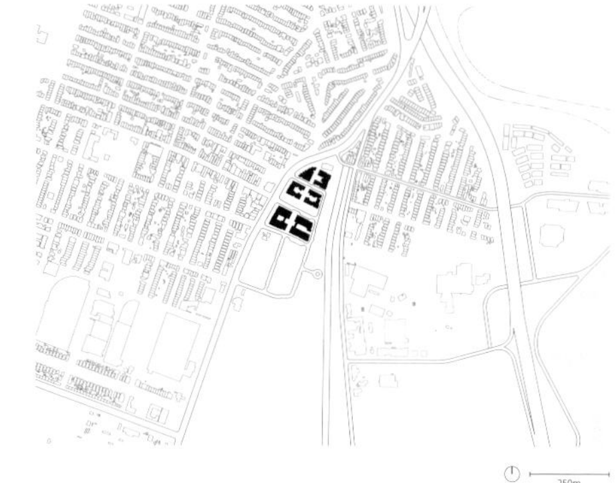

Site plan

A Vision for Sustainable Urban Renewal

Situated on an 8.1-hectare site in South San Francisco, the FOREST Community project occupies the historic Schlage Lock property, comprising nine blocks. The location, strategically positioned near US Highway 101 and just south of downtown San Francisco, is in a rapidly evolving neighborhood. Once an industrial hub, it now blends light manufacturing, commercial spaces, and emerging residential developments. The area's proximity to Silicon Valley has attracted tech professionals and immigrants, fostering a diverse community and an influx of high-density housing. With a Mediterranean climate and growing demand for sustainable living, this site is ideal for the FOREST Community, which aims to offer a dynamic mix of residential, commercial, and recreational spaces.

The project's goal is to revitalize a former industrial brownfield into a vibrant and sustainable urban district, addressing climate-change challenges and outdated development models.

SAN MATEO COUNTY
SAN FRANCISCO COUNTY

Site map

Schlage Lock old site

Street view

Mixed Community, Vibrant Block

The first phase of the project spans three blocks, with a total built area of 640,812 square feet (59,533 square meters), including 606,993 square feet (56,392 square meters) of residential space and 33,819 square feet (3,142 square meters) of commercial space.

This phase is based on the concept of a "Mixed Community, Vibrant Block," which aims to provide a high-quality living environment and a diverse, open neighborhood. The architectural layout of each block follows an enclosed design, creating continuous exterior interfaces while forming internal courtyard spaces for activities. Public spaces, such as green parks and street-facing shops, are integrated to encourage sharing and interaction. The residential buildings are assembled using modular units, with different assembly methods tailored to various living scenarios and dynamic interfaces.

Semi-bird's-eye view

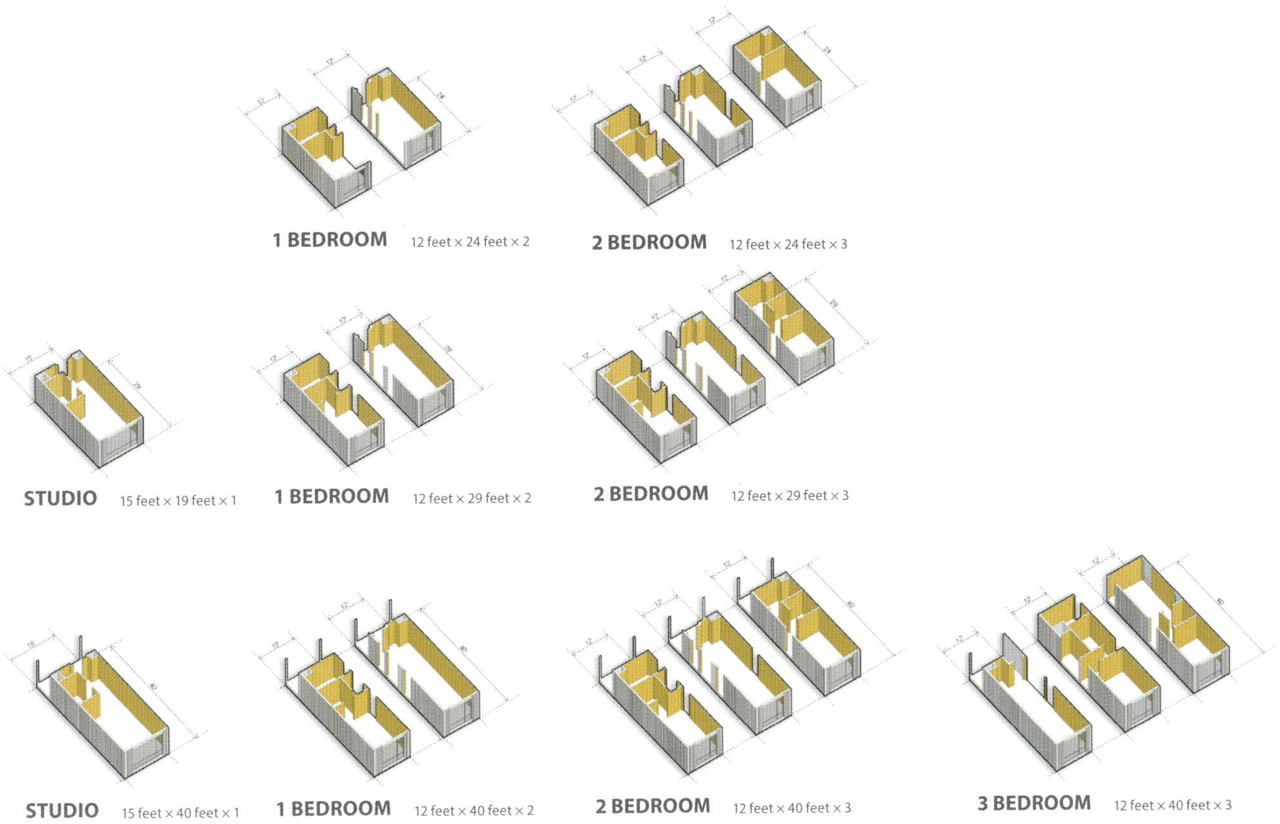

1 BEDROOM 12 feet × 24 feet × 2

2 BEDROOM 12 feet × 24 feet × 3

STUDIO 15 feet × 19 feet × 1

1 BEDROOM 12 feet × 29 feet × 2

2 BEDROOM 12 feet × 29 feet × 3

STUDIO 15 feet × 40 feet × 1

1 BEDROOM 12 feet × 40 feet × 2

2 BEDROOM 12 feet × 40 feet × 3

3 BEDROOM 12 feet × 40 feet × 3

Unit type

Residential unit model

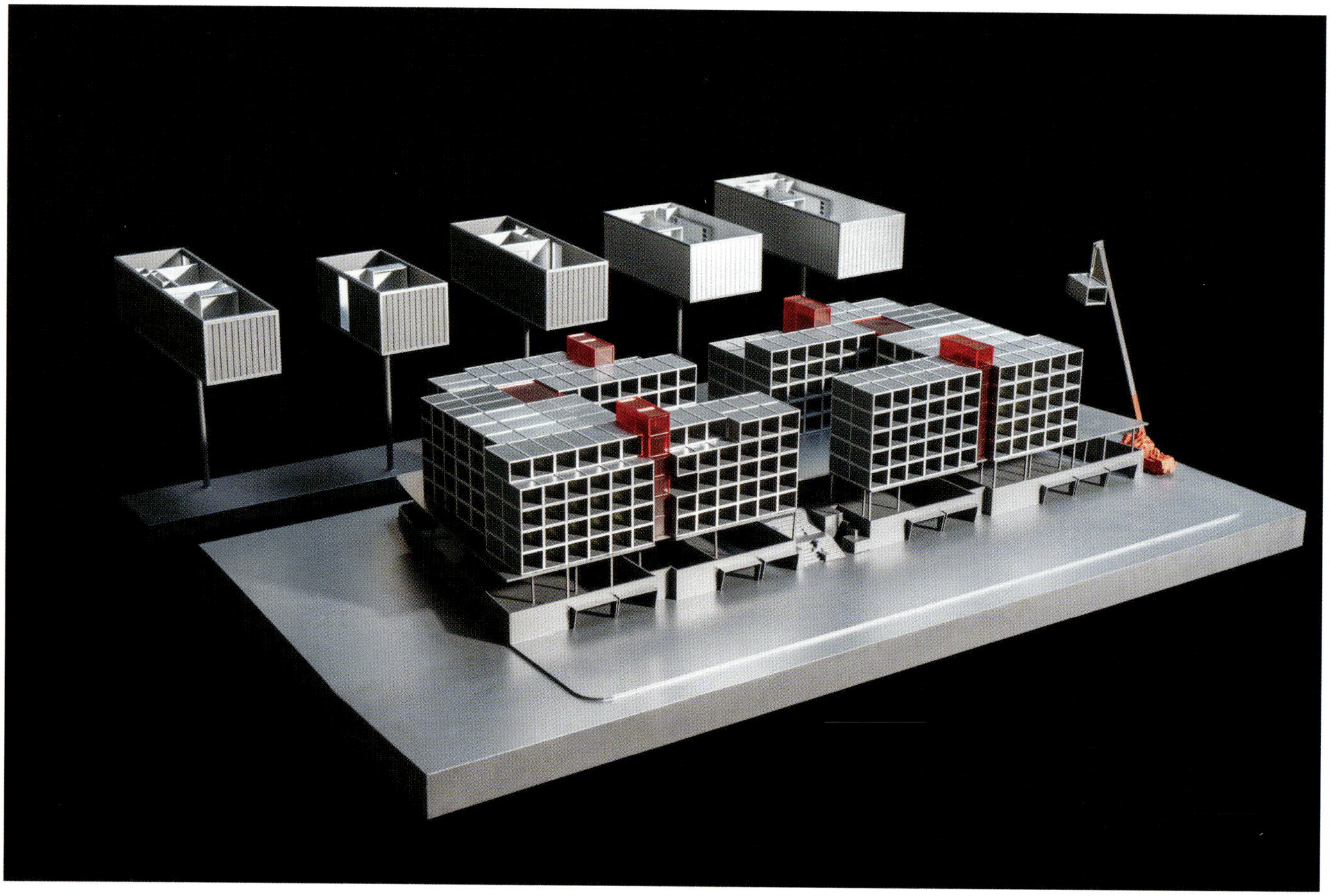

Modular construction model

Tech-Driven Resilience

Given the area's high seismic risk and population density, the local government and project owners have set rigorous safety standards for the buildings.

line+ studio set a full lifecycle zero-carbon target, integrating a global supply chain that includes design, materials, production, and transportation from around the world. The design adopts a systematic approach, combining information management with high construction standards.

Buildings are divided into modular units, sized to meet shipping and land transport requirements, addressing transportation challenges. The flexible, adaptable modular assembly method suits different site conditions and diverse living needs. Special connection nodes between modules ensure the buildings meet seismic requirements in high-intensity areas.

Street view

Residential façade

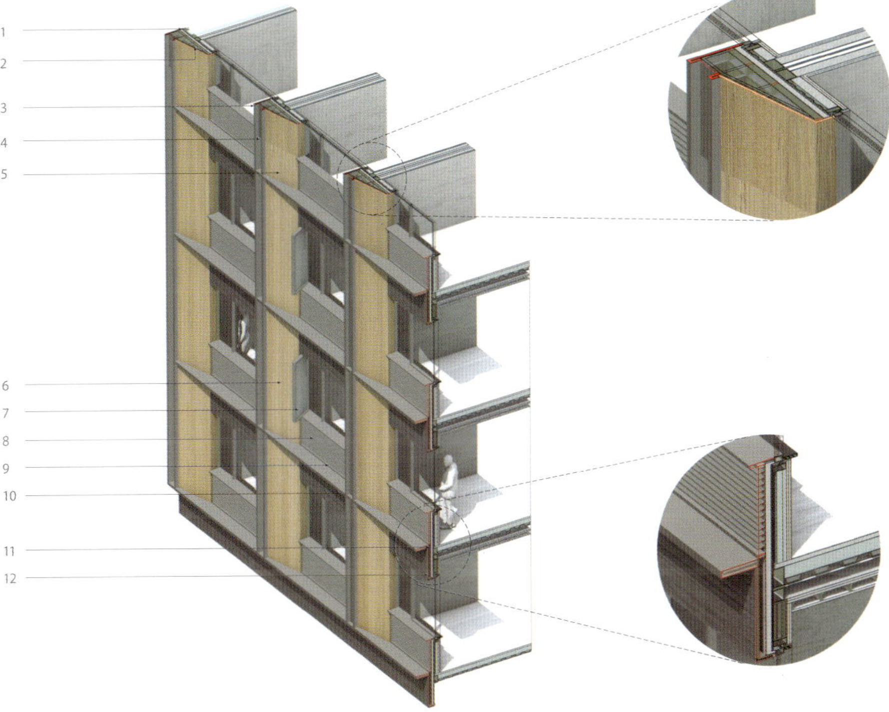

Residential unit wall section detail

1. Mineral wool
2. Curtain-wall frame
3. Formed alum panel
4. Perforated alum panel (for intake)
5. Fiber cement siding (wood texture)
6. Glass-mat gypsum sheathing
7. Operable window
8. Outside air intake
9. Metal louver
10. Formed alum panel
11. Curtain-wall frame
12. Fiber cement siding

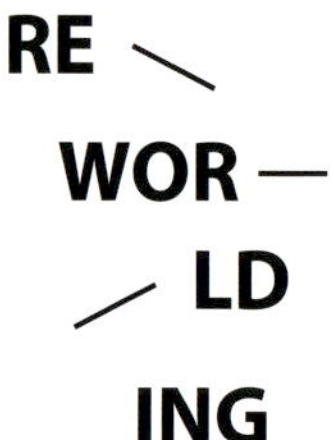

A New Model of Zero-carbon Living

The project has completed its horizontal design and received entitlement from the City of San Francisco. Over the next four years, line+ studio will collaborate with the developer and local design institutes to create the Bay Area's first mixed-use community aimed at achieving carbon neutrality. The community will serve as a forward-thinking, high-quality public waterfront garden for California and North America, exploring a new paradigm for contemporary urban renewal and the creation of high-quality habitats.

As a Chinese design institution, line+ studio integrates contemporary Eastern culture with Western practices to create a new model of zero-carbon living. The project emphasizes future-oriented pluralistic values while focusing on the human living experience.

Neighborhood-style living atmosphere

Residential façade

17th Venice Architecture Biennale, 2021: *How Will We Live Together?*

Rural Nostalgia and Urban Dream

In 2021, Meng Fanhao was invited to the 17th International Architecture Exhibition organized by La Biennale di Venezia at the Arsenale, Venice, Italy. This 17th Venice Architecture Biennale was curated by architect and scholar Hashim Sarkis. The theme of the exhibition, *How Will We Live Together?* attempted to establish a new "space contract" that calls on architects to imagine spaces within which we can generously live together in the context of widening political divides and growing economic inequalities.

Location: Arsenale, Venice, Italy
Design firm: line+ studio
Principal architect: Meng Fanhao
Design principal: He Yaliang, Xu Hao
Design team: Zhu Jun, Deng Hao, Ge Zhenliang, Wang Yubin, Xing Shu, Wang Xinyu, Tu Dan, Li Yinze
Project executive: Fang Yi, He Yalang
Documentary: ZuoJing Studio, Chen Xi Studio, Stray Birds Art Hotel
Video: Liu Xinhui, Chen Yufan, Shi Fancheng, Fang Sitao
Miniature model production: Shi Fancheng, Lou Shiyuan, Fang Sitao, Sun Yang, Xue Yuhui, Sun Shudi, Chen Yufan, Tao Sixu, Tao Siyan, Liu Yimin
Building model making: Hangzhou Tianhan Architectural Modeling Design Co., Ltd.
On-site executive: Yang Xiao
Area: 1,185 square feet (110 square meters)
Design period: July 2020–September 2020
Photography: Liu Xuanzhu, Chen Xi Studio

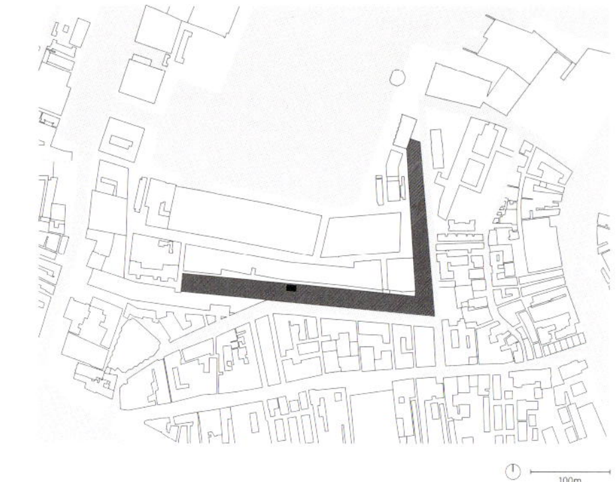

Site plan

The City and the Countryside

In undertaking various projects, the design team has worked in different geographical environments of the cities and villages in China, designing constructions of different scales and typologies for both urban and rural habitants. The urban-rural relationship in China is like a "fortress besieged"—urban dwellers are tired of the density and vertical developments in urban areas, and "returning to the countryside" has become a soothing balm for their frazzled mental and emotional states; rural residents on the other hand are attracted to the lifestyle and culture found in the city, and "going to the city" has become a popular trend. The spatial production based on the misaligned demands between the two groups has become an important vehicle for urban-rural interaction, and to a certain extent transforms the one-way flow of urban-rural connections into a two-way process of integration.

The *Rural Nostalgia and Urban Dream* installation was a reflection of the current status and development situation of contemporary China, as well as presenting an in-depth consideration of the exhibition theme, *How Will We Live Together?* From that angle, the studio explored architecture that would heal the rural nostalgia of city dwellers and fulfill the urban dream for rural residents. Three projects were exhibited to propose how different groups will live together, in response to the theme, from three perspectives: constructing a new type of community, reusing existing buildings, and creating public spaces. The installation showed the urban-rural relationship in contemporary China through different spatial forms, architectural functions, and construction strategies, while exploring new urban-rural hybrid models triggered by architectural space production.

Using models, digital videos, and graphic images of the three projects, the design team presented contemporary urban and rural lives in China in a European context in the Arsenale's exhibition space.

Arsenale in Venice

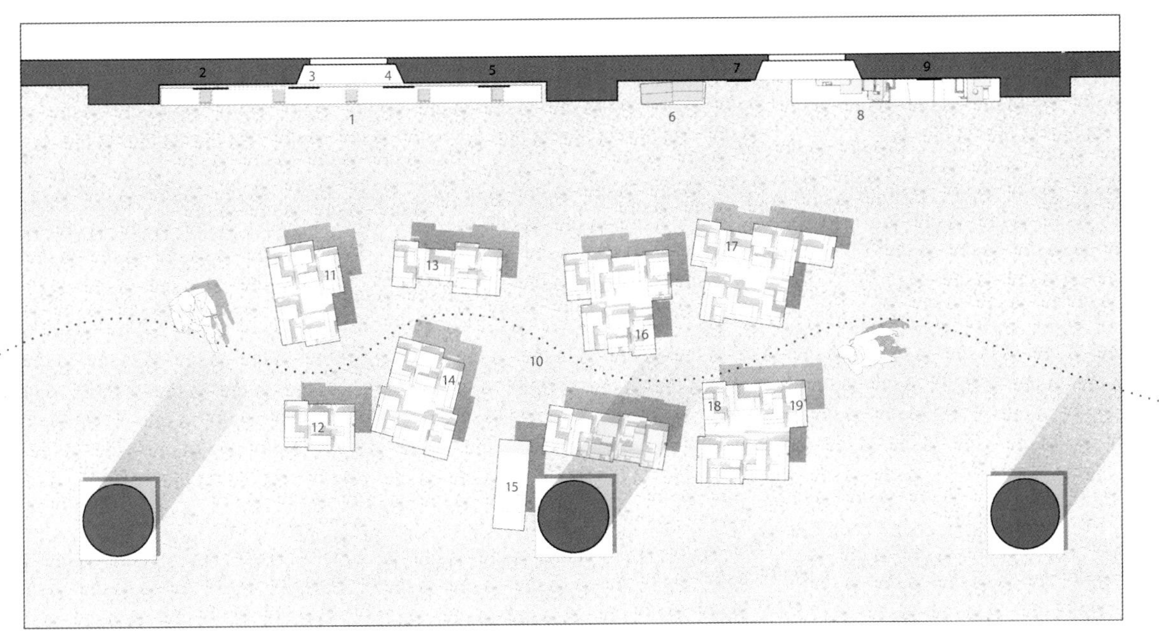

Ground-floor plan

1. Display stand
2. Photo of traditional Jiangnan houses
3. *My Jiangnan* by Wu Guanzhong
4. Photo: Dongziguan Village
5. Video: Dongziguan Village
6. Model: Stray Birds Art Hotel
7. Video: Stray Birds Art Hotel
8. Model: teahouse in Jiuxing Village
9. Video: teahouse in Jiuxing Village
10. 1:30 Model: Dongziguan Village
11. Model: house for the principal
12. Model: house for a seven-stringed Chinese instrument player
13. Model: house for a calligrapher
14. Model: house for a farmer
15. Model: Dongziguan Villagers' Activity Center
16. Model: house with a traditional kitchen
17. Model: bed-and-breakfast
18. Model: house of plants
19. Model: house of tea

Elevation

1. Exhibition rack
2. Photo of traditional Jiangnan houses
3. *My Jiangnan* by Wu Guanzhong
4. Photo: Dongziguan Village
5. Video: Dongziguan Village
6. Model: Stray Birds Art Hotel
7. Video: Stray Birds Art Hotel
8. Model: teahouse in Jiuxing Village
9. Video: teahouse in Jiuxing Village

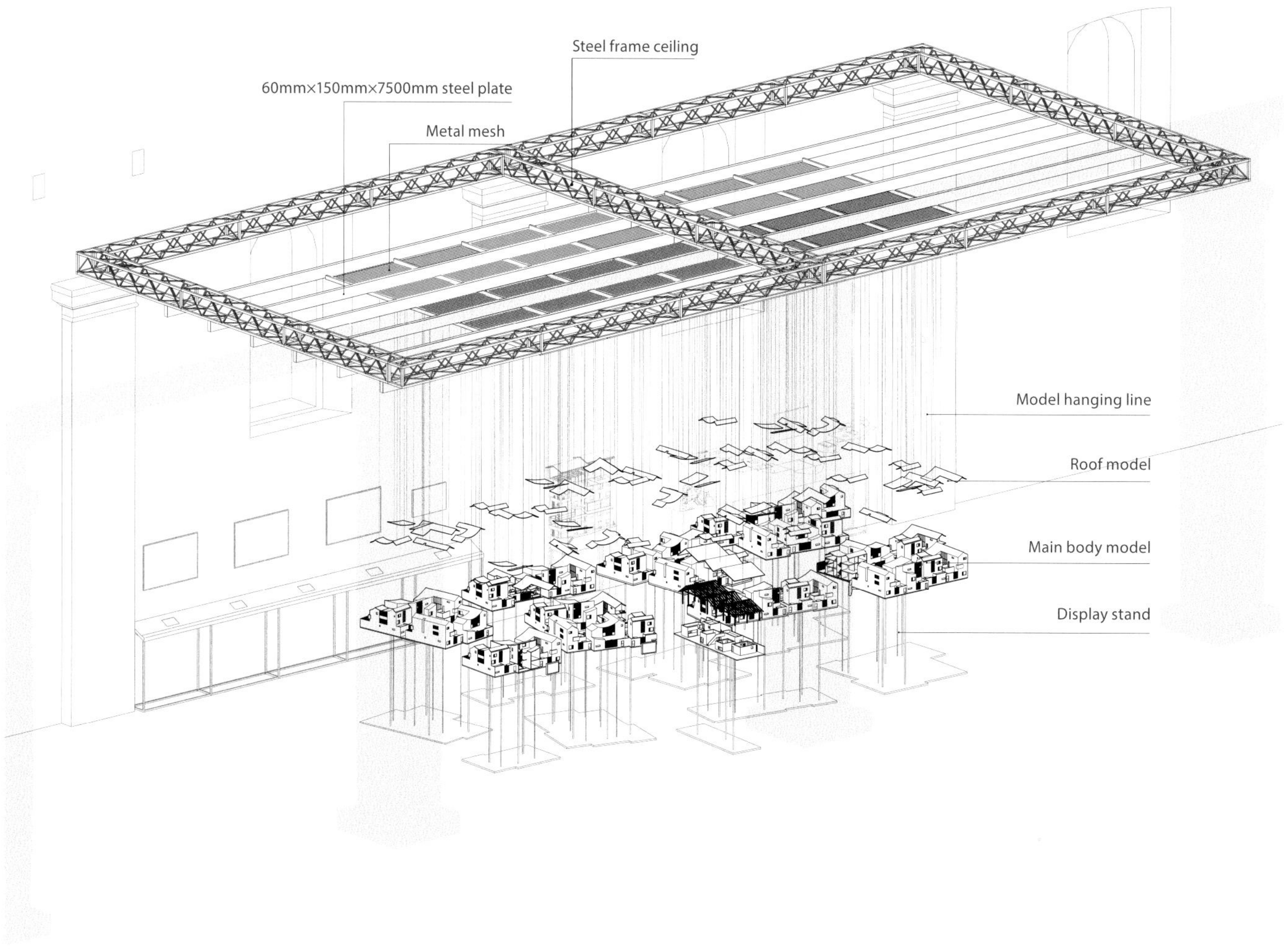

Axonometric sketch of exhibition space layout

Exhibition Design

For the 17th Venice Architecture Biennale, a miniature model of forty-six of the dwellings in Dongziguan Village, at a scale of 1:30, recreated the diverse clusters and organic village texture. Additionally, miniatures of eight typical family homes and the Dongziguan Villagers' Activity Center also showcased real-life scenes in profile view. The spacing between the cluster models was set at an appropriate ratio to tie the real-world structures with the scale of the exhibition, allowing visitors to walk freely among the streets and alleys to observe and feel the villagers' daily life from a human point of view, so as to establish an interactive relationship between the street space, local life in the village, and the exhibition experience. Additionally, in the exhibition model, the roof was extracted and suspended in mid-air to provide multiple viewing angles, enriching the vertical spatial dimension in the exhibition hall.

Urban-rural integration:
Over the past three years, Dongziguan Village has seen an unexpected influx of residents following enhanced media coverage, which has led to the creation of new businesses and industries, the return of some original residents, and the arrival of new people, including artists and young entrepreneurs. Together they formed a new model for a rural community—one that transcends urban and rural settlements.

Within the exhibition model, the design team placed images of eight typical families that represent different living conditions and cluster models as part of this new type of community: a guqin (Chinese zither) family, a vegetable planting family, a mud stove family, a bed-and-breakfast, the house of the principal, a calligraphy family, a plant family, and a teahouse family.

Visitors free to wander into the streets and alleys

Aerial view of Dongziguan Village

Extraction of village fabric

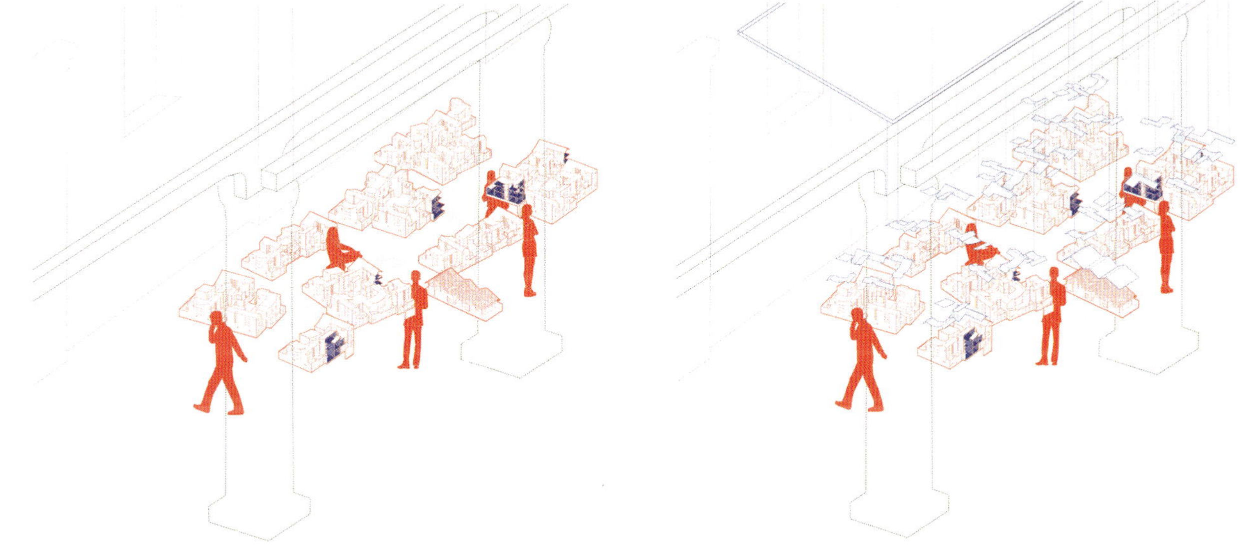

Exhibition installation

Exploded diagram of roofs

Experiencing scale relationships authentically from a human perspective

Exhibition venue

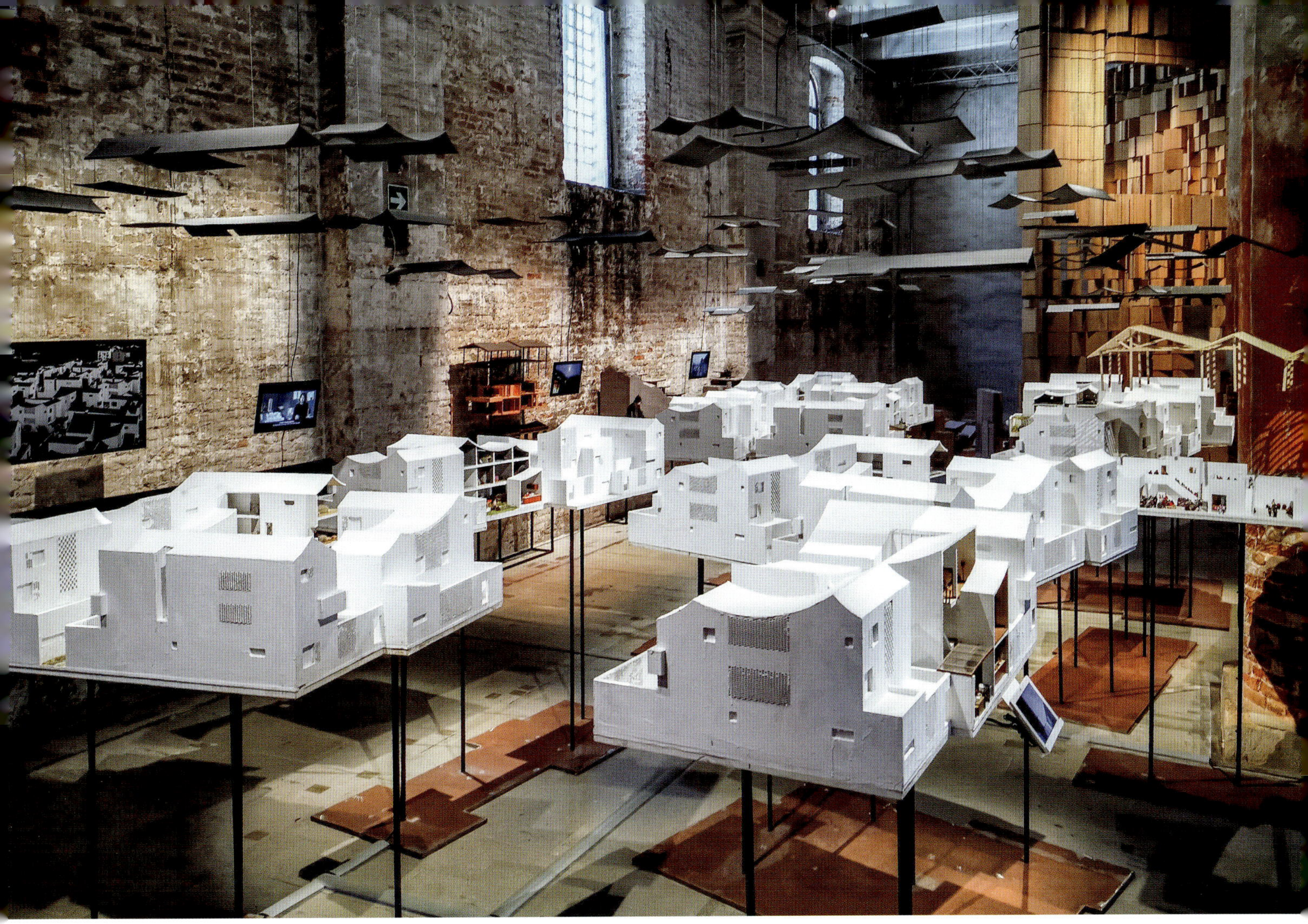

Installation view

Songyang Stray Birds Art Hostel model

A03 Guqin family

A06 Vegetable planting family

A22 Mud stove family

A53 Plant family

A32 House of the principal

A26 Calligraphy family

House for a seven-stringed Chinese instrument player: Supported by the local government, a traditional craftsperson from Shanxi Province rents a house in the village and produces traditional Chinese zithers here to spread traditional culture.

House for a farmer: The old couple plants vegetables in their garden and lives a simple rural life.

House with a traditional kitchen: The typical agricultural family does farm work in the yard and cooks on a traditional adobe stove, thus maintaining earlier living habits.

Bed-and-breakfast house: The B&B is a new form of business to the village and a new, self-managed way for local people to generate income.

House for the principal: The 60-year-old retired principal and his six family members live together. The interior decoration and layout of the unit follow a traditional Chinese style.

House for a calligrapher: In the artist's space that fulfills complex functions, the first floor is used for calligraphy and painting exhibitions, and the second and third floors are used for operating a guesthouse.

House of plants: A family of three lives here. The yard is full of plants, and the interior decoration follows the style of an exquisite urban model house.

House of tea: The urban couple left the city to live in Dongziguan, where they converted their residence into a teahouse to provide tourists with a place to enjoy a break.

A57 Teahouse family

A20 Bed-and-breakfast

A visitor looking at the house of tea

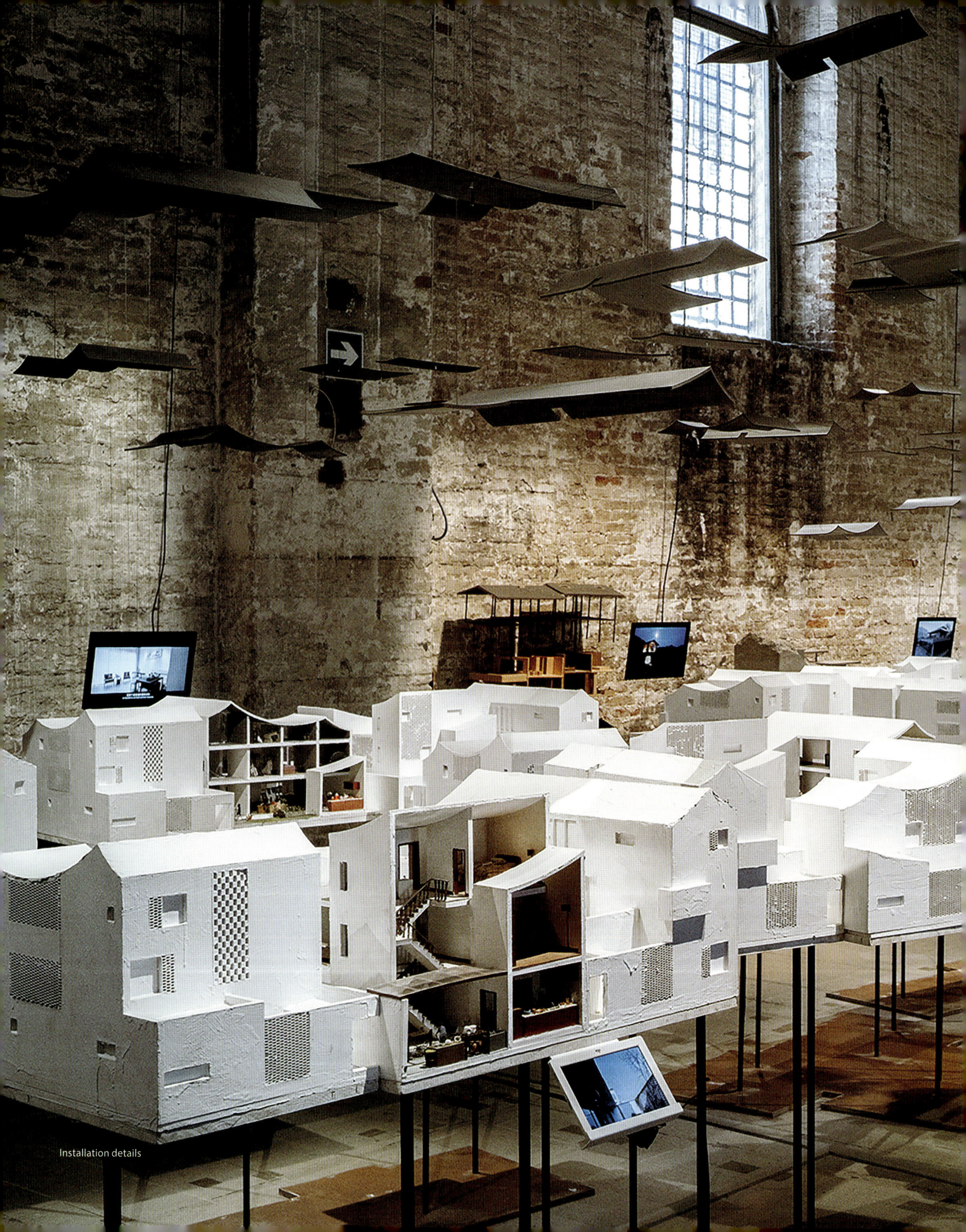

Installation details

RE ⟍
WOR —
⟋ LD
__ ING

How Will We Live Together?

In terms of population flow and spatial agglomeration that accompany the processes of urban-rural interaction and integrated development, urbanization depends on the integration of rural people, while rural construction similarly depends on urban people's longing for the countryside. The Rural Nostalgia and Urban Dream exhibitions do not merely represent spatial requirements and symbolic visions—they are the combined characteristic phenomena of an urban-rural connection, and the driving force for reconstructing the urban-rural relationship. Through the interaction between people's needs and architectural design, multifunctional places—where multiple groups with urban and rural backgrounds gather—are formed. In the process of creating spaces for this new pattern of urban-rural mixing, determining how to integrate and respond to the new demands for shared and cultural spaces used by hybrid groups has become a sustained focus for the architects.

Compared with the city, the countryside is a more complex ecological entity. In the countryside, the architect is no longer a passive, monolithic, unidirectional problem solver, but an active, composite, multidirectional organizer and guide who pushes for spatial empowerment driven by design. By going beyond the scope of architectural design and combining it with specific social contexts, integrating resources at all levels and establishing a complete set of project procedures—ranging from planning to design, construction, and the operation and marketing of a new place—this design team advances the innovation of the development paradigm through design. This is the team's reflection on and implementation in response to the 17th Venice Architecture Biennale's theme, *How Will We Live Together?*

View of installation

About line+ studio

line+ studio is an international innovative design studio founded by Meng Fanhao and Zhu Peidong in Hangzhou, China. "line" refers to the boundary in architectural design, while "+" refers to breaking through the clear boundaries of traditional industry and using cross-border thinking as a way to realize the boundless integration of planning, architecture, interior, product, operation, landscape, and fields outside of architecture. By adapting diverse strategies, line+ studio looks forward to sharing the value of design with our partners.

From the shaping of urban space to the revitalization of rural civilization, line+ studio always insists on critical thinking, thereby building design works rooted in geographical and cultural characteristics, and which respond to interpret the diverse connotations of contemporary culture. Within the premise of ensuring high-quality completion, the practice actively participates in various areas, such as urban public architecture, high-end residential projects, rural revitalization, cultural tourism, and so on, to deeply explore the potential value under business logic, as it strives to become a carrier between culture and commerce.

MENG Fanhao

Co-Founder and Chief Architect, line+ studio
International Awards for Excellence, RIBA
Gold Winner, ARCASIA Awards for Architecture
The 17th Venice Architecture Biennale
Young Architect Award, 2019-2020 ASC Architectural Design Award
2020-2022 RIBA China Architect 100
RIBA Charted Member
AIA International Associate Membership
Class 1 Registered Architect (PRC) / Professor-level Senior Engineer
Professor, College of Architecture and Urban Planning of Tongji University
Master of Architecture, Nanjing University
Design Tutor, Architecture Department of Zhejiang University
Visiting professor, Zhejiang Gongshang University

Mr Meng has long been committed to the architectural practice of both urban construction and rural revitalization, actively exploring and considering the possibility of urban environment improvement and rural revitalization under the current system and social development status. Through "form giving," he achieves memory continuity by delving into the innovative creation of architectural ontology in the context of contemporary architecture and construction logic; and through "space empowerment," he explores the greater potential of architecture in top-level areas such as society, economy, and culture.

He has been honored with numerous prestigious awards both domestically and internationally, including the RIBA International Awards for Excellence, the gold winner of ARCASIA Awards, ASC Young Architect Award, the First Prize in ASC Architectural Design Award, WA Design Experiment Award Highly Commended, and the winner of Dezeen Awards, etc.

He was selected as one of the RIBA China Architect 100, and was invited to participate in the 17th Venice International Architecture Biennale, 2017 Seoul / 2021 RIO / 2023 CPH World Congress of Architects Exhibition Chinese Architecture Exhibition, the Bi-city Biennale of Urbanism/Architecture, Shanghai Urban Space Art Season, Beijing International Design Week and other significant academic exhibitions at home and abroad. He was invited to deliver lectures and participate in teaching evaluations at renowned architecture schools, including Harvard University, University of Cambridge, University of Sheffield, Tsinghua University, Tongji University, Nanjing University, and Shanghai Jiao Tong University.

His works are published by Domus, DETAIL, THE PLAN, SPACE, THE Architects, World Architecture, Time Architecture and other well known publications. Additionally, they have garnered extensive attention and acclaim from major social media platforms, including CCTV, People's Daily, Xinhua News Agency, Phoenix TV, and Sanlian Life Weekly.

ZHU Peidong

Co-Founder and Chief Architect, line+ studio
Ph.D. in Architecture, Tongji University
Honorary Mention, ARCASIA Awards for Architecture
Highly Commended, World Architecture Festival
Perspective 40 Under 40
FA Emerging Architect Best Practice Award
Top 10 Outstanding Young Architects in Hangzhou
RIBA Charted Member
AIA International Associate Membership
Class 1 Registered Architect (PRC) / Senior Engineer
Design Tutor, Architecture Department of Zhejiang University

Dr Zhu Peidong employs a research-oriented approach and the thread of "Empowering Spaces" to actively and continuously engage in the forefront of design. He responds to the demands of contemporary architecture within its complex context and addresses societal issues. Continuously employing the method of "scenario configuration," he achieves the augmentation of spatial value and the equilibrium of societal value through architectural innovation and creation. This process fosters a symbiotic relationship among individuals, society, architecture, and nature.

He has garnered numerous prestigious awards and honors including the Perspective 40 Under 40, the 2020 FA Emerging Architect Award, and being named one of the "Top 10 Outstanding Young Architects in Hangzhou." His works have received accolades such as Honorary Mention of ARCASIA Awards for Architecture, AIA International Awards, the China Survey and Design Industry Award, the First Prize in ASC Architectural Design Award, WA Technological Innovation Award Winner, China Construction Engineering Luban Award, Archdaily Building of the Year Winner, Dezeen Awards, WAF Highly Commended, and Architizer A+Awards Jury Winner, among other significant domestic and international recognitions.

He was invited to participate in the 17th Venice Architecture Biennale Chinese Pavilion, the UIA 2021 RIO / 2023 CPH World Congress of Architects Exhibition Chinese Architecture Exhibition, Vicissitude of Vision: Inaugural Sino-Europe Invitational Architectural Exhibition 2020-2021, Beijing International Design Week, 2020 Industrial Architecture Innovation Forum and Color Trend, MindTalk Creative Open Class, Chinese Students and Scholars Association of Harvard School of Design, etc.

Many of his works and research papers have been published in prominent architectural journals both domestically and internationally, including DETAIL, Architectural Journal, Time Architecture, World Architecture, Architectural Technique and Architectural Practice. Additionally, his projects have garnered attention from public and social media platforms such as CCTV, People's Daily, and Zhejiang Daily.

Published in Australia in 2025 by
The Images Publishing Group Pty Ltd
ABN 89 059 734 431

Offices
Melbourne
Waterman Business Centre
Suite 64, Level 2 UL40
1341 Dandenong Road
Chadstone, Victoria 3148
Australia
Tel: +61 3 8564 8122

New York
6 West 18th Street 4B
New York City, NY 10011
United States
Tel: +1 212 645 1111

Shanghai
6F, Building C, 838 Guangji Road
Hongkou District, Shanghai 200434
China
Tel: +86 021 31260822

books@imagespublishing.com
www.imagespublishing.com

The Images Publishing Group Reference Number: 1629

A catalogue record for this book is available from the National Library of Australia

Title: Shaping Changes
Author: line+ studio
ISBN: 9781864709247

EU GPSR Authorised Representative: Easy Access System Europe Oü
Company Registration ID: 16879218 | Address: Mustamäe tee 50, 10621 Tallinn, Estonia
Email: gpsr@easproject.com | Tel: +358 40 500 3575

Printed by Everbest Printing Investment Limited, in Hong Kong/China